Lisa Chase &
Vern Grubinger

✢ *Food, Farms, and Community*

EXPLORING FOOD SYSTEMS

UNIVERSITY OF
NEW HAMPSHIRE
PRESS ✢ DURHAM,
NEW HAMPSHIRE

University of New Hampshire Press

www.upne.com/unh.html

© 2014 University of New Hampshire

All rights reserved

Manufactured in the United States of America

Designed by Eric M. Brooks

Typeset in Minion Pro and Fresco Sans

by Passumpsic Publishing

For permission to reproduce any of the material
in this book, contact Permissions, University Press
of New England, One Court Street, Suite 250,
Lebanon NH 03766; or visit www.upne.com

Library of Congress Cataloging-in-Publication Data

Chase, Lisa, author.

Food, farms, and community: exploring

food systems / Lisa Chase and Vern Grubinger.

    pages cm

Includes bibliographical references and index.

ISBN 978-1-61168-421-6 (pbk.: alk. paper) —

ISBN 978-1-61168-687-6 (ebook)

1. Food supply. 2. Food security.

I. Grubinger, Vernon P., 1957– author. II. Title.

HD9000.5.C488   2014

338.1'9 — dc23   2014035951

5 4 3 2 1

Contents

Acknowledgments vii

1 Introduction to Food Systems 1

2 Local Food Systems 16

3 The Business of Food and Farming 33

4 Values in Food Systems 54

5 The Agricultural Workforce 74

6 Farming and the Environment 88

7 Climate Change and Agriculture 108

8 Energy, Food, and Farms 123

9 Access to Healthy Food 138

10 Farm to School 149

11 Agritourism and On-Farm Marketing 165

12 Food Safety from Farm to Fork 182

13 The Next Generation of Farmers 195

14 Maintaining Farms and Farmland for the Future 212

15 Improving Food Systems 230

Notes 249

Figure and Map Credits 273

Index 279

Acknowledgments

We are grateful to the many people working in food systems around the country who were willing to be interviewed for this book, allowing us to share their experiences and insights. We also thank the following colleagues who reviewed chapters and provided insightful comments, guidance, and suggestions during the writing of the book: Selena Ahmed, Linda Berlin, Laura Brown, Mark Canella, Dan Chase, Kate Clancy, Doug Constance, Hans Estrin, Eric Garza, Bill Guenther, Susan Harlow, Joyce Hendley, Shoshanah Inwood, Fred Magdoff, Thomas Maloney, Tom Morris, Mary Peabody, Abbie Nelson, Londa Nwadike, Ellie Rilla, Rachel Schattman, Erin Shea, Arthur Schmidt, Bill Schmidt, Tatiana Schreiber, David Timmons, and Alex Wilson.

Special thanks to the Dean of the University of Vermont Extension, Doug Lantagne, and Associate Dean Dan Lerner, who provided support, financial and otherwise, throughout the writing of the book. In the Brattleboro Extension office we thank Carol Morrison and especially Gail Makuch, who tirelessly formatted references and kept us organized as we pulled the disparate pieces of the book together into a seamless whole. Thanks to Kristen Winstead, our graphic designer, who artfully reproduced many of the figures in the book.

Finally, we dedicate this work to our families, who supported us in so many ways and put up with the long hours we spent working on the book: Tracey Devlin, Sam and Nick Grubinger; Bob Ethier, Hazel and Iris Chase Ethier. We hope that our children, their children, and the generations that follow will be nourished by sustainable food systems.

1 ∾ *Introduction to Food Systems*

Food systems are extremely complex. If they were linear, at one end of the human continuum would be farmers, or producers, and at the other end would be consumers. Or food waste managers could be at the far end, and if some of them were composters, they'd connect back to the farmers, creating a circular food system. But food systems aren't linear, nor are they circular. They are webs of people and the resources and behaviors they affect. Producers, consumers, processors, distributors, wholesalers, and retailers interact with people working in education, social services, research, and other areas. These people may be advocates, entrepreneurs, or employees of institutions and businesses; they function in the for-profit and nonprofit sectors. Some deal directly with food and some deal with infrastructure; they offer technical assistance, manage natural resources, provide inputs such as fuels and fertilizers, or develop and implement policies and regulations. Together they create a food system, which can be broken down into myriad smaller systems.

Food System Models

A food system has been defined as

> an interconnected web of activities, resources and people that extends across all domains involved in providing human nourishment and sustaining health, including production, processing, packaging, distribution, marketing, consumption and disposal of food. The organization of food systems reflects and responds to social, cultural, political, economic, health and environmental conditions and can be identified at multiple scales, from a household kitchen to a city, county, state or nation.[1]

Individual perspectives determine how that web will be envisioned and described. A relatively simple depiction, for example, considers only the various types of markets for food (fig. 1.1). This reflects the economic measures that are often used to evaluate food systems: how much is produced, how much is sold, and how much is sold to which markets. Alternatively, a food system

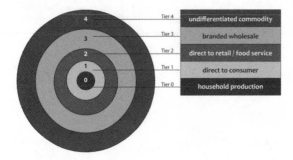

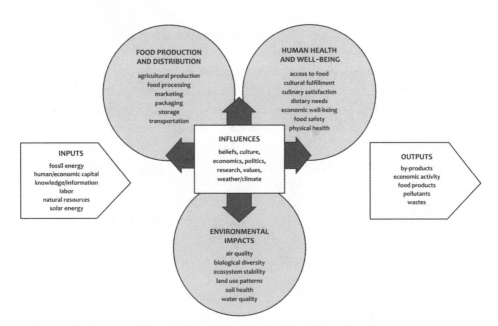

FIGURE 1.2 Complex diagram of a food system. This view focuses on food, people, and the environment, as well as factors that influence their interactions in the system, which uses inputs and generates outputs.

can be depicted as a much more complex and broad-reaching set of interactions that go far beyond the production, processing, and distribution of food to include the connection of food to the health of people and the environment (fig. 1.2).

When human and environmental interactions are included, the economic impact of a food system is much greater than the market value of the food sold. Holistic assessments of the food system may reveal many other kinds of positive economic impacts, such as improved nutrition and ecosystem services. They may also reveal negative impacts not accounted for by simple

FIGURE 1.3 Human health and food systems. This view focuses on dietary behavior and human health. Note that food production and distribution are depicted as a small part of this system, just one of many practices, whereas in Figure 1.2 they are shown as a primary part of the system.

market prices, such as the effect on health care costs due to excessive consumption of low-quality foods or the cost of cleaning up water pollution resulting from agricultural runoff. The positive and negative impacts that are not captured by the market are known as externalities.[2]

There is widespread concern about negative externalities from the food system, in particular the impact of a poor diet on human health. Efforts are under way to understand how the food system can be changed to alleviate food-related illness. From the perspective of people for whom the effect of dietary behavior on human health is a priority, it's important to describe a food system in a way that captures the "ingredients" they can work with to improve the situation (fig. 1.3).

In response to concerns about human health, many initiatives have been introduced to strengthen local and regional food systems. In these cases a primary consideration is often which facets of a system can be influenced by local or regional policies. Thus the descriptions of food systems in these plans usually focus on the governing unit's "sphere of influence," such as the activities of various industries and markets, rather than human behavior or environmental outcomes (fig. 1.4).

Another way that food systems can be described is in terms of desired outcomes for a healthy community (fig. 1.5). This doesn't provide details about how a system actually functions, but it articulates a set of broad, interrelated results that can then be stated as measurable goals.

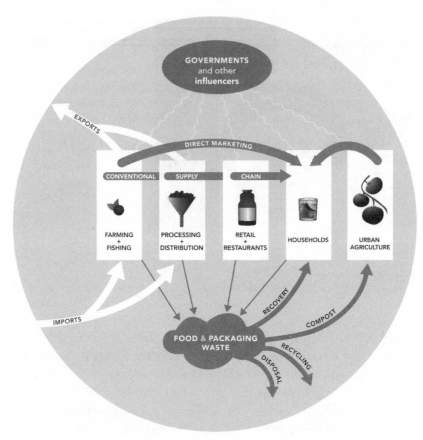

FIGURE 1.4 Food system components affected by policy. This view focuses on industries and activities that can be influenced by local and regional government policy.

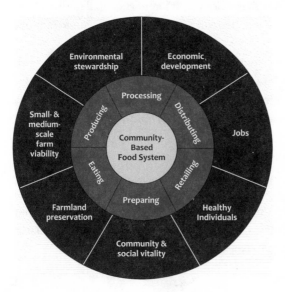

FIGURE 1.5 Food system community outcomes. This view emphasizes the goals a community may have that are related to food.

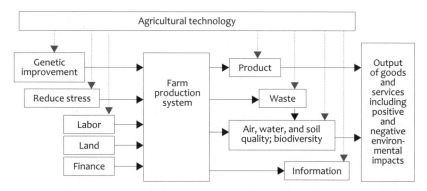

FIGURE 1.6 A farming system. This diagram depicts how a farm functions, without reference to larger systems outside the farm that affect the supply of inputs, demand for outputs, and interactions with the environment.

Systems within a Food System

Systems have hierarchies. That is, within an overall food system is an array of smaller systems. These include farming systems, agricultural ecosystems, economic systems, and social systems. Within those are further subsets of water systems, energy systems, financing systems, marketing systems, policy systems, culinary systems, and so on. If you are accustomed to organizing your files on a computer, it may be helpful to think of the larger systems as directories that contain an overview of the more detailed files, which are the smaller systems. For example, farming systems describe the manner in which natural, technological, and human inputs are managed on farms that use a certain set of practices to produce desired outputs as well as environmental impacts and wastes (fig. 1.6).

Within a farming system (a system "file" in the food production "directory") there are "sub-files" that address its components, such as the soil system, the pest system, the labor system, and the waste system. That's the level where most people work, on relatively focused, incremental change in the food system. Working higher up in the system, for example on redesigning an entire farming system, can lead to more transformational change, which is much harder to achieve.

Environmental or ecological systems overlap with food systems, and they can be explored at different levels, from a single field, to a whole farm, to the local, regional, or global food system. The flows and cycles of carbon, energy, nutrients, pollutants, water, and a host of other features can be described as individual systems. Most of these flows occur both inside and outside the food system. Figure 1.7 illustrates one of these cycles, the nitrogen cycle.

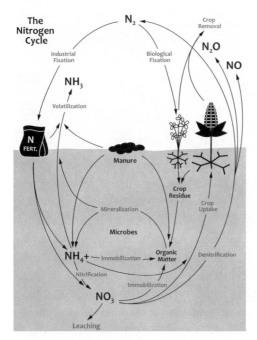

FIGURE 1.7 The nitrogen cycle. The flow of nitrogen (N) in this system takes place both on and off the farm. On the farm it is affected by activities such as fertilization, manure application, and crop harvest, as well as by biological processes such as mineralization (the release of plant-available forms of N from carbon-based compounds). Off the farm the N cycle includes atmospheric and watershed-level phenomena.

Economic systems within larger food systems are powerful drivers of decisions and measures of success. We have many tools for assessing short-term, market-based economic value, and very few for understanding other forms of wealth. For example, clean water has value but market mechanisms often fail to monetize that value, so it is a positive externality without a "price." Polluted water is a negative externality of some farming systems; it has economic impact but there is no market "cost" associated with it. Regulations, fines, and taxes may be used to account for negative externalities and hold those responsible for their costs. Some mechanisms have also been developed to reward farmers and others for positive externalities such as ecosystem services. For example, hayfields in the northeastern United States provide nesting grounds for migratory songbirds like bobolinks and eastern meadowlarks. The Bobolink Project uses community contributions to pay farmers to manage their hayfields in order to provide habitat for grassland-nesting birds.[3] Creating market mechanisms for externalities helps society capture the "true" values of different farming and food system practices, by placing them in a traditional economic context. Figure 1.8 illustrates this economic system of exchange of money for products and services.

Social aspects of a food system include culinary, dietary, and cultural fac-

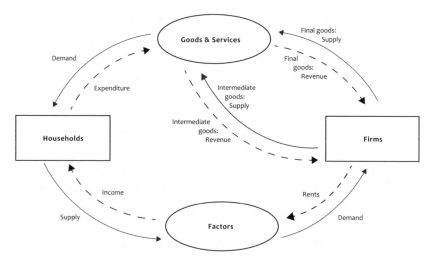

FIGURE 1.8 The economic system. This diagram depicts the economic system as the flow of household labor and capital to firms (industries), in return for payment as wages and capital income. Households also receive goods and services from firms, in exchange for payment.

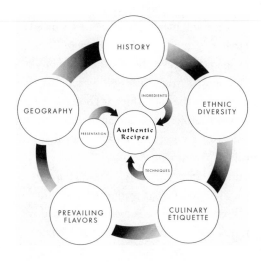

FIGURE 1.9 Factors that create a region's food culture. This diagram depicts the interaction of history, prevailing flavors, and culinary etiquette, which are cultural aspects of a food system.

tors. Figure 1.9 shows how a variety of factors interact to form a region's food culture. There is often a disconnect between people working on these aspects of the system and those working on production and economic issues. This is slowly changing as scientists and policy makers start to recognize the advantages of systems thinking that is not limited to the perspective of a single subject matter discipline.

Using Systems Thinking to Analyze Food Systems

While a system is a set of things that are connected to work together, systems thinking is aimed at understanding the underlying structure of the connections, not just the individual parts. It's an approach that focuses on interactions, cycles, flows, and patterns rather than characteristics of separate pieces. This can reveal leverage points for change and inform decisions that lead to desired outcomes instead of unintended consequences.

Systems thinking has been used for thousands of years, perhaps as the most common form of human thinking until the development of Western rational thought.[4] Many indigenous people integrated an appreciation for systems into their cultural traditions and ways of life, especially around nature. Today, the need for systems thinking is clear if modern society is to learn how to protect the systems that make up the natural world. However, specialized, reductionist thinking (which simplifies complex ideas to the point of distorting or obscuring them) is deeply entrenched in many organizations and professional disciplines. People don't switch easily from reductionism to systems approaches.

It can be a challenge to apply systems thinking to something as complex as a food system. Any action in the system will inevitably generate a side effect or an unanticipated consequence that may or may not be acceptable. Thus the system as a whole can't be tightly managed, even though that may be one's intent. For example, changing a cropping system to no-till agriculture may reduce soil erosion and conserve carbon in the soil, which is good for the environment; but it may also require more herbicide use and alter soil chemistry so that the quantity of greenhouse gases generated is greater than that produced by tillage, which is bad for the environment.

Systems thinking is useful for understanding the larger context of a problem or a proposed solution. It is an approach that recognizes the inherent difficulty of managing complex sets of interactions. For people charged with managing some part of a system, the idea is to try to anticipate the consequences of an intervention, keep an eye out for surprises once it's made, and then makes adjustments.

All systems have certain characteristics; these are present whether one is looking at a business system, a food production system, or an ecosystem. *System boundaries* define what area one is analyzing or trying to affect; this determines which parts of the overall system are left in and which are left out. For example, one may be trying to improve a dairy farm's economic system. The boundary could be at the cow level (genetics, feed management, etc.), the farm level (cost and returns from various inputs, management skills of the farmer, etc.), or the societal level (milk supply and demand, land use, labor, etc.).

The overall system of dairy farming comprises a *hierarchy of systems* with different boundaries. The cow is a living system, and it is part of the dairy herd, which can be analyzed as a system. The herd is part of the farming system, which includes crop, land, and facilities management. The farm is imbedded in the local or regional dairy farming community, which is a system within the national dairy industry system.

Systems are not usually closed; they have *inputs and outputs*. Sticking with the dairy farm example and simplifying: feed, fuel, sunshine, and water come in; manure, milk, and nutrients go out. Money is both an input (income) and an output (expenses). Systems have *feedback loops*, too. For example, when the price of milk is high, farmers may increase milk production so they can make more money. They make more milk and more money for a while; then the additional supply of milk causes the price to drop, and farmers react to that.

Emergent properties of a system are characteristics that appear at a certain level of complexity but do not exist in smaller parts of the system, lower in the hierarchy. The cow is alive but its component parts, such as the reproductive system or digestive system, by themselves are not. The farm generates revenue but that property emerges as a result of the cows, the crops, farm infrastructure, and the market.

Levels of Food Systems

Food systems function at the individual, household, local, regional, national, and global levels (fig. 1.10). The levels, or scales, in this hierarchy are

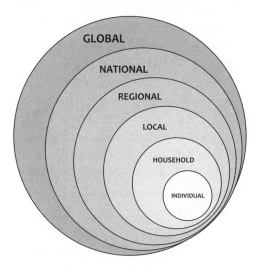

FIGURE 1.10 Levels of a food system. A food system has a hierarchy of levels, or scales, and each reflects and responds to social, cultural, political, economic, health, and environmental conditions, whether in a household kitchen or through a nation's food policies.

often operational at the same time, and they interact. For example, consider coffee. More than half of American adults choose to begin their day with a cup of coffee.[5] Some coffee drinkers prefer free-trade organic coffee, and they are willing and able to pay more for it. They might buy coffee at a local café that buys its beans from a regional distributor. That distributor may in turn buy from regional grower cooperatives in Latin America and Africa. Other coffee drinkers' household budgets might limit their spending on coffee, so they buy inexpensive national brands at a supermarket owned by a global corporation. Those brands contain beans purchased as a commodity traded on the international market. Any decisions made about a morning "cup of Joe" have the potential to affect one's individual health and well-being, a household budget, the revenues of local, regional, and national companies selling coffee, and the livelihoods of coffee producers and their communities on different continents. The same is true for almost everything we eat and drink.

INDIVIDUAL FOOD SYSTEMS. This level of a food system is focused on personal decisions about food, which include how to acquire, prepare, serve, give away, eat, store, and clean it.[6] These decisions and resulting behaviors are influenced by many factors, including life experience, cultural and social factors, and the need to balance different values such as affordability and quality. The decisions a person makes about food can differ depending on the situation, and they can change over time. For example, when people eat out, their diet is often different from the one they follow when they cook at home, and few middle-aged people eat the same way they did as a teenagers.

There are many ways to categorize people's eating habits and interactions with the food system. For example, in the United States, 5 percent of people consider themselves vegetarians, and 2 percent say they are vegans.[7] About 3 percent of Americans buy kosher food.[8] Although only 4 percent of all food and beverage sales are for organic products,[9] 75 percent of U.S. consumers say they use organic products.[10] In western North Carolina a survey found that more than half the respondents spent at least 10 percent of their food budget on local food.[11] A statewide study in Florida found that 53 percent of respondents purchased local foods at grocery stores, and 62 percent purchased local foods at farmers' markets, roadside stands, or U-pick operations.[12] About 15 percent of Americans are served by SNAP, the Supplemental Nutrition Assistance Program, formerly called the food stamp program.[13] Individual decisions about food can be aggregated at the household level, helping us understand how families interact with food systems.

HOUSEHOLD FOOD SYSTEMS. Most households are groups of people, often related, who live together and function as a unit. In terms of food, they may eat together, share a household food budget, and affect one another's eating behaviors, especially in the case of parental influence on children. The household food system can be described by a variety of measures. For example, about 15 percent of U.S. households are food-insecure sometime during the year, and nearly 6 percent have very low food security, meaning that their food intake is disrupted at times because they lack money or other resources for food.[14] Twenty percent of households with children are food-insecure.[15]

As income rises, households spend more money on food, but food expenses are a smaller portion of their total income than in poorer households. Households in the middle of the income scale spend an average of $5,620 per year on food, or 12 percent of their annual income, while the lowest-income households spend $3,547 on food, or 36 percent of their income.[16] Almost one-third of all U.S. households participate in food gardening, and about 3 percent of all households raise chickens.[17] These measures help us understand food systems at the household level, and they can help us paint a picture of food systems on a larger scale, at the local, regional, and national level.

LOCAL FOOD SYSTEMS. Although there is a lot of interest in local food, there are many different definitions of it. With no universally accepted definition of a local food system, the label "local food" is often based on a geographic concept related to the distance between food producers and consumers.[18] In addition to geographic proximity of producer and consumer, local food may also be considered to include certain social and production characteristics, such as fair treatment of workers and sustainable production methods.

Local food systems are frequently associated with direct marketing from the farm to the consumer or to retailers and institutions in the same geographic location as the farm. Direct-to-consumer markets include farmstands, farmers' markets, and community-supported agriculture, while direct-to-retailer sales include convenience markets, supermarkets, and restaurants. Institutions include colleges, hospitals, prisons, schools, and senior centers.

A recent analysis of the Los Angeles County food system found that it produces $326 million dollars of fresh produce annually and is home to 1,734 commercial farms. It also contains 1,261 urban agricultural sites. Looking beyond a single county to the ten-county foodshed within two hundred miles of downtown Los Angeles, the analysis found 23,000 farms that sell $16 billion of crops. This food system (it could be called local or regional, depending on one's definition) employs 1.3 million people in farmwork, food processing, distribution, food service, and retail, accounting for 1 in every 7.5 jobs in the area.[19]

REGIONAL FOOD SYSTEMS. These systems are place-based, as are local food systems, but "place" is conceived more broadly.[20] There is no bright line, no distinct boundary between local and regional food systems. "Local" is often thought to mean a city, town, or a few counties—but to some it is a state. "Regional" may also mean a cluster of counties or a cluster of states. In general, regional food systems aggregate smaller local communities in order to accommodate larger scales of production and economic activity. In a regional food system, direct marketing is not paramount; rather, regional identity has value in the food marketplace to consumers and producers. As Kate Clancy and Kathryn Ruhf explain:

> An ideal regional food system describes a system in which as much food as possible to meet the population's food needs is produced, processed, distributed, and purchased at multiple levels and scales within the region, resulting in maximum resilience, minimum importation, and significant economic and social return to all stakeholders in the region. This is known as "self-reliance"—as opposed to "self-sufficiency" wherein everything eaten is supplied within the target area. . . . local is a necessary but not sufficient component of a regional food system. Regional is larger geographically and in terms of functions—volume/supply, food needs, variety, supply chains, markets, land use, and policy. A regional food system includes multiple "locals" within a state, and those that cross state boundaries.[21]

Regional food systems can be delineated and measured in many ways; one such measure is the nature of their agricultural production. The U.S. Department of Agriculture (USDA) has identified nine "resource regions" of the country that share patterns of farming, financial performance of farms, and economic well-being of farm households.[22] These commonalities within a region, and differences among the regions, stem from the effects that climate, soil, water, and topography have on the types of crops and livestock that thrive in a region. For example, the Heartland region, with its deep soils and open spaces, contains 27 percent of all U.S. cropland and 22 percent of all farms, and it accounts for 23 percent of the value of all farm production, mostly as grains and cattle. The Eastern Uplands region located in Appalachia features mountainous terrain that limits farm size and production. It contains the smallest farms of any region, 15 percent of the nation's total. Many of these are part-time and produce cattle, tobacco, and poultry. The Fruitful Rim is a non-contiguous region that spans the milder climates of the coastal West and South. It accounts for 22 percent of U.S. farm production value, largely from high-value fruit, vegetable, nursery, and cotton farms. Together, regional food systems within the United States make up the national food system.

NATIONAL FOOD SYSTEMS. The food system of a country is easier to define than a local or regional food system because the geographic boundaries are clear. In addition, many features of the food system as a whole, such as most food policies and regulations, are set up on a national basis. In the United States, farm labor, food safety, pesticide use, and product labeling are all guided by federal regulations to which regional and local food systems must adhere. Cooperative Extension, the Department of Agriculture, the Department of Health and Human Services, the Department of Labor, the National Institute for Food and Agriculture, and many other national entities have enormous influence on lower levels of food systems. Market agreements for certain commodities like apples and milk affect supply and prices on the national level. A common platform for advertising, language, labeling, packaging, and transportation creates a relatively uniform playing field for food system actors across a huge geographic area.

Characteristics of national food systems can be described and compared by their agriculture, dietary intake, and much more. For example, about half the land in China, Mexico, and the United States is used for agricultural purposes, while in Canada, Egypt, and Sweden less than 10 percent of the land is arable.[23] The United States, Austria, and Greece lead the world in caloric intake per capita at more than 3,500 calories per person, while people in the Democratic Republic of the Congo, Eritrea, and Burundi consume the fewest calories, fewer than 2,000 per day.[24] All nations combined make up the global food system.

THE GLOBAL FOOD SYSTEM. Food at this level can be measured by overall production, its movement around the planet, and food security of the world's population. For example, total world production of corn is about 900 million metric tons (MMT) annually; wheat production is about 700 MMT, rice and oilseed crops average about 500 MMT, and soybean production is in the range of 250 MMT.[25] The total cost of imported food is about $1.1 trillion, $675 million of which is for developed countries and $415 million of which is for developing nations. Globally, well more than 800 million people, or 12 percent of the world's population, do not have a diet that meets their metabolic energy requirements.[26] The vast majority of hungry people live in developing regions. Some progress has been made to alleviate hunger over the past twenty years as food availability has risen faster than the average dietary energy requirements, and the quality of diets has improved.

Even in the days when all food systems were primarily local, hundreds of years ago, efforts were made to import spices and exotic foods that were not available nearby. The list of imported foods has, of course, greatly expanded to include many high-value imported products such as coffee beans, cocoa/

chocolate, oils, seafood, fruits, and vegetables. Imports of agricultural products to the United States exceed $100 billion annually.[27] Meanwhile, U.S. exports of agricultural products have tripled during the past decade to nearly $140 billion. Grains, oilseeds, and livestock products top the list of exports; China, Canada, and Mexico are currently the largest buyers.

Clearly, just about everyone is a participant in the global food system, and this has a significant influence on the diets, economies, environmental quality, and policies of national food systems, as well as on the lower levels of food systems within each nation.

Why Study Food Systems?

Food systems in the United States today provide unparalleled productivity. However, this has led to concerning levels of diet-related health problems, foodborne disease, hunger, and agricultural pollution. A quick look at the numbers shows some of the problems with this system:

- 67 percent of U.S. adults are overweight and 34 percent are obese;[28]
- 17 million households have difficulty obtaining enough food at some time during the year;[29]
- Food-borne illness affects an estimated 76 million people each year.[30]

Meanwhile, the agricultural landscape in the United States is under threat, seriously challenging the sustainable production of food: 42 million acres of farmland have been lost since 1987, and just 2.6 percent of all farms now account for 59 percent of the nation's gross agricultural sales.[31] This consolidation means that we're highly reliant on fossil fuel for transportation and storage and vulnerable when that fuel supply is threatened or becomes prohibitively expensive.

Likewise, food safety risk is amplified by aggregating food. Just think of how many people can be made ill by the meat of one contaminated cow when it's pooled with meat from thousands of other cows to produce ground beef. In addition, runoff from fertilizer- and pesticide-intensive agriculture is responsible for polluting 48 percent of the nation's river-miles and 41 percent of lake-acres; 18 percent of U.S. estuaries have impaired water quality.[32]

The range of food system issues having significant economic, environmental, and social consequences for society is staggering, with both positive and negative outcomes. New approaches are needed that use systems thinking to redesign major food system components in order to avoid undesirable side effects. Part of this thinking involves accounting for and placing value on externalities not captured by the current market value of food.

Working to Improve Food Systems

Food systems are enormous, complicated entities. They can be thought of and analyzed from many perspectives. Combining these perspectives to understand the interactions and connections among different components requires systems thinking. Food systems also include a wide range of scales, from individual people and their households, to local and regional communities, to nations and global trade. Activities at these scales overlap and affect one another, so it is simplistic to discuss them as if they functioned independently.

Clearly, it's a challenge to understand a complex food system, let alone act to improve it. Focusing on one facet at one time can be helpful, but each facet is connected to many other parts of the system. To be effective, focus must not lead to reductionism. This book describes a wide range of specific issues related to food systems, while remaining cognizant of how they are interconnected. Each chapter provides background on an issue, summarizes the key concerns, and describes opportunities and actions taken to address it. These actions are often, if not always, at the local level. While the book emphasizes local food system efforts to improve sustainability, we recognize that these take place in the context of regional, national, and global systems. The issues covered in this book all have an impact on economic viability, environmental health, and social well-being, but in different ways. Case studies are provided to illustrate successes, challenges, and realities of on-the-ground work that enhance the sustainability of food systems.

The goal of the book is to help readers develop a more comprehensive understanding of food systems by summarizing the relevant history and current data on key issues, as well as by presenting the personal perspectives of a variety of people working in and on such systems. The issues we address are commonly discussed in the media or in agricultural and food texts, but many times important details are omitted, details that are needed to mitigate dogmatic perspectives. Equipped with a broader and more nuanced understanding of these issues, students, educators, researchers, activists, and the general public should be better able to take action toward healthier food systems in the future.

2 ∽ *Local Food Systems*

Local food is all the rage and that may be a good thing. Local food is cred-ited with conserving energy, making better use of environmental resources, contributing to local economies, being fresher and tastier than other food, providing greater nutritional value, and building community.[1] On the other hand, it has been argued that local food systems are not inherently good, and they may be as just or unjust, sustainable or unsustainable, secure or insecure as other food systems at other scales, depending on their context.[2]

Local food has had some documented positive impacts, such as creating marketing opportunities for small farms. Direct sales of local food have in-creased in recent years, and small farms account for the vast majority of these sales.[3] Another positive impact attributable, at least in part, to the "local food movement" is the explosion in food system analysis and planning by com-munities across the country. These thoughtful examinations are likely to lead to a wide array of concrete actions aimed at creating a healthier food system.

The extent of other benefits provided by purchasing local food depends on the specific context being considered, and many of them, like improving peo-ple's diets, are a function of diverse factors that are not all related to the source of food. In short, there are limits to what a local food system can accomplish. Taken out of proportion, enthusiasm for local food can be a distraction from a wide range of issues that need attention when it comes to how all of our food is grown, marketed, and consumed.[4] Local food systems exist within the context of regional, national, and international food systems, so they should not be managed, promoted, or evaluated in isolation.

What Is Local Food?

The most local food of all comes from our own home gardens and back-yard animals. Or does it? When you make raspberry jam in the summer, you might use your own fruit, but you probably also use sugar—a commodity that's traded on a global scale. The eggs that come from your family's small flock of hens are local. Or are they? Perhaps you buy their feed from a nearby farm supply store, but it's grown somewhere in the Midwest Grain Belt. The tomatoes growing in the garden that you pop in your mouth, fresh off the vine and warm from the sun, are local. But to what extent? Where did the seeds come from? What is used to fertilize them?

Local food systems are one level in the overall food system hierarchy, and they interact with the smaller individual and household levels as well as the larger regional, national, and global levels. For example, at the national level, large food companies such as Whole Foods and Walmart launched "local food" purchasing initiatives in response to growing public interest in the source of their food, and McDonald's and Frito-Lay ran advertising to introduce their customers to some of the farmers they buy from. These efforts suggest that behaviors, relationships, and markets that have flourished in a relatively few local food systems have far-reaching effects once they reach a "tipping point" of consumer engagement.

Across the nation, interest in local food with an "identity" is evidenced by the recent boom in direct-from-the-farm markets. This interest is not equally distributed: local food sales tend to be stronger in the Northeast and the Northwest, and weaker in the South and Midwest (map 2.1).[5] Some states — for example, California, Michigan, and Vermont — are devoting considerable energy to the implementation of plans aimed at promoting stronger local and regional food systems. The size and scope of the food systems in these states vary considerably, along with the types of food produced.

Buying local food entails knowing something about the farm that produced it, the business that processed it, and the production practices that were used along the way. To many people, a local food is one that comes from a known location close by. If you pass a farm on your daily travels and can see firsthand where the crops are grown or the livestock raised, you'll surely consider it to be local. But what about a farm that's located on the other side of a state, hundreds of miles away? That may be considered local to some people, but not to others.

Local food can also be associated with scale of production. Most people who live next to an industrial meat processing plant probably don't tout it as a source of local food. In part that's because it's doubtful they can buy products directly from that plant. They may not be able to get those products unless a nearby supermarket stocks them. Even then, the product label may not reveal its point of origin. If you live in certain parts of California or Florida, thousand-acre fruit or vegetable enterprises could be your local farms, and they may sell only to wholesale markets and have no interest in local marketing.

Local food is associated with direct-to-consumer retail sales because pro-

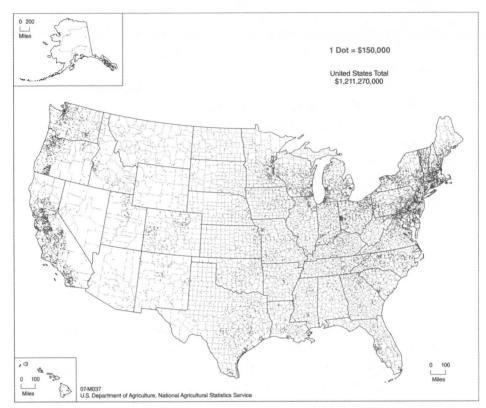

MAP 2.1 Value of agricultural products sold directly to consumers. Direct sales of food occur throughout the nation. More dots on the map indicate more direct sales from farms to consumers. Direct sales are strongest in the Northeast and on the West Coast, with some areas of concentration in the Midwest.

ducer and buyer proximity is required when products are purchased directly from farms, with the exception of Internet sales and mail order. Proximity also typifies certain markets where farms are separated from the consumer by just one distribution step, such as food sales to restaurants, general stores and food co-ops, or institutions like hospitals and schools (fig. 2.1). Local (and regional) food is also associated with "value chains" that aggregate food from multiple farms in order to deliver a large volume of food to nearby wholesale buyers or to support a processing enterprise. Typically a local or regional food value chain provides information about the nearby producers on the product label.

From place to place, there are very different ideas about how geographic proximity, connection to the farm, and scale of production connect to the concept of local food.[6] As more attention is given to strengthening these sys-

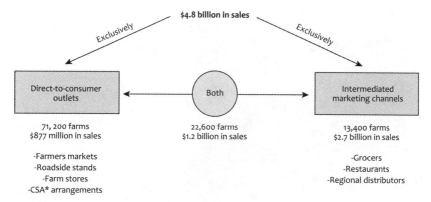

FIGURE 2.1 Annual sales of local food in the United States. Sales of local food from farms that sell only direct to consumers are less than $1 billion, while sales of local food from farms that sell only to intermediate buyers "one step removed" from consumers are nearly $3 billion. Sales of local food from farms that use both types of markets are $1.2 billion annually. (*CSA denotes community-supported agriculture.)

tems, it's important to examine what exactly "local" means—and what drives people to want local food. At the same time, we need to understand the benefits and promise of local food systems as well as their limitations.

Defining Local Food

The basis for calling a food "local" is sometimes a legal definition, and sometimes it isn't. In the 2008 Farm Bill, the federal government's key agriculture and food policy tool, Congress defined locally produced agricultural food products as those that are "raised, produced, and distributed in the locality or region in which the final product is marketed, so that the total distance the product is transported is less than four hundred miles from the origin of the product, or within the same state where the product is produced."[7] Three years later, Congress used a slightly different definition when it enacted food safety legislation that included an exemption for small, local producers, which were defined as those selling the majority of their food directly to consumers, restaurants, or retail food establishments located in the same state or not more than 275 miles from the farm.[8] These two definitions could also be considered appropriate for regional rather than local food systems, since they describe areas that extend several hundred miles. The distinction between local and regional food is not always clear.

The geographic boundary of a few hundred miles for a local food system supports the notion of food that can be delivered to the consumer by

FIGURE 2.2 Workers filling orders at a food hub. Food hubs aggregate, distribute, and market source-identified food from local and/or regional producers. The size of area served by food hubs varies, as do definitions of local and regional food, which in some cases overlap.

ground transportation within a day's time. It suggests, but does not guarantee, a shorter supply chain with a reduced number of transactions from producer to consumer than for food from farther away. This connects to the notion that storage, handling, and energy demands associated with local foods could be lower than for "commodity" foods (fig. 2.2). Conducting business in a small geographic area can also make it easier to form mutually beneficial relationships among different actors in a food system because they're more likely to share a common cultural, political, and regulatory environment.

It's not just the U.S. government that has developed regulatory criteria for local food. At the state level, a Vermont statute requires that foods labeled "local" must originate within the state or within 30 miles of the place where they are sold, measured directly, point to point.[9] In Illinois, local farm or food products are defined in statute as "products grown, processed, packaged, and distributed by Illinois citizens or businesses located wholly within the borders of Illinois."[10] Canada defines local foods in federal statute as manufactured, processed, produced, or packaged in a city, metropolitan area, town, village, municipality, or other area of a local government unit and sold only in that unit or adjacent units.[11]

Those who advocate eating locally grown food, dubbed "locavores" or "localvores," don't always depend on statutory definitions of local food; many have invented their own boundaries to define the limits of a local food system. The "100-Mile Diet" was popularized by two Canadian writers who pledged to eat only food produced within a 100-mile radius of their home in Vancouver.[12] The online magazine articles they wrote led to the publication of a book that topped the non-fiction bestseller list in Canada and inspired a reality television show, *The 100-Mile Challenge*, on Food Network Canada. Others have advocated for closer boundaries. Food activists in Athens County, Ohio,

www.jerseyfresh.nj.gov

FIGURE 2.3 Logos of programs promoting local foods. These logos may appear on products, at farms, or at stores and other locations where food is sold. They help consumers identify foods that meet a geographic criterion for being considered "local."

are championing the 30-mile meal. Individuals such as writer Vicki Robin have tested a 10-mile diet, making exceptions for oil, spices, and caffeine. In the best-selling book *Animal, Vegetable, Miracle*, writer Barbara Kingsolver and her family documented their attempts to grow most of their food themselves, buying other provisions from nearby farms and farmers' markets with just a few exceptions like spices.

"Buy Local" campaigns that promote local and regional food programs are also geographically based, but they tend to have flexible boundaries. Such programs often focus on building consumer awareness of an area's food system and increasing demand for food products from that area to promote farm viability and economic development; they're less concerned with specific distances that food travels. Buy Local campaigns are widespread in the United States, and their scale varies considerably. Some are statewide, like those in Maine, North Carolina, and Georgia. Others focus on a county or multi-county region; examples are "Appalachian Grown" in the mountain counties of North Carolina, Tennessee, Virginia, and Georgia and "Be a Local Hero, Buy Locally Grown" in western Massachusetts, which has the distinction of being the longest-running Buy Local campaign in the nation (fig. 2.3). Some programs focus on specific crops, like the "Jersey Fresh" program, an advertising, promotion, and quality-grading program aimed at informing consumers about the availability and variety of fruits and vegetables grown in New Jersey.[13]

LOCAL "PLUS." Besides a geographic framework for identifying food, there are social, environmental, or production practices that can create connections between consumers and food products. These connections may or may not be based on geography or proximity, although there are many instances in which location and desirable food attributes are combined—for example, seafood that is "Gulf of Maine Responsibly Harvested,"[14] Eco Apple labeling for northeastern apples grown using integrated pest management,[15] and pasture-raised beef from Ozark farms in northwest Arkansas (fig. 2.4).[16] Organic food labeling is regulated on a national basis by the USDA, but

FIGURE 2.4 Logos of foods that combine information about geographic location and production attributes. This information makes consumers aware of the point of origin and helps them to understand the sustainability of the production practices used to produce local food.

certification is carried out by USDA-accredited certification agencies, which may be state-based organizations or nonprofits. Thus, certified organic foods have both the USDA organic label and the label of the certification agency, like "Montana Certified Organic" or "Pennsylvania Certified Organic."

Local food is often considered to be a part of sustainable agriculture, which emphasizes community connections to farming and the food system. In places where commodity production (which involves farms selling undifferentiated products in bulk) has been in decline, one often sees the emergence of more diversified, smaller-scale farms that cater to markets closer to home. In many cases these markets have helped sustain farms that were struggling in the commodity market, in part because they can get a better price for their products and in part because local food is rooted in place-based commerce that is strengthened by social connections. When customers know their food producers (or their cousins, employees, etc.) personally, or their kids play on the same soccer team or attend the same school, they may be more motivated to buy the producers' products. This type of social connection may be the most powerful attribute of a local food system: shared experiences, common norms, and mutually beneficial transactions that reinforce trust and shared values and create allegiances in the marketplace. In other words, the underlying value of a local food system has a lot to do with positive relationships among people.

Sustainable Agriculture and Local Food Systems

Sustainable agriculture emphasizes place-based management that benefits farmers, consumers, their communities, and the environment. Unlike organic

FIGURE 2.5 Sustainable Agriculture Research and Education (SARE) program. This program of the U.S. Department of Agriculture and the National Institute of Food and Agriculture has funded many projects over the past twenty-five years that have helped move "alternative" farming and marketing practices into the mainstream. These practices include cover cropping, direct marketing, farm-to-school programs, management intensive grazing, and organic production.

agriculture, sustainable agriculture does not involve a set of standards, but like organic agriculture, it emphasizes ecological management on the farm over the use of purchased farm inputs like pesticides and fertilizers. Off the farm, sustainable agriculture recognizes the important connection between healthy farms and supportive communities that can be expressed not just through markets but also in land use, food access, food culture, and more. Any type or size of farm, including large-scale commodity producers, can be more sustainable, but much of the focus of sustainable agriculture programs has been at the local and regional levels, in part as a response to the challenges posed by the commodity food system.

To promote sustainable agriculture, Congress created the Low Input Sustainable Agriculture program, or LISA, in the 1980s. After several years, LISA was renamed SARE, for Sustainable Agriculture Research and Education (fig. 2.5).[17] The name change came about because sustainability isn't promoted by simply reducing farm inputs; it requires the use of different types of inputs, like biological processes and mutually beneficial market relationships. The SARE program funds research on and education about practices like using cover crops in place of fertilizers to provide nutrients and maintain soil organic matter, intensive pasture management to produce livestock at lower cost without having to till the land for row crops, and a range of market approaches that build ties between farmers and their communities, such as farmers' markets, community-supported agriculture, food hubs, and farm-to-institution programs. The success of sustainable agriculture practices is measured not only by traditional yardsticks—yield, sales, and profit—but also by their impact on things like soil health, water quality, farm viability, and farmer satisfaction.[18]

In some ways sustainable agriculture is like the practice of human medicine; just as farms are place-based, healing is person-based. Each local food system, like each patient a doctor examines, has unique needs and resources. There may be general concepts that apply to the whole population, but their application is something best done up close and personal. Another similarity between sustainable agriculture and medicine is that there isn't a regimented way to practice them. The goal is to thoughtfully pursue health and sustainability, not to perfect a set of instructions. We want doctors and nurses to spend their time caring for patients, not arguing about definitions of health. Farmers and consumers too should work to make the food system healthier, without getting bogged down in labels and geographic boundaries.

Who Buys Local and Why

A great many concerns and desires drive both sustainable agriculture practices and the local food movement. Many have to do with a growing awareness of the problems related to what we eat and how it's produced. It's doubtful that many individual consumers are aware of, or motivated by, more than a few of these issues. When they buy local food, a lot of consumers are driven by personal interests, whether culinary preference, health, greater confidence in food safety, or a positive experience associated with the market environment itself. These personal motivations for buying local food can be reinforced by a desire to have a positive impact on the local community.

A recent USDA Economic Research Service report on local foods looked at a number of studies and concluded that local food consumers are demographically diverse, yet they are very similar in their motivations for buying local food.[19] People value freshness, supporting their local economy, and knowing the source of the products they buy. Some studies found that education and income level did not affect whether consumers were likely to purchase local food, while others found that people with more education and above-average incomes were more likely to be local food buyers.

Data from a recent national survey of nearly 1,000 food shoppers indicated that the strongest factors associated with buying local food were enjoyment of cooking, shopping at health food stores, and purchasing organic food; attitudes or behaviors related to the environment and health were not much of a factor.[20] Another national survey of 1,300 shoppers found that freshness was the most important food-buying criterion, followed by price. Local sourcing came third, ahead of organic or natural sourcing,[21] suggesting that shoppers may have more confidence in local food being sustainably produced than they do in organic food. Across all income levels, shoppers were willing to pay more for local food; 71 percent of affluent families would pay more, as would 57 percent of low-income families. However, the local premium was small: only 8 percent of shoppers would pay more than 10 percent extra for local food. Farmers' markets and farm stores were the most trusted sources of safe local food, while big-box retailers and online grocers were least trusted.

Local governments may also prefer to buy local products, including food, to reinvest taxpayer dollars in their own economies. But just like individual shoppers they have limits on how much extra they can pay. Since government spending is regulated, statutes with specific criteria are needed to guide local purchasing decisions. Some states have vague criteria that are not likely to be effective if, for example, they simply state that public agencies should buy local products when they can. A variety of more specific approaches are being used by states to more forcefully promote local food buying (see box 2.1).

A recent study in Nova Scotia explored local food-buying perceptions among personnel working in wholesale food procurement for institutions (health care facilities, hospitals, prisons, and schools) and industry (distributors, food service companies, and suppliers).[22] There were commonalities as well as differences in the benefits and barriers to procuring local foods that these people identified. Food freshness and support of the local economy were identified as benefits of local food by people in all sectors of both institutions and industry. Institutional personnel also identified sustainability as a benefit. Benefits identified by industry personnel were customer service and a sense of community.

Barriers identified by all institutional and industry personnel were internal habits, distribution, supply, and price. Distribution barriers included the problem of multiple deliveries needed to obtain local food; supply barriers had to do with the amount, variety, and seasonality of local food availability. Health care and academic institutions were more concerned about liability than were other types of buyers, so they had concerns about quality assurance. Industry personnel felt that their needs and requirements concerning local food could be better communicated. This study shows that, even within a similar group of stakeholders in the food system, many factors affect local food-buying behavior. People who do buy locally often have the perception that this will have a beneficial impact on the environment, the local economy, or people's health — whether this is true or not.

Impacts of Local Food

LOCAL FOOD, ENERGY USE, AND GREENHOUSE GAS EMISSIONS. It's easy to assume that because local food travels a smaller distance to market than non-local food, energy use and greenhouse gas (GHG) emissions would be lower per unit of food. That is, assuming all other things to be equal in a

2.1 *State Policies That Promote Local Food Purchasing*

Many state governments have enacted policies that promote local food purchasing, using one or more of the following methods to favor local producers:

- Tie-breaker preference. When two producers (one out-of-state and one in-state) submit identical bids, the in-state producer receives the preference and is awarded the contract. Bids must be identical on price, quality, quantity, and availability.
- Price "reasonably exceeds" preference. When two producers (one out-of-state and one in-state) submit bids that are equal on everything but the price, the higher-priced, in-state producer will receive a preference so long as the in-state producer's price only "reasonably exceeds" the out-of-state producer's price. "Reasonably exceeds" is generally defined as a price that is both "reasonable" and one that can be covered by the purchaser's existing budget.
- Price percentage preference. When two producers (one out-of-state and one in-state) submit bids that are identical on everything but the price, the higher-priced, in-state producer gets a preference so long as the in-state producer's price is only a certain percentage higher than the out-of-state producer's price.
- Reciprocal preference. When two producers (one out-of-state and one in-state) submit bids that are identical on everything but the price, the higher-priced, in-state producer receives a preference if the out-of-state producer would receive a price percentage preference in his or her home state.
- Quotas. A certain percentage of the food purchased by schools is required to come from in-state producers by a certain date.
- Grants. Schools can apply for grant money to help cover the costs of purchasing food from in-state producers or for kitchen equipment and trainings necessary to purchase and prepare local foods.

Meghan Scully, *Preferences That Support Local Farmers: A 50 State Review* (Denver: Prevention Services Division, Colorado Department of Public Health and Environment Government Purchasing, 2012).

supply chain, more food transportation would require more fuel for vehicles and more electricity for storage. However, the supply chains for local food and conventional food from farther away involve very different methods of production, marketing, transportation, and storage, so an honest comparison requires life-cycle analyses that account for as many aspects as possible of the processes that get food from field to plate. Transportation by itself is a small part of the overall food system.

A number of studies have evaluated food transportation energy use and

FIGURE 2.6 Community-supported agriculture pickup at the farm. CSAs have the potential to reduce energy use in several ways. The use and disposal of food packaging are avoided or minimized, refrigeration is avoided when produce is harvested shortly before customer pickup, and the farmer uses no fuel to make deliveries.

GHG emissions, and they do not agree on whether local food systems are more energy- and emissions-efficient.[23] Different conclusions can result from the use of different boundaries on the systems that are analyzed, differences between local and long-distance supply chains, and variation among local food markets considered by the studies (fig. 2.6).

The type of food eaten by consumers appears to have a more significant influence on energy use and GHG emissions than whether food is local or not. Using life-cycle analysis, Weber and Matthews found that 83 percent of the average U.S. household's annual GHG emissions associated with food came from its production, transporting food accounted for only 11 percent of GHG emissions, and final delivery from producer to retail contributed only 4 percent. However, different foods varied greatly in the intensity of their GHG emissions, with red meat being about one and a half times more GHG-intensive than chicken or fish. Thus a dietary shift may be a more effective means of lowering an average household's food-related climate footprint than buying local.[24] Consumer choices within a local food system can have a large influence on energy use and GHG generation (box 2.2).

ECONOMIC BENEFITS OF LOCAL FOOD. Studies suggest that local foods can have a positive impact on local economic activity.[25] This occurs when purchases of local food replace purchases of food imported from outside the area, increasing revenues for local food businesses, which in turn spend more money on local labor and production supplies from within the area. Shifting to local purchases can also increase the circulation of dollars in the local economy if additional functions such as advertising, financing, packaging, storage, and transportation are localized.

However, unless the total population consumes more food, increasing the economic activity of local food systems must reduce economic activity in the location(s) where the food was formerly produced or processed. From a national policy perspective, creating economic winners and losers by shifting food to a more local system may be justifiable if other benefits result from more local food consumption, such as improved health and nutrition or greater food security.

LOCAL FOOD AND HUMAN HEALTH. There are two ways that local food can improve human nutrition and health: by improving the quality of food that people are already consuming and/or by increasing the availability and thus the consumption of healthier food.[26] If food is fresher and has not traveled far, it may contain more nutrients than the same food that comes from

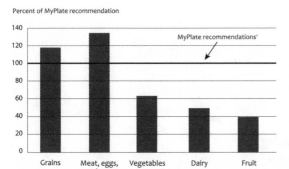

Percent of MyPlate recommendation

FIGURE 2.7 Average amounts of foods consumed compared with nutrition recommendations in the United States. Many people in this country do not eat the recommended quantities of fruits and vegetables.

farther away, though our modern food transportation system tends to move food relatively quickly and optimize storage conditions in order to minimize reductions in food quality. Conversely, a local system that does not sell its products in a timely fashion or fails to control the storage temperature and humidity may offer no benefit in quality compared with more distant foods.

Many local food programs try to improve the type of food people eat. These programs rely on locally based relationships to increase consumer interest in, and consumption of, healthy local food. Examples include farm-to-school programs, farmers' market coupons through the WIC (Women, Infants and Children) program, and subsidies offered for community-supported agriculture memberships where low-income families and seniors in some locations receive weekly allotments of fresh vegetables, fruit, and other farm products. In some areas, consumer food co-ops also play an important role in connecting farmers to consumers and influencing the types of food their members eat.

When education, marketing, and policy aimed at promoting local food also make healthier food choices more available, affordable, and desirable to a wide range of people, they can be important tools for addressing diet-related health problems. Since more than half of all local food sales are of fresh produce,[27] it may be that stronger local food systems can increase the availability of these foods and help improve dietary behavior (fig. 2.7).

LOCAL FOOD AND FOOD SECURITY. Food security can be thought of in terms of access to food by individuals and families or as the ability of a locale such as a community or region to maintain a supply of food. Today, many people are food-insecure, and some go hungry even though they live in areas with an abundant food supply. Poverty is a big reason for this. Local food efforts that increase the supply of food without addressing the economic constraints that people face in obtaining food will not do much to improve

FIGURE 2.8 Passively cooled crop storage. Supermarkets may have empty shelves during a major storm event if long-distance transportation of food is impeded. A local food supply can provide a measure of "food security" in such situations. If the local food storage is resilient in the face of power outages that often occur during severe storms, it further enhances food security. This passively cooled underground vegetable storage requires no electricity to keep crops cool.

individual or family food security. Similarly, accepting payment through Electronic Benefit Transfer (EBT), formerly known as food stamps, which subsidize purchases for low-income families) at farmers' markets may increase access to fresh food but will not increase the amount of food people can buy unless the prices are lower than at other locations where they shop. Low-income farmers' markets where farmers agree to maintain affordable prices have been developed to address this issue.

Food security at a larger scale has not been well studied. It seems likely that more local and regional food production, processing, and distribution systems offer greater resilience in the face of disruptions due to extreme weather, shortages of fuel or electricity, a pandemic flu, or other events that could lead to a rapid decline in food availability should supermarkets run out of food or be forced to close (fig. 2.8). Large corporate entities that distribute food to most of our stores have the ability to cope with short-term disruptions using technology to anticipate storms and to track and reroute products.[28] However, in the face of more widespread or longer-term disruption, it is important to maintain some food-producing capacity closer to home, with the aim of feeding people with less reliance on interstate transportation and fossil energy. This strategy could help enhance community food security and emergency preparedness across the nation.

Local Food and Community

The embedding of local agriculture and food production in the community has been termed "civic agriculture" by Thomas Lyson.[29] Civic agriculture has at its heart a network of producers and consumers bound together by place-based local institutions and organizations. Civic agriculture differs significantly in its structure and goals from "conventional" food systems, which have become increasingly consolidated and controlled by large corporations. Rather than focusing on financial returns from the mass production and mass retailing of vast quantities of standardized food, civic agriculture filters the economic imperative to make a profit through a set of cooperative and mutually supporting social relations in order to also solve community problems (box 2.3).

While geographic proximity between consumers and producers can help foster sustainable agriculture and civic agriculture, it is not essential to fulfilling many of the societal goals articulated by these approaches. That's because every food purchase one makes—from a local, regional, or international source—is an endorsement of the conditions under which it was produced. The majority of food products today keep consumers in the dark; their labels don't reveal the farms they come from, the communities they were produced in, or the practices that were used to produce them. As a result it is hard to make informed decisions about what one is endorsing when "investing" food dollars. Supporters of local food are making an effort to fight that anonymity, and their effort extends to products from distant places as well. For example, coffee and chocolate (which many of us intend to consume even though they are not local) sometimes have labels in the marketplace that encourage consumers to support the well-being of their producers and local communities — despite the fact that they are far away.

As we celebrate local food, let's not lose sight of the need to support much wider changes in food systems. We want our own communities to have healthy local food systems, but an equally compelling goal, given our engagement in the global economy, is to support markets that provide a fair price to farmers, encourage stewardship of natural resources, and promote community well-being all over the world.

3 ∾ *The Business of Food and Farming*

Food and agriculture are big business. Together they contribute well over $700 billion to the U.S. gross domestic product, or about 5 percent of the nation's economy.[1] The majority of food-related economic activity comes from food services, followed by manufacturing, and then farming. More than 16 million jobs are related to agriculture and food, or about 9 percent of all employment. More than 10 million people work at eating and drinking places; 2.6 million work on farms, and 1.5 million work in food manufacturing.

The business of food is not just big; it's also complicated. It involves many relationships in the supply chains that deliver food from the farm to the consumer (fig. 3.1). Simply defined, a supply chain is the sequence of steps involved in the production and distribution of a product. Supply chains may be relatively short, as with direct-to-consumer sales of products from the farm, or they may be long, as with processed foods that require a variety of raw ingredients and are sold to a variety of buyers in different locations.

Food Consumption and Waste

Food supply chains are developed to meet the demand for food, and in the United States that demand is growing. Consumers, businesses, and government spend about $1.3 trillion on food and beverages each year, which is about twice as much as we spent twenty years ago (fig. 3.2).[2]

Although we spend more money than ever on food, food spending as a proportion of household income has declined. Food expenditures currently account for less than 10 percent of disposable income for the average American household; in 1960 it accounted for more than 17 percent (fig. 3.3).[3] Households with high incomes spend more money on food than low-income households, but as income rises, food costs represent a smaller portion of disposable income (fig. 3.4). Of the money people spend on food, very little goes to food producers; most goes to other parts of a food system, such as food services, processing, retailers, finance, energy, packaging, and transportation (fig. 3.5).

The mix of foods purchased by the average consumer does not meet the

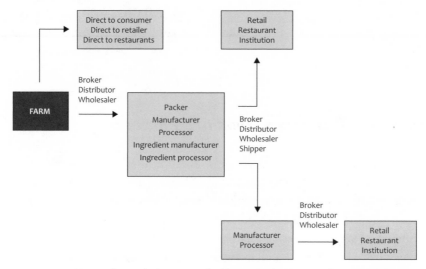

FIGURE 3.1 Diagram of a supply chain. Once food leaves the farm, it can take a variety of paths to the final consumer.

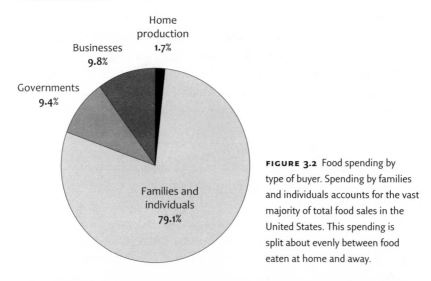

FIGURE 3.2 Food spending by type of buyer. Spending by families and individuals accounts for the vast majority of total food sales in the United States. This spending is split about evenly between food eaten at home and away.

USDA's recommendations for a healthy diet that is high in fruits and vegetables, whole grains, and low-fat meat and dairy products.[4] Consumers allocate too much of their food budgets to less healthy foods that are high in sugars and refined grains. On average, households in the Northeast and the West purchase healthier foods than those in the Midwest or the South. As income rises, households make slightly healthier food choices, but households at all income levels have a long way to go to meet current dietary recommendations (fig. 3.6).

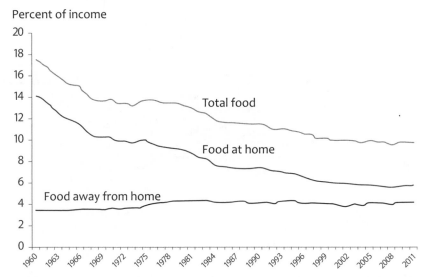

FIGURE 3.3 Percentage of per capita disposable income spent on food in the United States. Over the past half century, the cost of food for Americans in terms of percentage of disposable income has steadily declined. Most of the decline has been in the cost of food purchased for home consumption; there has been a slight increase in the percentage of disposable income spent on eating out.

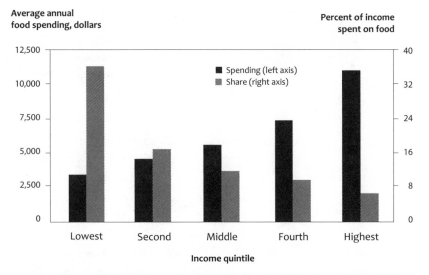

FIGURE 3.4 Average food spending and household income. The highest-income households in the United States spend an average of more than $10,000 per year on food, which is less than 8 percent of their disposable income. The poorest households spend an average of about $3,500 per year on food, or about a third of their disposable income.

FIGURE 3.5 Breakdown of the consumer food dollar. Of a typical dollar spent by U.S. consumers on domestically produced food, 31 cents goes to food service establishments, 22 cents to food processors, 12 cents to food retailers, and only 11 cents to food producers and agribusiness.

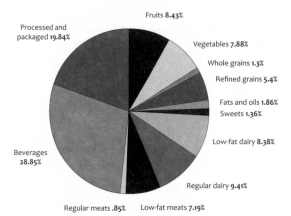

FIGURE 3.6 Different types of food purchased by consumers at grocery stores, as a percentage of total food purchases. The average U.S. household spends about half of its food shopping dollars on beverages and packaged foods.

Americans now consume an estimated 2,538 calories per person per day, up from 2,064 calories forty years ago.[5] Over the course of one year, a typical American adult eats an average of 58 pounds of chicken, 54 pounds of beef, and 33 pounds of cheese, in addition to 86 pounds of tomatoes and 83 pounds of potatoes, much of this as canned tomatoes, pizza, and french fries. People also consume an average of 10 pounds of bananas, 9 pounds of apples, and 130 pounds of sweeteners, evenly split between refined sugar and corn sweeteners.[6]

Most food that is not consumed by people or animals goes to waste. It's estimated that 133 billion pounds, or almost one-third of the 430 billion pounds of food available for human consumption in the United States each year, is not eaten.[7] The retail value of this waste is $162 billion. Some food loss is inevitable during cooking and when perishable food must be discarded to ensure food safety. In addition, there are costs associated with recovering food that would otherwise be wasted. However, much food waste is avoidable. For example, in-store food losses, which are estimated to be more than 40 billion pounds each year, result in part from discarding perfectly edible food due to overstocking and expired "sell by" dates. Only about 10 percent of available, edible wasted food is recovered each year in the United States.[8]

There are many motivations for addressing the problem of food waste. Uneaten food rotting in landfills, where it accounts for a large portion of our nation's methane emissions, is the single largest component of U.S. municipal solid waste.[9] Recovery of just 15 percent of food that is now wasted would be enough to feed more than 25 million Americans, at a time when one in six Americans lacks a secure supply of food.

Food Marketing

There are two general categories of food products and two general categories of food markets. Food may be either a commodity or a differentiated product.[10] Markets may be direct to consumers, or they may involve intermediaries between the producer and the consumer.

Commodities are undifferentiated products; they have no unique identity in the marketplace. Every unit of a commodity is just like another to potential buyers, so tons of pork bellies or bushels of hard red winter wheat can be comingled from many different farms, and the price that the farmers get paid for these commodities will be the same. Farmers in this case are price-takers since they can't set the commodity price; it fluctuates in response to global and national demand. Commodity producers are not direct competitors, although one region may compete against another for market share; for example, Maine may compete with Idaho for the market share of potatoes. Generally speaking if the price of a commodity is higher than farmers' production plus transportation costs, they make money; if the price is lower, they lose money. Farm profitability depends on the average price, average costs, and volume of production over time.

Differentiated products are those that can be distinguished from similar products offered by other producers. The goal of producers is to offer a better product, or, more specifically, to get buyers to believe their product is better than the competition's. Producers set their own prices, but only within reason. The price of a differentiated product can be higher than that of similar products only if buyers perceive it has more value. Otherwise the product will be perceived as too expensive, and it won't sell. Consumers' "willingness to pay" a certain price for a certain food is affected by both real and not-so-real attributes of that food. It may actually taste better, be better for you, or not. Many food claims are not regulated by law. Advertising is generally aimed at differentiating products by persuading consumers, using fact or fiction, that one product is a better value than other products. Having a brand identity for a differentiated product allows consumers to locate it in the market and helps cultivate loyalty through marketing messages that strengthen their perception of a product's value.

DIRECT-TO-CONSUMER FOOD MARKETS. These markets include community-supported agriculture, farmers' markets, farmstands, and pick-your-own operations. Internet and mail-order sales are also direct to the consumer, without requiring face-to-face contact.

Community-supported agriculture, or CSA, allows consumers to "join" or "subscribe" to a farm as "members" entitled to a "share" of food in exchange for a payment, usually on an annual basis. The price of a CSA membership ranges from a few hundred dollars for a seasonal vegetable share in rural areas to several times that in more urbanized upscale locations, or for shares that offer produce plus other foods such as eggs, meats, and prepared foods. Some CSAs offer shares for different seasons: summer, fall, and winter. Others offer add-on options to a standard vegetable share for cut flowers, fruits, and other products.

Some CSAs are small, serving just a few neighborhood families; the farmer may be part-time, or the CSA may supplement other marketing methods. Other CSAs are quite large, some serving more than a thousand families. Large CSAs usually have several different distribution days, and either the farm is located near a lot of people or the shares are delivered by truck to sites in more populated areas, which may take hours each way. Multi-farm CSAs allow smaller farms, or larger farms specializing in just a few products, to aggregate goods and thus offer diversity over the season.

Successful CSAs have a well-organized production plan to maintain a steady and varied supply of products, whether they come from one farm or many farms. They also know how to assess and meet the needs of their members to retain them from year to year. The Robyn Van En Center, based at Wilson College in Pennsylvania, maintains a national database that now includes more than 1,650 CSA farms.[11]

Farmers' markets are places where groups of farmers and other vendors gather to sell directly to consumers. New Hampshire statute defines a farmers' market as "an event or series of events at which 2 or more vendors of agricultural commodities gather for purposes of offering for sale such commodities to the public. Commodities offered for sale must include, but are not limited to, products of agriculture."[12]

To participate, marketers pay a fee or percentage of sales for their booth or table space. Market managers coordinate the operation and promotion of the market. Managers may be volunteers in small markets or paid for their services in larger markets. Bona fide farmers' markets are different from flea markets, where anyone can sell just about anything; they have restrictions on who can participate, the types of products that may be sold, and where they come from. Successful farmers' markets have guidelines that address these and other issues (box 3.1).

Since the USDA's Agricultural Marketing Resource Center began tracking farmers' markets in 1994, the number has grown from 1,755 to 8,144 in 2013.[13] The states with the most farmers' markets include California (759), New York (637), Illinois (336), Michigan (331), and Ohio (300). Total annual sales at U.S. farmers' markets are estimated at $1 billion.

Farmstands, also known as roadside stands, roadside markets, or farm stores, may be located on a farm or at a nearby site with better means of access for customers, such as a well-traveled, paved road. These markets range from simple self-serve tables to sophisticated grocery-like facilities with a wide range of fresh and prepared food products. Like farmers' markets, farmstands may offer all kinds of products with no restriction on origin, or they may specialize in on-farm products from a specific geographic area.

States and localities vary in their regulation of farmstands. In addition to building codes and zoning issues that address construction, road setbacks, parking, lighting, and time of operation, there may be marketing regulations. In some jurisdictions, farms that sell processed or other value-added products are considered "retail food facilities," so they must comply with the same health and safety requirements as any retail food business, which can be costly.

Michigan recently passed a law exempting some farmstands from building codes that require plumbing and electric power.[14] To qualify, a farmstand cannot be larger than 400 square feet, it must be used only for seasonal retail trade in agricultural products, and at least 50 percent of the agricultural products offered for sale must be produced by the farmer who owns the farmstand.

The North Carolina Certified Roadside Farm Market program promotes roadside farm markets that sell primarily horticultural crops grown by the operator and other local farmers.[15] To qualify for certification, a roadside farm market must sell primarily agricultural commodities direct to the public, with a minimum of 51 percent of total sales from farm products grown by the market operator.

Good data are lacking on the number and type of roadside markets across the country. However, one USDA report stated that of all the farms engaged in direct marketing of local food, 32 percent used roadside stands and 10 percent used on-farm stores.[16]

Pick-your-own (PYO) or *U-pick operations* take place primarily on fruit farms where customers are able to harvest crops when they are ripe. PYO is often available at apple, blueberry, and strawberry farms where some customers are keen to get fresh fruit at a price that is lower than retail since the farmer saves on harvest costs. The reduced need for hired harvest labor is one advantage of PYO marketing for farms, but farm laborers may still be needed to park cars, direct pickers to the right location, and collect payment. PYO farms offer customers an outdoor experience, and this can enhance the farms' other marketing methods. PYO can complement sales at a farmstand, or it can supplement wholesale markets, as is the case for many apple orchards. The success of PYO is dependent in part on a farm's location: the farm needs to be close enough to a customer base that is sufficiently large to pick a lot of fruit when it is ripe. As with farmstands, good data are lacking on the number of farms that offer PYO and the sales that result.

Internet and mail-order sales depend on shipping rather than face-to-face contact with consumers. Product information is conveyed and relationships are developed through websites and/or catalogs. Some food products are better suited for shipping than others depending on their perishability and weight, both of which can affect packing and shipping costs for the producer.

INTERMEDIARY FOOD MARKETS. These markets include food service establishments, retail food stores, and wholesalers.

Food service establishments include commercial and non-commercial enterprises, such as restaurants and institutions. The U.S. food service industry has sales of about $600 billion in food each year, comparable to food retailing sales.[17] Commercial food service establishments include full-service restaurants, fast food outlets, caterers, hotels, recreational facilities, and cafeterias in places like retail stores. These markets account for the vast majority of food service sales. About three-quarters of all these commercial sales are those made by restaurants, evenly split between full-service and fast food operations. Non-commercial food services do not sell food directly to the general public; they include airlines, colleges and schools, day care centers, hospitals, military facilities, nursing homes, prisons, and senior centers. They serve about $100 billion of food annually.[18]

Retail food stores include grocers, supermarkets (grocers with annual sales of more than $2 million), and superstores (supermarkets larger than 30,000 square feet) as well as drugstores, warehouse stores, and small corner stores or general stores.[19] There are more than 200,000 retail food stores in the United States, which sell about $600 billion of food and non-food products. Groceries, supermarkets, and superstores account for more than 90 percent of these sales, convenience stores account for about 5 percent, and specialized food stores account for the rest. Twenty retail food chains sell two-thirds of all the groceries in the United States, and the long-term trend is for increasing concentration of sales among the largest grocery retailers.[20]

Food wholesalers assemble, store, and transport food to customers, including institutions, restaurants, retailers, other wholesalers, government, and other types of businesses. There are three types of food wholesalers: merchant wholesalers (or third-party wholesalers), manufacturers' wholesalers, and brokers. Merchant wholesalers buy groceries from manufacturers or processors and then sell them to retailers, institutions, and other businesses. Their sales account for about a third of all wholesale grocery sales.[21] Manufacturers' wholesalers are operations run by grocery manufacturers so they can market their own products; their sales account for about one-fifth of all grocery wholesale sales. Brokers and agents buy and sell wholesale products for a commission; they don't hold or physically handle products. They account for about a fifth of wholesale grocery sales.[22]

Food wholesalers are further classified by the type of products they distribute. Broad-line or full-line grocery distributors handle a wide range of food products. Specialty distributors focus on a narrow range of items such as dairy products, fresh produce, frozen food, and meats.

Farm Numbers, Income, and Production

Agricultural data have been collected by the U.S. Census of Agriculture dating back to 1840. Initially the census was taken every decade, but soon it was done every five years. Some of the parameters have changed over time (slaves on farms were counted until the Civil War), but others, such as the total number of farms, the area of land in farms, and total gross sales of raw products by county and state, have been consistent. In recent decades, new measures have been added, such as direct-to-consumer sales, income from agritourism, sales of organic products, and use of renewable energy on farms. While the census does not fully describe the diverse value of agriculture to society, it is useful for identifying trends in farming and food production.

The number of U.S. farms peaked in 1935 at 6.8 million, then declined sharply until the early 1970s, due largely to increases in agricultural productivity and non-farm employment.[23] Farm numbers declined slowly in the 1980s and leveled off in the 1990s. Average farm size went from 155 acres in 1935 to about 400 acres in 2012. Slightly more than 2 million farms are currently in operation. The first increase in the number of farms in modern times was reported in the 2007 census, which showed a 4 percent gain over the previous five years.[24] Most of the growth came from small, diversified farms. Large producers of single commodities, including grains, horticulture, and cattle and hog operations, continue to increase in size but decline in number. Small farms now account for about 90 percent of all U.S. farms and more than half of the land in agriculture. The USDA recently adjusted its definition of a small farm to be a farm with gross sales of less than $350,000, up from the $250,000 cutoff established nearly fifteen years earlier.[25]

In the first part of the twentieth century most small farmers appeared to be poor by today's standards, but back then the need for disposable income was not as great as it is today. Most of the population lived on small farms, and these farms typically provided subsistence food supplies for the household, along with a small income from a cash crop or two, perhaps some livestock, and other products. In some ways, diversified small farms have not changed that much over time, but the larger economy and household income requirements have.

Today, the economic well-being of most U.S. farm households depends on income from both on-farm and off-farm activities. More than half of all farm operators also work off the farm, and on-farm income accounts for just one-fifth of the total household income of U.S. farmers, down from one-half of total household income in 1960.[26] Of course, these data are affected by the fact that there are many extremely small farms with operators who have no

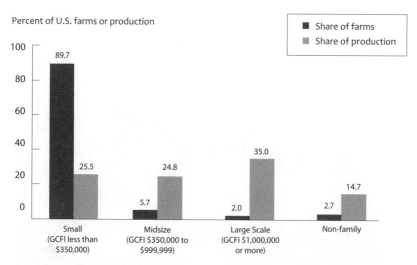

Percent of U.S. farms or production

■ Share of farms
▨ Share of production

100

89.7

80

60

40

35.0

25.5   24.8

20
                                                                14.7

5.7
0   2.0   2.7

Small   Midsize   Large Scale   Non-family
(GCFI less than   (GCFI $350,000 to (GCFI $1,000,000
$350,000) $999,999)   or more)

FIGURE 3.7 Size classes of farms and their share of production. The USDA currently defines small farms as family farms with annual gross sales of less than $350,000. Small farms account for about 90 percent of all farms and a quarter of U.S. food production. Midsize family farms, with $350,000 to $1 million in sales, constitute less than 6 percent of all farms but also produce about a quarter of U.S. food. Large family farms with sales of more than $1 million account for only 2 percent of all farms but produce a third of U.S. food. Non-family farms are counted separately by the USDA. Farms with annual sales of more than $1 million (the combination of large family farms and large non-family farms) produce more than half of all food in the United States.

intention or expectation of making a living from farming because they either are retired or have a primary occupation other than farming.

The revitalization of small farms is important for stabilizing the total number of farms and maintaining farmland and rural communities. At the same time, large farms have become increasingly important for food production, and they now produce most of our food. Thirty-seven percent of very large family farms and 13 percent of non-family farms have annual sales of $1 million or more.[27] (Non-family farms are those not owned primarily by a farm family, such as corporate farms, and they are counted separately.) These very large farms make up about 2 percent of all U.S. farms, yet they account for half of all production (fig. 3.7). They dominate the production of high-value crops (vegetables, fruits, nuts, nursery, and greenhouse products), hogs, dairy, poultry, and beef.

FARM PRODUCTION. The cash income of America's farms is about $440 billion per year (fig. 3.8). Of this, about $223 billion comes from crops, $166 billion from livestock, $34 billion from other farm enterprises, and $11 billion

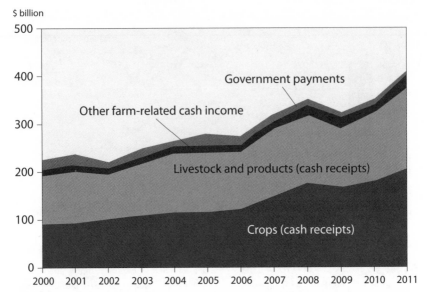

FIGURE 3.8 Gross cash income from farming. Since 2000, cash receipts for livestock and crops have risen significantly; government payments vary from year to year but in general account for only a small percentage of farm income.

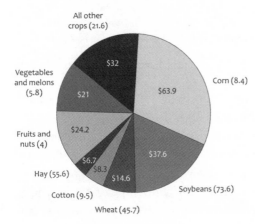

FIGURE 3.9 Annual crop production in the United States. The cash value of crops ($223 billion total in 2011) is shown in the pie chart and their acreage (300 million acres total) in parentheses. Corn and soybeans account for about half of crop sales and acreage; fruits, vegetables, and nuts account for about a quarter of crop sales from only 2 percent of crop acreage. Hay and wheat produce relatively low sales per acre.

from government payments.[28] After expenses of $305 billion, net farm income is about $134 billion annually.

A variety of crops and animals are produced all over the United States, but the majority of some products come from specific locations (fig. 3.9).[29] California produces the most food of all fifty states; it is number one in the production of many horticultural crops as well as milk. Illinois, Iowa, Minnesota, and Nebraska lead in corn and soybeans. Washington typically leads the country in apple production; Florida is the largest producer of oranges.

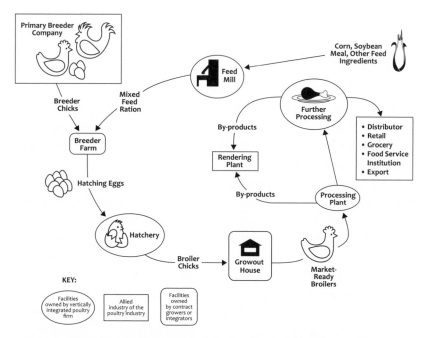

FIGURE 3.10 Vertical integration of poultry production. The supply chain for contract chicken production and distribution includes components owned by the vertically integrated poultry firms and those owned by other industries such as poultry breeders and food marketers. The integrator controls the feed, the hatchery, and the processing; farmers simply raise chicks to market-size broilers.

Texas, California, Iowa, Kansas, and Nebraska lead in cattle production. Georgia leads in poultry production, followed by North Carolina. Vermont is the number one maple syrup producer.[30]

Vertical integration has come to be a dominant feature of livestock production. For example, today more than 90 percent of all chickens raised for human consumption in the United States are produced by independent farmers working under contract with integrated chicken production and processing companies (fig. 3.10).[31] Most of the other 10 percent of chickens are raised by company-owned farms, and less than 1 percent are raised by individual growers. An important purpose of contracting systems is to standardize production practices with the goal of producing a homogeneous commodity.

Economics of Food Systems

When considered in its entirety, from "farm to plate," food has a significant economic impact throughout the United States, and so does farming, but all too often agriculture is considered in isolation, making it appear somewhat insignificant relative to the overall economy. The reality is that agriculture does not exist in economic isolation, nor do the range of businesses that add value from "farm to plate." Together they make up a working food system, and this is best analyzed by considering all its components and their interactions. Value in the food system may begin to be generated through sales of raw products from farms, but it continues through food processing, packaging, transportation, storage, distributing, and retailing businesses—all of which buy additional products and services, pay wages and taxes, and reinvest in their communities.

A recent study of six northeastern states (Connecticut, Massachusetts, New Hampshire, New Jersey, New York, and Rhode Island) found that the 65,000 farms in the region have a farm-gate output (the net value of a product when it leaves the farm) of about $17 billion (of which 9 percent is from forestry and fishing), and this supports an additional $54 billion in processing output.[32] In Washington State, $9.5 billion of agricultural production leads to $23 billion in additional economic impact through value-added food processing, wages, tax revenues, and the effect of money earned through agriculture being spent throughout the state's economy.[33] In Utah, $1.5 billion in direct farm output results in $16.3 billion in total economic output, or nearly 15 percent of the state's economy.[34] In Delaware, $1.1 billion in farm-gate sales translates into $8 billion in economic activity.[35] In California, the state's $36 billion in direct farm production leads to $340 billion in economic activity when distribution, processing, and support services are accounted for along with industry purchases and employee spending.[36] Some states are well known for their agricultural productivity and outputs; others are not. But all states recognize the economic importance of food systems when examined in their entirety.

The Economy of Vermont's Food System: A Case Study

Using data pertaining to Vermont, we can explore in more detail the economy of one state's farm and food system (fig. 3.11). According to the U.S. Census of Agriculture, Vermont farmers sell about half a billion dollars of products annually, which is only the beginning of the story. Farmers also grow a lot of their own animal feed (hay, corn, pasture), raise their own young stock, and produce many other products that they don't have to buy, such as compost, plant nutrients from cover crops, and on-farm fuel from wood and anaerobic digesters. With the value of on-farm consumption considered, Vermont farmers generate about $700 million dollars a year of "farm production."[37]

Of the food sold from Vermont farms, only a small portion goes directly to consumers. However, direct marketing gets a lot of attention, since it is highly

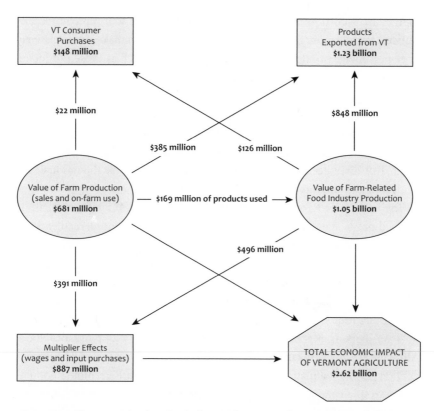

FIGURE 3.11 The economic value of agriculture in the context of Vermont's larger food system. The total economic impact is estimated to be $2.6 billion annually.

visible and people can easily participate in it. The value of direct-to-consumer sales from farms has increased dramatically in recent years, up to $22 million dollars annually, and the number of farms selling direct to consumers has also increased.[38] Enthusiasm for direct market sales has made Vermont the top state nationally in terms of per capita purchases of agricultural products direct from the farm. Oregon is the number two state, but most of the top ten are in the Northeast. The average Vermonter spends $37 per year on food bought directly from farmers, compared with $15 in Oregon and just $5 per year nationally. Vermont's lead sounds impressive, but $37 of buying per year from farmers' markets, farmstands, and CSAs doesn't seem like much. Vermonters spend more than $2 billion a year on food purchases,[39] so even when the $126 million in purchases of locally processed food is added to the $22 million of food bought through direct markets, Vermonters spent only $148 million, or about 7 percent of their food dollars, on "local" food.

The small portion of total farm production that is sold directly to consumers (slightly more than 3 percent of total farm sales) makes up a relatively large percentage of sales for certain types of farms, such as those producing fruits, vegetables, and ornamental plants. In addition, direct markets are especially important for the creation of new farms, especially those with horticultural or value-added products like cheese, which usually start small. Low-investment direct market opportunities provide small farmers with a chance to test "proof of concept" in both production and product development. This direct feedback loop with customers can provide the rationale for owners to take the leap and expand their business.

The vast majority of food made in Vermont, about $1.2 billion worth, is shipped out of state in bulk at wholesale prices by distributors, retailers, and food manufacturers. Some of this, about $385 million, is in the form of raw products that will be processed, packaged, and stored out of state. Most of it will be sold elsewhere, though some products like fluid milk will return for retailing in the state. Another $848 million worth of food processed inside the state boundaries — for example, ice cream and cheese — will then be exported to larger markets. Many Vermonters are striving to use a lot more local food. Although their efforts can help the state's food economy, it will still be dependent on nearby population centers in other states because Vermont's population is so small and so much of what is produced is a commodity: fluid milk. Thus the health of the local farm and food system relies on regional markets within a day's drive, where tens of millions of consumers in nearby states patronize supermarkets and other retail food outlets.

Both farming and food processing generate so-called multiplier effects, which benefit the local and state economy above and beyond the revenues recorded by the sale of the food itself. You've got to spend money to make money, paying for things like wages, supplies, energy, services, and transportation, all of which put money back into circulation. As a result, farming and food processing create nearly $900 million of revenue for other people and businesses in Vermont. Taken together, farming, food processing, and their multiplier effects contribute more than $2.6 billion to Vermont's economy every year.[40]

There is even more economic value that's not directly measured as farming or food production. Consider the restaurants, hotels, hospitals, schools, and senior centers that serve tens of thousands of meals every day. And the food distributors and truckers and salespeople who serve those institutions. And the people who sell and service the stoves and refrigerators, work in the kitchens and dining areas, and haul the waste that's generated. The Farm to

Plate Initiative, created by the Vermont legislature and guided by the Vermont Sustainable Jobs Fund, has added up all this economic activity as part of a ten-year strategic plan for food and agriculture. It estimates that almost 18 percent of all private jobs and 12 percent of all private business establishments in Vermont are engaged in some part of the state's food system.[41]

Some other economic benefits are harder to quantify, but are just as real. One is the value of household food production. From hunting to gardening to raising backyard chickens, Vermonters generate a lot of food value, and they purchase a variety of inputs in order to do so, including equipment, seeds, transplants, feed, and fertilizers. Few attempts have been made to measure the dollars involved in home food production, but one study in Maine looked at vegetable gardening and found that a well-run 1,600-square-foot garden generates about $2,000 worth of food at local retail prices.[42] A conservative guess is that there are five thousand such gardens in Vermont, yielding about $10 million of food and generating an unknown but significant amount of spending at local businesses.

A much larger food- and farming-related economic activity is tourism, which creates an estimated $1.5 billion a year in direct spending in Vermont.[43] How much tourism actually results from Vermont's reputation for family farming and related culinary delights? Clearly these things attract people — from the cheese, ice cream, apples, and maple syrup to, more recently, wine, artisan bread, and grain products, along with the working landscapes of cows, crops, barns, and fields that produce them. Since the data are lacking, let's estimate that 10 percent of tourism revenues are attributable to these products and landscapes. That adds another $150 million, plus or minus, to the value of the state's food system.

So the real economic value of food and farming in Vermont turns out to be well over $4 billion annually, compared with the half billion dollars or so typically reported on the basis of farm-gate sales only. Much of the difference is a function of the mutually beneficial relationships that businesses have developed along the way from field to table, creating new markets for fresh food, processing to add value to it, and connecting food to marketable experiences like tourism. Some of these collaborative relationships are informal, even unacknowledged, between independent business entities, but others are at the core of normal business structures, such as farmer cooperatives.

Farmer cooperatives provide one way for producers to work together to develop brand identity and control some of their destiny in the wholesale marketplace. The Deep Root Co-op of vegetable growers, from Vermont and Quebec, is an example. They aggregate their fresh produce for sale to natural food groceries. Another example is Cabot Creamery, a cooperative of dairy farmers from New England and New York that produces a full line of value-added products like cheeses, spreads, and butter to sell to supermarkets and distributors. These co-ops ultimately allow individual famers from rural areas to aggregate, brand, and sell their products in population centers hundreds of miles away, and beyond.

Cooperatives at their very root are ownership structures, so farmer-owners own stock or equity in the business. That creates a mechanism for farmers to get some of that investment back through annual dividends or sale of their equity when they retire. In many ways, farmer cooperatives embody the traditional values of rural communities: people working together for mutual economic benefit and security, creating jobs and boosting a place-based reputation for high-quality food along the way.

Cabot Creamery Cooperative

One of Vermont's renowned farm and food businesses started as a small creamery in the town of Cabot in 1893. It became a cooperative in 1919. The creamery hired its first cheese maker in 1930 and had developed a line of butter, cheese, and sour cream by the time bulk tanks and refrigeration were introduced in the 1950s. Cabot began developing a brand in southern New England in the 1980s, but the turning point for its brand recognition was in 1989 when it won an award for best cheddar at a cheese contest in Green Bay, Wisconsin. It was the first time a cheese from east of the Mississippi River had won, and it put Vermont cheeses on the map (fig. 3.12).

Today, Cabot has farmer-members in all six New England states and upstate New York. Of the 1,250 member farms, about 300 are in Vermont, constituting about one-third of the state's dairies. All farms have equity in the co-op. The majority of its members are multigenerational farms, which is a good sign for the future.

Cabot has evolved to a point where it is primarily exporting cheese from Vermont. Its cheese is sold all across the country, but the strongest market is the Northeast. Clearly it is good business to sell products to Vermonters, but in a small state a relatively large company like Cabot needs bigger markets, so it distributes to areas where there are a lot more customers. It has developed the critical mass of product needed to sell to regional supermarket chains and to justify the slotting fees that are charged for shelf space. These fees can be substantial.

To some of Vermont's small-scale cheese producers, Cabot is a Goliath. Cabot's director of sustainability, Jed Davis, puts the size of Cabot in perspec-

FIGURE 3.12 Local cheeses. Artisan cheeses are a popular local food item in many locations. For producers seeking to scale up their businesses, it can be a challenge to meet the quantity, quality, and price requirements of wholesale buyers beyond a local market.

tive: "People within the borders of the Green Mountain State think of Cabot as a huge food company. The minute you step outside Vermont, we're a gnat." Cabot's brand recognition is strong and so are its sales. Jed explains:

> We have markets for our members' milk and we have opportunities to grow our branded products. Our biggest challenge has more to do with national dairy policy. The dividend that we return is helpful to our farmers but we can't be profitable enough to make up for ongoing low milk prices. We augment the price with market premiums since we would rather our farmers receive bigger milk checks than Cabot have a bigger profit. That's the difference between Cabot and big companies we compete with. If all you're doing is manufacturing dairy products, you want milk to be priced as low as possible and you don't care where it comes from. As a cooperative first and foremost, we want dairy farmers to get a fair price for their milk. We care about the future of our farmers. But at the end of the day, there needs to be a solution aimed at the base milk price.

Strengthening the Food Economy Close to Home

Like many places around the country, Vermont is blessed with innovative farmers, businesses that pay fair prices for farm products, and a public affection and respect for agriculture. These qualities are not as widespread in the United States as they could be, and cultivation of each component is needed to sustain agriculture and the state's food system over the long haul. Even that will not be enough. In the end it will require an engaged citizenry that actively supports agriculture and food businesses and sees their unique connections to the greater public good.

One obvious way that people can help farms thrive is to buy local food directly from them. A related but less obvious way requires paying quite a bit of attention to the food you buy in the supermarket. Cabot cheese and

Ben & Jerry's ice cream are household names to Vermonters who know that these companies use local milk in their products. But there are plenty of other brands that use local ingredients yet are not household names. The same is true in other states, where companies committed to using local and regional ingredients deserve consumer support. Across the nation, schools, hospitals, and other institutions are increasingly using local and regional food, spurred on by interest from their customers, the high quality and healthfulness of the products, and the desire to support the economic well-being of their communities.

Purchasing practices are important, but policies are also needed that can help sustain agriculture at the local, state, and national levels. At the national level, it's important for people to stay informed and to let federal agencies and representatives know how they feel about policies. At the local and state levels, it's equally important to support policies that encourage the prosperity and longevity of farms and their partners in food.

At the level of town governance, one way to start the policy discussion is to ask the question, does our town have ordinances that are farm-friendly? There is a checklist, developed by the University of New Hampshire Cooperative Extension, to help answer that question.[44] Items on the list address issues like agricultural zoning, farm signage, and accessory uses.

At the state level, a wide variety of policies can be put in place to encourage the viability of food and forestry systems, including use-value taxation and support for the purchase of farmland conservation easements. Many states have property taxation rules that allow the assessment of working land at its "use value" rather than its value for development. This keeps taxes down for eligible farmers and forestland owners. That's a fair thing to do, when you consider that land with farming and forestry enterprises does not require the same level of expensive public services as land whose use has been converted to housing, shopping malls, and office buildings. Cows don't go to school, collards don't commit crimes, and tomatoes don't dial 911.[45]

Use-value taxation is not unique to Vermont, but the funding mechanism for land conservation just might be. A modest tax on property transfers was set up more than thirty years ago, with proceeds going to the Vermont Housing and Conservation Board, which uses the money to assist with both affordable housing and the purchase of conservation easements on productive farm- and forestlands. A portion of that funding also goes to a statewide Farm Viability program that provides business planning programs for farms. Funding for land conservation has been leveraged by the Vermont Land Trust and other organizations to obtain federal and philanthropic support for the program. Other states have used similarly innovative approaches to support farms and farmland.

Farming and food businesses play a far bigger role in the U.S. economy than many people realize. This economic impact goes well beyond the value of farm products to include a variety of food businesses, recreational activities, and tourism. In addition, benefits that are harder to measure include the maintenance of open space, a working landscape, healthy ecosystems, and cultural traditions.

Too many people today know the price
of everything and the value of nothing.
Ann Landers

4 ∾ *Values in Food Systems*

Food systems are driven by the decisions people make, and those decisions are affected by values. People's values shape their perception of something's importance or worth, whether a tangible item that can be bought and sold or an aspect of quality of life that can only be experienced. How much is a bushel of corn or an acre of land worth? You can check out recent sales data to get an answer. How important is clean water? What is the worth of vibrant rural communities? Things like these are valuable but not easy to put a price on.

Economic, environmental, and social values all play key roles in food systems. They are interwoven, sometimes reinforcing and sometimes conflicting. Markets are driven by monetary worth. Even though people may value a clean environment and social well-being, these are usually undervalued in the marketplace because we lack widely accepted, systematic approaches to recognizing their worth. The positive and negative impacts that are not captured by the market are known as externalities.[1]

People seek out low prices for items like cars, clothing, computers, and food. They are not willing to pay more than "necessary" for such items, yet they also value environmental quality and probably don't want products they buy to contribute to water pollution or soil erosion. They probably also value fairness and don't want people to suffer unhealthy or exploitative working conditions when they make the products. Lacking information about anything else, market price becomes the primary influence on consumer behavior. The same can be said of commercial enterprises. A restaurant chain that sells chicken sandwiches probably spends a lot more time seeking out the lowest-cost chicken than it does determining how poultry farm waste is managed or how poultry processing plant workers are treated.

In the food industry, economies of scale, yield maximization, and short-term profitability drive most of the thinking and practice. At the same time alternative, locally oriented food systems are emerging that give more recognition and support to environmental and social values. Deeper consideration of non-market values in food systems is just beginning to gain credibility among policy makers, financiers, and scientists who are intellectually invested in mainstream financial models and technologies. To change their views and decisions, as well as those of food producers and consumers, will require a robust analytical framework that allows environmental and social values to be part of the calculation.

As Marty Strange put it: "Everyone wants to earn more, to buy more, to have more. They discount the influence of other values — community, loyalty, love of the land, and continuity, for example. But these values are real, and they are economic values because they influence economic behavior."[2]

Food System Consolidation
and the Narrowing of Values

A small number of economic entities wield tremendous power at every level of modern food systems, from farmers' inputs, such as seeds and fertilizers, to the distribution of raw commodities, such as grains and meats, to the processing of those commodities into branded products, to the retailing of those products by supermarkets and fast food chains. In each food system sector, the market is dominated by an oligopoly, or a cartel, where a small number of corporations have disproportionate influence, not only on prices, but on the types of products available. If a new company comes along with a successful product or process, it is likely to be out-competed or purchased by one of the larger entities. As the few corporations with marketplace dominance grow in size and scope of offerings, they gain additional market control and political influence. The result is entrenched consolidation of food systems, driven by short-term profits. In other words, food system decisions are aimed at achieving profits and continuous growth without substantive consideration of other values that are tied to well-being. Non-market values are dwarfed by the prime objective: to make money, and lots of it. Making money is arguably a good thing, but many problems arise because that objective is out of balance with values that are harder to put a price on.

Within a food system sector, the names of the largest businesses and the proportion of total sales they represent vary from year to year, but marketplace domination by a relatively few companies is now the norm. For example, the global commercial seed market is worth about $35 billion annually; the top three companies account for more than half of all sales. and the top ten companies control 75 percent of that market (fig. 4.1). Ten companies control almost 95 percent of the $44 billion global market for pesticides; six of these are also among the largest seed companies. Seven firms, all subsidiaries of multinational drug companies, control 72 percent of animal drug sales. Four firms account for 97 percent of poultry genetics.[3] Similarly, four companies control the majority of beef packing in the United States, and the same

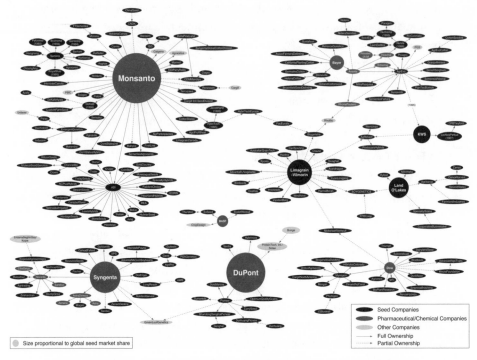

FIGURE 4.1 Consolidation of the seed industry. The seed industry is one example of consolidation in a food system. Many small regional seed companies have been purchased by large global companies in recent years.

is true for pork and poultry processing. Just three companies dominate flour milling and soybean crushing.[4]

Oligopoly is the norm not just for food production and processing but for food retailing as well. The ten largest U.S. food retailers account for about two-thirds of all grocery store sales (fig. 4.2).[5] In the largest one hundred metropolitan areas, four retailers control nearly three-quarters of grocery sales.[6] The ten largest fast food chains generate more than $95 billion in annual sales,[7] which is more than 20 percent of the $469 billion that Americans spend at eating and drinking places.[8] The ten largest food and beverage processing companies in the United States have annual sales of about $200 billion,[9] which is about one-third of the market for all manufactured food sales.

By some accounts, our food systems are working well regardless of consolidation. After all, food is relatively inexpensive in historic terms, when measured as a proportion of household income spent on it. But this perspective ignores the true costs of food. It doesn't account for what is paid through taxes to fund farm price supports, crop disaster payments, highways to trans-

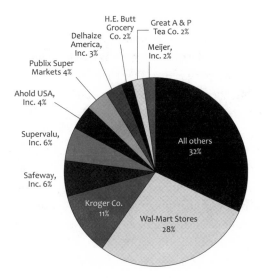

FIGURE 4.2 Supermarket share of grocery sales. Ten supermarket chains account for 68 percent of all grocery sales in the United States.

port food, and water systems to irrigate arid regions to grow crops. Simple analyses also fail to capture the environmental and social costs associated with industrial farming and food processing, such as those that result from water pollution, soil erosion, greenhouse gas emissions, diabetes, food insecurity, and low wages paid to farmworkers. These negative externalities add up to a large expense for society.

Improvements in food systems can be achieved by a variety of methods that address both market and non-market values. Regulations can rein in practices that are detrimental to people or natural resources. Research and education can identify and disseminate approaches to improving human health, and market forces can provide powerful incentives for a variety of practices that benefit people and the planet. However, if market forces are to help improve food systems, consumers need to know what's really going on. And therein lies the rub: many aspects of food systems lack transparency. As a result, consumers often invest their food dollars in practices that don't match their values. A lot of the people who want an inexpensive hamburger would be willing to pay a few dimes or even dollars more for that burger if it meant cleaner water and healthier cows and pastures. Many people who want low-cost milk would pay a bit more to help keep family dairy farms in business or to support the vitality of rural agricultural communities they visit as tourists. But absent information on the indirect effects of their food choices, people make their purchasing decisions on the basis of attributes they can directly assess, like product appearance, flavor, and price.

Valuing More Than Money

Values shape every step of a food system, from practices on the farm, to marketing messages, to consumption patterns and food waste management. Further, values shape the policies and perspectives that affect economic decisions, environmental stewardship, the pursuit of "efficiency," and the ability to achieve fairness and justice in the food system. Values are the basis for a framework of behavioral norms and governmental regulations that set limits on the exploitation of natural and human capital. Over the years, a wide variety of people have articulated the importance of valuing not just the economic but the environmental and social well-being of agriculture and the larger food hierarchy. This view is not an aberration; it has been a consistent theme of thoughtful people throughout history, although it is often pushed aside in the pursuit of profits. The following is a sampling of people whose ideas have challenged us to change the food system for the better.

Henry Wallace was secretary of agriculture under President Franklin D. Roosevelt. A visionary public servant, Wallace promoted increased agricultural output but also the conservation of natural resources and the well-being of rural communities. Under his leadership the Department of Agriculture established the food stamp and school lunch programs, which greatly aided low-income Americans during a time of economic and social stress.

Aldo Leopold, in his 1949 book, *A Sand County Almanac*, described a land ethic whereby people have a duty to protect the natural world, even as they manipulate it. He wrote: "We abuse land because we see it as a commodity belonging to us. When we see land as a community to which we belong, we may begin to use it with love and respect."[10]

In her 1962 book, *Silent Spring*, Rachel Carson articulated that we have an ethical responsibility to produce food without poisoning the environment. She helped change public policy and corporate behavior by exposing the damage caused by toxic approaches to pest control. Once people understood what was at risk, many were motivated to shift away from the overuse of pesticides because they valued a clean environment.[11]

César Chávez led a social movement and started a farmworkers' union in the 1960s aimed at stopping worker exploitation. His movement sought fair wages, decent working conditions, and the protection of fieldworkers from pesticide exposure. He was responsible for bringing public attention to the fact that the farmworkers who were essential to cultivating and harvesting much of our food often had little money or food for themselves.

In 1971 Francis Moore Lappé popularized the notion that our individual diets could influence food systems as well as our own health. In *Diet for a*

Small Planet she argued that in the United States too much grain was used for feeding meat animals, given that so many hungry people in the world could eat that grain. She advocated a vegetarian diet as a way to directly address personal health as well as problems with an industrial agriculture oriented to livestock production.[12]

In 1990 Wendell Berry wrote that "eating is an agricultural act."[13] Berry has articulated the importance of community as a cradle of social and environmental values that are the basis for how people think about the role of government, industry, and science. He argued that these values express themselves in the types of agriculture and food systems we develop.

Fred Magdoff, soil scientist at the University of Vermont, wrote about the connection between ecological production practices and social and economic justice. He described how agribusiness in collaboration with agricultural science has contributed to a production and marketing system that leads to many negative environmental and social effects. This is the result of a reductionism in which individual problems are addressed in isolation from all others. The outcome, he contended, is that "large-scale, highly mechanized agriculture is probably the greatest threat to the existence of billions of people."[14]

Michael Pollan, in *The Omnivore's Dilemma*, argued that the industrial food system obscures relationships and the connection between how food is produced and its environmental and social impacts. He wrote, "The more knowledge people have about the way their food is produced, the more likely it is that their values — and not just 'value' — will inform their purchasing decisions."[15]

Paul Thompson, philosopher at Michigan State University, described the industrial ethic and the agrarian ethic that are at the core of two competing sets of values that shape how people view agriculture and the larger food system.[16] The industrial ethic views agriculture as just another part of industrial society, in which commodities are produced at the lowest cost possible. The trend toward the consolidation of farms and food firms is just economies of scale at work. This industrial system must be applied globally to ensure sustainable food production for the world. Landscapes are viewed in terms of the commodities they can produce, and while there are some concerns over the well-being of communities, environment, labor, and livestock, any negative impacts can be addressed without a severe departure from the industrial model. From this viewpoint, sustainability is about producing more, with fewer inputs. In contrast, the agrarian ethic values the multifunctionality of agriculture and views it as having important environmental and social functions beyond the efficient production of commodities. These functions include providing positive ecosystem services (benefits that people get from a healthy environment) and enhancing the quality of life for people and local communities involved with agriculture. Advocates of this view argue for fair trade, fair labor, animal welfare, and a major departure from the conventional agriculture model because that model is extractive and not sustainable.

The agrarian ethic aligns with the modern-day "alternative agrifood movement," which is a synthesis of many ideologies and their values.[17] These include traditional agrarian values of independence, hard work, and family-based farming; community food security values of self-reliance and self-sufficiency; the agroecological value of using nature as a model for farming system design and management; and the social justice values of inclusion, equal participation, and shared power—not just for farmers and consumers, but for farmworkers, food processors, and people of all economic classes, races, and genders.

Networks and Value Chains

A lot of food is "anonymous" to consumers. That is, it comes without information about its origin and impact. Such anonymity can decouple food-buying decisions from the wide range of values that people hold. Low prices trump clean water, healthy soil, fairly paid farmworkers, and stable rural communities if all we know about a product is what we can personally observe or obtain from marketing information that may or may not be accurate and complete. Thus anonymity in the marketplace leads to uninformed purchasing decisions by consumers who unwittingly support food system characteristics that are in conflict with their values. Within the mass food market, anonymity is fostered by geographic distance and long, opaque chains of custody between producers and consumers. Minimal labeling requirements, comingling of ingredients from many sources, and products christened with imaginary farm names further hide the provenance of food. In other words, food systems "distance" consumers from their food not just by physical distance from the source, but also through processing and packaging.[18]

Anonymity and distancing are powerful symptoms of what's fundamentally wrong with food systems. At the core of many problems is the way relationships among people are structured. To transform our food system so it is significantly healthier will require changing the structure of relationships so they are built around more than prices and profits. They must be shaped by shared values that support a "triple bottom line" for individuals and society: economic, environmental, and social benefits. One way to restructure relationships in a food system is to promote horizontal rather than vertical networks of people.

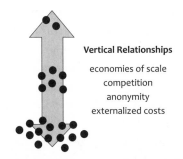

Horizontal Relationships

economies of scope
collaboration
transparency
truer cost accounting

Vertical Relationships

economies of scale
competition
anonymity
externalized costs

chain stores, industrial processors, commodity markets   farmers' markets, CSAs, producer co-ops, value-chains

FIGURE 4.3 Vertical and horizontal networks in a food system. The dots represent people in the two types of networks. In the vertical network, power is held by a few people at the top who have little direct connection to those involved in distributing, marketing, and consuming products. In the horizontal network, power is more evenly shared among participants, and activity is aimed at achieving both economic and non-economic benefits.

Vertical networks are largely impersonal and opaque. They focus on the exchange of goods and services for money. They are hierarchical, with most of the authority held by decision makers at the top; their decisions flow through distributors, wholesalers, advertisers, and retailers to a base of consumers at the bottom. In contrast, horizontal networks are people-oriented and transparent; they are established to provide mutual benefits and shared prosperity; they lack a powerful central authority and instead use shared governance approaches.

Horizontal networks are not exclusively local, although proximity can create a common context that facilitates their development. Horizontal networks, like local food systems, are not inherently good. The outcomes they produce depend on the people involved and the agendas that are empowered. Horizontal networks and local food systems do not exist in isolation; they have links and interdependencies with both vertical and more distant networks,[19] often leading to a mixture of relationships, which makes sense given the complexity of our food system.

Although food systems would benefit from more horizontal networks, it will continue to involve, and perhaps require, a blend of vertical and horizontal networks. Take tractor production, for example. Unless and until small-scale manufacturers figure out how to build these complex machines, rural agricultural communities across the country and the world will need a relatively vertical network of factories and their distribution chains so that farmwork can be appropriately mechanized. Creating more horizontal networks associated with tractor production may not be a top priority right now. But in some other areas there appears to be stronger motivation to shift to more horizontal approaches. In the case of seed production, while a few multinational companies dominate this activity, there has recently been a resurgence of much smaller companies with strong connections to local and regional farmers and their specific needs. Such companies are often characterized by alternative corporate governance, such as employee ownership, cooperatives, and nonprofits. Johnny's Selected Seeds, Fedco Seeds, and High Mowing Seeds in New England are examples, along with the Family Farmer Seed Cooperative in the Northwest and Native Seeds/SEARCH in the Southwest.

Horizontal approaches within a business sector that has become increasingly vertical are possible. In fact, domination by just a few companies may increase consumer and producer interest in alternative products and business approaches. For example, although just a handful of companies dominate the U.S. beer market, the number of craft breweries has increased to well over two thousand in a short amount of time, and that number continues to grow.[20] The same holds true for food (some people consider beer to be a food), as many people seek out small-scale food alternatives, such as farmers' markets and CSAs, to experience some balance with the vertical, corporate world of supermarket chains. For most shoppers, the two are not mutually exclusive.

While local food systems generally rely on horizontal networks that support both market and non-market values, local food has its limits as a focus for improving the overall food hierarchy. The problem is that it's viable and beneficial only under certain conditions. These typically include a geographic cluster of diverse farms and processors of a scale that allows them to market to a nearby population of sufficient size and wealth to buy their products. It can be more challenging if you live in the middle of the Wheat Belt, next to an industrial-scale meat processing plant, in an urban food desert, or in a climate that is hostile to food growing. Then, local food may not be feasible for consumers and producers.

For many "ag in the middle" farms, a focus on local food may not be helpful. These farms are described as small and midsize operations grossing less than half a million dollars annually, with farming as their primary occupation. They are often unable to sell their food directly to local end users because they produce too much, don't raise the right products, or are located too far from the markets. At the same time, these farms are typically too small to compete individually in wholesale or commodity markets, where much larger farms dominate. As a result these "farms of the middle" have been disappearing for decades.[21] An alternative to selling locally for these farms is to tap into values-based supply chains that promote horizontal networks scaled to accommodate the volume of their supply and the demand from comparably sized markets.

Values-based supply chains, such as Shepherd's Grains (see the next section), can create new markets for farms of the middle by connecting the producers, processors, and buyers around high-quality, differentiated products with an unmet market demand (box 4.1). These markets are typically regional, though they may be of any geographic scope. Partners all along the supply chain work in cooperative (horizontal) rather than hierarchical (vertical) networks where the performance and well-being of all partners are equally important. Through the fair distribution of profits and shared decision making, this business model codifies the social value of making commitments to the welfare of all strategic partners in the chain, including the farmers, rather than treating them as interchangeable with other potential suppliers.

Shepherd's Grain: Building a Regional Value Supply Chain around Sustainability

While policy makers and scientists are developing indicators of progress, entrepreneurial farmers are taking matters into their own hands by implementing production and marketing practices that reflect their values and work toward self-defined goals of sustainability. Shepherd's Grain in Washington State is a leader in this movement (fig. 4.4; box 4.2).

One of the founders, Karl Kupers, grew up on a wheat farm in Washington, the son of a sharecropper. Fifty years later he is still growing wheat on that same land—but in a very different way. This is how Karl describes his experience:

FIGURE 4.4 Shepherd's Grain logo. Karl Kupers and Fred Fleming founded Shepherd's Grain in Washington with the goals of sustainability for environmental health, social justice, and economic profitability.

In 1982, over half my income as a wheat grower came from subsidies. Trying to make a living at the mercy of volatile commodity prices, I was on a roller coaster that wasn't good for the farm, the consumer, or the environment. In 1985 I decided to create a farm that didn't need subsidies. For wheat production that meant diversifying and caring for the long-term health of the soil using no-till and crop rotation. I was heading towards environmental sustainability, but I needed a marketplace for my crops outside of the commodity markets. So I created Shepherd's Grain with my partner, Fred Fleming. Our goal was to reconnect the farmer to the consumer through relationships with a focus on all three parts of sustainability.

Sustainability is never an end; it's a goal and you're constantly seeking new ways to achieve it in all three areas. Focusing on sustainability was a radical shift when we first proposed it. As businessmen, Fred and I knew we needed to think about the economics of selling wheat. When it came time to figure out the pricing, we got some bakers in the room to find out what would work for them. It turned out the volatility in wheat prices from commodity markets was just as difficult for them to deal with as it was for us, and they would welcome stable prices. The commodity market wasn't based on real business numbers. We went back to the basic business premise of covering our costs plus a reasonable profit. The wheat-buying community understood that and was very accepting of the change. But some farmers who were used to taking prices from the commodity markets thought we couldn't set the price; we had to take what the market would give us. But they were wrong.

4.2 Shepherd's Grain Sustainability Goals

- Environmental health: taking care of the land, soil, and animal life that exists on the land
- Social justice: developing relationships to inform and educate customers
- Economic profitability: maintaining a pricing structure derived from the producer's cost of producing crops

Being transparent about our costs and making sure we cover them has been an amazing part of the success of Shepherd's Grain. We developed two important policies for Shepherd's Grain: First, set the price depending on what would cover costs; de-commodify what had become a commodity. Second, reconnect the farmer to the consumer. To do that, we focused on identity preservation through the chain of custody so that our grain can be traced back from a bag of flour to the farm itself. Every year it's become more important to have that traceability. Our customers know and trust their farmers through the relationships we've developed.

When I look back at my values over time, I realize that they have not changed but rather have been validated. I always knew something was wrong with relying on subsidies and not managing the land for environmental health over the long term. But I didn't have a chance to act on those values. Now I have the opportunity to be self-motivated by values and more importantly to share them and to see how they can have a positive impact on society. It's not my values exactly that I'm sharing; it's the value of doing the right thing for the land and the people.

The model we've used for developing Shepherd's Grain is transferable to other products. I'd love to see all agricultural producers receive the cost of production plus a reasonable rate of return. If producers are transparent, then buyers can make informed decisions. Buyers feel good about the fact that the farmer is receiving a fair and equitable price and they are willing to pay more to support transparent profits.

How does the price of Shepherd's Grain wheat compare with commodity prices? Sometimes our wheat is a little more expensive and sometimes it is less expensive. Our buyers appreciate the stability we're providing with our pricing structure. There are tremendous costs for both the bakers and the growers who have to deal with the volatility of commodity markets."

This isn't rocket science. We were just a couple of farm boys trying to do something different to address a problem in the best way we knew how. It's simple but it requires following your dreams and passions and having commitment to stick to a set of values.

The need for more values-based food supply chains extends to global commerce. If you like to drink coffee or eat chocolate, as many of us do, our food choices have a long reach. Those of us in northern climates who consume tropical and subtropical products have an obligation to communities far away that also desire and deserve well-being. We need to think beyond local and regional food systems to build horizontal relationships across cultural barriers and geographic distances. Fortunately, this can be done without much difficulty in the age of information. Many of us already support coffee farmers or cocoa producers and their villages or cooperatives, thanks to the work of values-driven marketing entities and companies oriented toward fair trade. But a lot of work is still needed to build horizontal networks for many more crops, food products, and agricultural communities around the globe.

Sustainable Harvest Coffee: An International Value Supply Chain

For roasters and cafés wanting to feel good about the cup of Joe they offer to customers, companies like Sustainable Harvest provide an answer.[22] Sustainable Harvest imports specialty-grade coffee from nearly a hundred producer organizations in seventeen countries in Latin America, East Africa, and Asia. The company acts as a link between roasters and growers while importing beans.

Founded in 1997, the company has thirty staff members working from offices in Colombia, Mexico, Peru, Rwanda, and Tanzania, along with a headquarters in Portland, Oregon, that provides importing, shipping, and warehousing logistics to ensure the timely delivery of specialty coffee to roasting companies. Members of the company's "story team" provide details about specific farmers to roasters and retailers to strengthen the value chain, which the company calls Relationship Coffee.

Sustainable Harvest secures contracts for coffees and oversees delivery, as well as tracking for the roasters. The company introduces growers to loan institutions catering to midsized farmer enterprises, which then use Sustainable Harvest's contracts with roasters as collateral against the loan. This step enables coffee co-ops to pay farmers during harvest, making the supply chain less vulnerable to onetime coffee buyers toting cash, as well as other socioeconomic and environmental forces that compromise stability in an industry with tight margins.

Sustainable Harvest receives a small portion of the retail price of its coffee (fig. 4.5) and invests two-thirds of its operating expenses in farmer training and development activities. These programs train farmers to increase crop

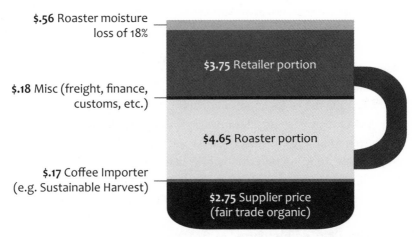

$.56 Roaster moisture loss of 18%

$3.75 Retailer portion

$.18 Misc (freight, finance, customs, etc.)

$4.65 Roaster portion

$.17 Coffee Importer (e.g. Sustainable Harvest)

$2.75 Supplier price (fair trade organic)

FIGURE 4.5 A coffee value chain. In this scenario, a pound of coffee sells for $12.06. This retail price comprises all the monetary value in the supply chain, from the producer to the consumer. The $2.75 that the coffee grower receives is based on the commodity market price of $2.25, plus the $0.30 premium for organic and the $0.20 fair trade premium. Sustainable Harvest as a specialty coffee importer receives $0.17 to pay for quality control, sourcing and importing the coffee, financing the coffee from port until paid by the roaster, managing the relationship between buyers and growers, farmer training, sales and marketing, fulfilling orders, import services, and conducting programs that benefit coffee-growing communities.

yields and manage risks such as coffee plant diseases. They also help growers diversify crops, through, for example, household vegetable production, beekeeping programs, and the cultivation of mushrooms from the pulp discarded from coffee processing, in order to provide greater food security. In addition, Sustainable Harvest shows growers how to evaluate their coffee for the qualities that coffee buyers want. A "train the trainer" approach is used to build community capacity rather than reliance on outside expertise.

Sustainable Harvest hosts an annual private gathering that brings together members of the entire supply chain to develop and deepen direct personal relationships and conduct business in an inclusive business environment. The event, called Let's Talk Coffee, is held in a different coffee-producing country each year. At the most recent gathering in El Salvador, coffee growers and roasters from twenty-two countries came together to receive training, share information, and trade 11 million pounds of organic, fair trade coffee over three days.

Sustainable Harvest focuses on connecting all the stakeholders involved in producing high-quality organic, fair trade coffee to create a sustainable and resilient supply chain. By building direct relationships and investing a significant amount of money in farmer communities, Sustainable Harvest is conducting business in a way that benefits the people who grow the coffee and the environment in which it is grown. This business model brings tools, financing, and professional training to the farmer cooperatives so they can better serve their members. By bridging the gap between growers and roasters and facilitating direct communication and better business practices at both ends of the supply chain, the business becomes more efficient and viable for all involved while also ensuring a reliable source of coffee.

As people work to build more horizontal networks, we should be clear about what constitutes long-term success. It isn't unfettered growth, which simply cannot be sustained. What we need instead are measures of *progress*.

Values-Related Measures of Progress

There's a time for sheer growth, and there's a time for different types of development. This is probably true of any living thing, from an organism to a society. Here's a simple example. Until they are sixteen or seventeen, when children go to the doctor for an annual checkup, increases in their height and weight are marked on charts that have lines representing the median and the "normal" range for their age. As children grow, they are expected to get bigger by a certain percentage every year. But once adulthood looms, a steady increase in growth is no longer desirable. Instead, the focus shifts to measures of how well health is maintained—for example, blood pressure, cholesterol level, and a stable weight. Parents may also try to assess attributes of adult well-being that are harder to measure, like responsibility, tolerance, creativity, and happiness.

Food systems need to take an analogous approach. Once a desirable level of capacity is achieved, how well are food production, distribution, and human nutrition sustained rather than increased? What quantities of energy, soil, and water are used per unit of production? What is the extent of waste product utilization? How stable is the supply of labor, land, and capital? What is the level of job satisfaction among food producers? How equitable is the distribution of wealth that's generated along the value chain? All these questions make more sense as measures of a mature food system than those that simply track gross production and revenues. Box 4.3 lists possible indicators of "good food."

Tools are needed that enable people to plan, track, and account for the attributes that define strong communities, sustainable food systems, and healthy populations. Many of these attributes are hard to measure, but if they

4.3 Indicators and Measures of "Good Food"

Suggested indicators of "good food" were developed to reflect social and environmental values—that is, food that's healthy, fair, green, and affordable. Although many possible indicators were considered, priority was given to those that could be measured using data that are valid, reliable, and transparent.

HEALTH INDICATORS

- Death rates associated with major diet-related diseases are decreasing.
- Adult overweight and obesity prevalence is decreasing.
- Fruit and vegetable consumption meets current U.S. dietary guidelines.
- The prevalence and cost of food contamination are decreasing.

FAIRNESS INDICATORS

- Farmworkers receive wages for full-time work that are sufficient to support a household.
- The percentage of farmworkers hired through labor contractors is declining.
- Food system workers have safe, healthy working conditions.
- Average net farm income of small and midscale family farms matches or exceeds median national household income.
- Acreage of midscale family farms is holding stable.
- Farmers retain a consistent proportion of the food dollar.

ENVIRONMENTAL QUALITY INDICATORS

- Farmland is remaining in production.
- Soil quality is improving.
- Water contamination by pesticides in agricultural areas is declining.
- The nitrogen balance of farming systems is declining.
- Agricultural production emits lower amounts of greenhouse gases.

AFFORDABILITY INDICATORS

- The prevalence of household food security is increasing.
- Increases in wages and salaries are equal to or greater than increases in food prices.

Adapted from Molly Anderson, "Charting Growth to Good Food, Developing Indicators and Measures of Good Food," final project report, Wallace Center at Winrock International, Arlington VA, 2009.

aren't measured, their value in the formulaic world of business and policy making will be ignored or underestimated. This concept of a broad, holistic set of measures to guide decision making is not new. Genuine Progress Indicators (GPIs) have been developed in recent decades as an alternative to Gross Domestic Product (GDP), which accounts only for the monetary value of goods and services.

GPIs use quantitative tools to recognize the interdependence of economic well-being and the quality of the natural environment and social relationships.[23] One challenge is to identify key attributes for which data can be readily and consistently collected and analyzed so as to inform ongoing decisions. There is no perfect way to do this, and there will be different approaches taken before commonly accepted practices are established. This is evidenced by the variation in GPI approaches taken by the few governmental entities that have adopted them. For example, Minnesota has used forty-two GPI indicators and Maryland has used twenty-six.[24] Nova Scotia has used more than a hundred indicators for twenty key areas of health, environmental sustainability, quality of life, equity, and economic security.[25]

What indicators should be used to assess the well-being and viability of farms? Average net income over time is important, as it integrates the demand and market price for a product, the cost of producing it, and the management capacity and natural resources of a farm or farming region, as well as weather and other unpredictable conditions. The number of new farmers may be an important factor in assessing future farm viability because it indicates the success of transferring farmland to new farmers and whether sufficient training and capital are available to support the next generation of farmers. The percentage of agricultural fields covered with living plants over the course of a year could be an indicator of vulnerability to soil erosion, loss of plant nutrients, impacts on water quality, and long-term stewardship of soil health. The ratio of fossil fuel energy consumed to food calories produced could shed light on the extent of energy-efficient production practices and resilience in the face of fossil energy price hikes or shortages.

There is a large body of literature having to do with development, use, and validation of indicators of agricultural sustainability, though social indicators have not been studied in as much detail as agronomic, economic, and environmental indicators.[26] Deciding which indicators to use to measure progress in achieving goals is more a political than a scientific question in some ways. The combination of science, policy, and values is needed to develop widely used indicators for measuring progress toward sustainable food systems.

Market-Based Approaches to Diverse Values

What approaches are needed to allow food consumers to act in accordance with their values for a wide range of products, on a scale that significantly affects food systems? Part of the answer lies in increased access to information. Consumers need to know more about how their food is produced, by whom, and who benefits — without taking on a research project for every purchase. They need access to the types of food that align with their values, while farmers and companies making this food need access to the consumers who want to buy it. There are several marketing methods that provide the type of food and information needed to help shift the balance of values in our food system: direct markets, cooperatives, value chains, and food hubs.

Direct markets are the low-hanging fruit of a more values-driven food economy, because they are relatively easy to develop and engage in. When consumers meet farmers and food producers (or their employees) in person, a rich flow of information opens up. Even with direct Web-based sales there is the opportunity for lots of transparency and interaction. Farmers' markets, CSAs, farmstands, and Internet sales provide farmers with a chance to cultivate customer loyalty through personal relationships and disclosure of relevant information. However, direct markets account for less than 2 percent of all agricultural sales and involve only 5 percent of the nation's farms.[27] So even as direct markets grow, this approach must be complemented by wholesale market strategies in order to increase the values-oriented portion of our food supply. These strategies include wholesale cooperatives, values-based supply chains, and food hubs.

Cooperatives are by definition horizontal. By sharing decision making and profits with their members, they fulfill a social mission that is different from returning value to outside investors. The key difference is that members are likely to make decisions and use profits in a way that strengthens the cooperative over the long term, first by simply staying in business, and second by reinvesting in their business.

There are many ways that agricultural cooperatives can be organized. For example, a group of dairy farmers can work together to brand and sell their milk as a marketing or producer cooperative. Such cooperatives often highlight non-economic values like environmental stewardship as part of their marketing strategy. If these farmers also own a processing plant to make their milk into cheese, they are also a value-added agricultural cooperative. Farmers who buy equipment, fertilizer, seeds, and consulting services together are part of a purchasing cooperative.

Values-based supply chains may be legally organized as cooperatives, yet they go beyond the common activities of co-ops by creating partnership across the supply chain. In other words, it's not just the farmers working together; it's also the businesses that process and market and distribute their products. This requires the development and branding of "differentiated products" for wholesale markets. Differentiation can take the form of culinary product attributes such as superior flavor, production attributes such as organic or sustainable methods, and social attributes like family farming and/or fair trade. This differentiation, if it resonates with consumers, can have a positive influence on the bottom line for farmers and their partners, while also supporting environmental and social goals.

Food hubs, another avenue of cooperation among producers, and often buyers, are formed to facilitate the aggregation and distribution of products in a community or region (box 4.4). Food hubs are not necessarily formal cooperatives; they have a variety of business structures, both for-profit and nonprofit. Many provide wider access to institutional markets for small to midsized producers. Many, if not most, are also mission-driven, with the goals of increasing access to fresh healthy food for consumers, providing higher-quality food for underserved and at-risk populations, helping maintain the working landscape, and/or creating new economic opportunities for farmers using sustainable production practices. Food hubs often have their own brand, and many use online platforms to facilitate connections between buyers and sellers, as well as to support educational or technical services they may provide. Food hubs typically are engaged with other organizations that promote local food and entrepreneurship in some way, including agritourism, farm-to-school programs, food safety training, and urban agriculture.

Incremental changes in our current methods of production and consumption will only temporarily sustain an otherwise unsustainable food system dominated by a focus on short-term profit rather than long-term, multi-faceted well-being. The development of compelling and consistent measures of progress will help drive wider consideration of the environmental and social values embodied in food. These values are best supported through horizontal networks composed of mutually beneficial, durable, and transparent relationships all along the value chain, from farmer to consumer.

Ag employers don't have many options.
Most U.S. citizens don't want to do farm
work, forcing many farmers either to hire
workers they suspect might be illegal or to
use the safety net of the H-2A program—
even though that safety net is so small
and tattered it can barely catch anything.
Craig Regelbrugg, Co-chairman
of the Agriculture Coalition for
Immigration Reform

5 ∾ *The Agricultural Workforce*

Food systems start with farmers—and the people working on their farms. However, farms and their workers, especially at the national and regional levels, are largely anonymous. A package of frozen vegetables or a carton of milk from the supermarket may have an iconic image of a farmer in overalls in a field or next to a barn, but that picture is not complete without the farmworkers who harvest the crops or milk the cows.

Sustainable food systems are supposed to be built on relationships that strengthen communities and build social capital. "Know Your Farmer, Know Your Food" is a slogan of the USDA that urges consumers to get to know the farmers they buy from. But even consumers who do get to know a farmer probably know little or nothing about the workers on the farm. Out in the fields or inside barns and packinghouses, most farmworkers are hidden from consumers. Everyone knows that working on a farm is hard work, but hardly anyone knows who is actually doing that work.

Of the approximately 3 million people working in agriculture, about 1 million are estimated to be hired farmworkers (fig. 5.1). The other 2 million are self-employed farmers and their families.[1] Hired farmworkers are either "local" or come from somewhere else in search of work, thus the term "migrant." Migrant workers may be legal, or they may be "undocumented." It is likely that there are many more hired farmworkers than government data suggest, since both the legal and the undocumented migrant farmworker populations are difficult to count. In fact, there may be more than 3 million migrant farmworkers in the United States.[2] Migrant farmworkers are essential to our nation's agriculture, especially those industries that require a lot of

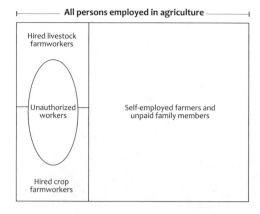

FIGURE 5.1 Types of people in the agricultural workforce. This diagram depicts the results of a study which found that self-employed farmers and their unpaid family members made up two-thirds of the farm workforce, while hired farmworkers made up the other third. About half of the hired workers lacked legal authorization to work in the United States.

manual labor, such as fruit and vegetable farms, dairy farms, and — one step removed from the farm — meat and poultry processing plants.

There are about twice as many hired workers on farms focused on growing crops than there are on those that produce livestock.[3] Of course, livestock production can range from grazing sheep to milking cows and includes a wide range of labor requirements. On dairy farms, which generally need a year-round workforce, local labor shortages have led to increased hiring of Hispanic workers. More than 40 percent of dairy farms in the United States now depend on foreign labor.[4] Every state relies on migrant farmworkers to some degree, with California, Texas, Washington, Florida, Oregon, and North Carolina hiring the most farmworkers, respectively.[5]

Farms spend a lot of money on hired labor. On average nationwide, it's about 17 percent of variable operating expenses, but on those farms that produce labor-intensive crops like fruits, vegetables, and nursery products, it's closer to 40 percent of operating costs. Hired labor is needed to help with everything from preparing fields, planting crops, milking cows, managing pests, picking fruits and vegetables, processing, marketing, and other activities that have to get done in a timely and skilled manner if a farm is to be successful. Typically this work is physically challenging, often it's seasonal, and in general it's low-paying compared with many other professions.

With all the attention given to immigration policy and its impact on migrant farmworkers and the labor pool available to farmers, it's all too easy to overlook the fact that there is a local workforce that is also very important for agriculture. They may be a small proportion of Americans, but some people can and will work for hire on farms. These are often people who like being outdoors and enjoy physical labor; they may feel connected to the land,

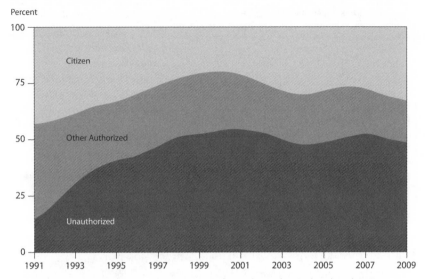

Percent

Citizen

Other Authorized

Unauthorized

FIGURE 5.2 Change over time in the proportion of unauthorized agricultural workers in the United States. In the 1990s undocumented workers became an increasingly important part of the U.S. farm workforce.

to animals, or to the importance of making a product that has meaning and value in a fundamental way: food. In some cases they are people with the goal of owning their own farm, so they work for other farmers to gain experience while saving money and/or looking for their own place.

It's also important to recognize that while many in the agricultural community do not think there are enough capable local workers to replace foreign workers, another view is that foreign workers take local jobs and that they send local money out of the country. Of course, foreign workers also spend some money on living expenses while here, and they may pay into the Social Security system even though they are not likely to collect any benefits. The issue of foreign agricultural labor, legal and illegal, is complicated (fig. 5.2).

As with any other business, farmers who understand labor management principles and follow "best practices" are better able to attract and retain high-quality workers. Sure, farmers have every right to expect a reasonable level of productivity, reliability, and respect for their farming operation, but they also need to value the opinions and feelings of workers, provide positive feedback when warranted, honor the terms of employment agreements, be courteous and consistent, and provide opportunities for advancement over time.[6] Specific human resource management practices that would help some farms increase their "local" workforce include offering a shorter work week, increasing employee benefits, and improving working and living conditions for employees.[7]

In 2010 the median pay for a farmworker in the United States was $18,970 per year, or $9.12 per hour.[8] So besides the labor management issues, there is an economic reason that many farmers have trouble finding workers. Considering how difficult it is for farms to find affordable labor from the pool of available legal workers, it is only logical that they would turn to other laborers who are willing to do the work at the prevailing rate of pay. The methods farmers use to cope with this problem vary depending on the type of farm, and they include hiring interns, legal migrant workers, and undocumented migrant workers.

Internships and Farm Apprenticeships

On small farms, including many that grow organic vegetables, interns are commonly hired. Well, not exactly hired. In exchange for labor, these workers, typically young people interested in learning more about agriculture, get room and board for the growing season, and often a modest stipend. They also get hands-on education, so quite often they're eager to accept this arrangement.

One common way that interns and small farms connect is through nonprofit organizations that do the "matchmaking." In the United States, statewide organic farming associations often offer this service, recruiting both farm hosts and potential interns to enroll in a database. Several thousand such internships across the United States and Canada are listed in an online database titled "Sustainable Farming Internships and Apprenticeships," a program of the National Center for Appropriate Technology (NCAT). The website lets farmers post their internship offerings, and they can be searched by state or province. NCAT makes clear that the listings are provided only as a public service, and it is the responsibility of the farm or organization offering internships to be aware of federal and state labor laws related to such positions.

In the United States, these arrangements may not conform to labor laws, because interns in the for-profit private sector who qualify as employees rather than trainees are supposed to be paid at least the minimum wage.[9] There are some circumstances that allow private-sector internships without that level of compensation, according to the U.S. Department of Labor criteria for internships (box 5.1).[10]

To directly address this issue, Washington State implemented a pilot program that allowed interns to learn about agriculture while working on small farms for less than the legal pay rate, while still having workman's compensation coverage. The program stipulates that participating farms have annual gross sales of $250,000 or less, host no more than three interns at a time, pay into a worker's compensation account, and submit a curriculum and description of the program—which the intern has to agree to.[11]

Internships on farms are available in many countries. The World Wide Opportunities on Organic Farms (wwoof) network links interns or volunteers, known as wwoofers, with organizations that work with organic farms throughout the world. The organizations have connections to the farmers, who provide food, accommodations, and learning experiences in organic production. In exchange, wwoofers provide about four to six hours of labor per day, which is described as fair exchange for a full day's food and accommodation—and an international educational experience.

H-2A Guest Worker Program

Many medium- and large-size horticultural farms rely on migrant workers to meet their labor needs. Some of these farms take part in a program known as h-2a, an agricultural guest worker program that establishes a legal means for agricultural employers who anticipate a shortage of domestic workers to bring foreign workers to the United States to perform temporary or seasonal labor, typically for less than ten months. It's not the first program to do this; the bracero contract labor program allowed several million Mexicans to come to the

United States between 1942 and 1964 to do farmwork. They gained U.S. work experience, and some continued to work illegally after the program ended.[12]

H-2A is not so easy for farmers utilize. It requires the involvement of three federal agencies. The Department of Labor issues the labor certifications and oversees compliance with labor laws; U.S. Citizenship and Immigration Services approves the individual petitions from workers; and the Department of State issues their visas through oversea consulates.

The H-2A program is open to workers from more than fifty countries, many in the Caribbean. Between 40,000 and 60,000 agricultural workers enter the United States each year on H-2A visas, with North Carolina, Florida, Georgia, Kentucky, and Louisiana among the states to receive the most H-2A certifications.[13] In total, H-2A provides only about 2 to 3 percent of the seasonal labor force in U.S. agriculture. While it's an important program for many farms, it hardly makes a dent in the overall need for foreign farmworkers in the United States. Critics of the H-2A program cite the low levels of participation as evidence that the program is not able to meet the needs of agricultural employers. Low participation may be due in part to the administrative hassles and financial costs of the program; others blame the availability of undocumented workers, who receive lower wages than legal workers.

In Vermont, more than four hundred people, mostly Jamaican men, are hired annually through the H-2A program. They spend the growing season working long hours on apple orchards and vegetable farms. Some of these men have been returning to the same farms for decades, and most have good relationships with their employers, who appreciate their work ethic and their reliability. The majority of H-2A workers come from Jamaica because the United States has a treaty with several Caribbean nations enabling their citizens to come here without a visa; thus the application process is quicker for them than for people from other countries.

The Story of H-2A at Mazza's Farm

Hepburn Montague has been working at Sam Mazza's fruit and vegetable farm for twenty-seven years, even though he lives almost two thousand miles away. Hepburn is from Manchester, Jamaica, and every year he travels to and from this farm in northern Vermont (see fig. 5.3).

Gary Bombard is the farm's co-owner and production manager. He works side-by-side with about two dozen Jamaican men each year to plant, maintain, and harvest a wide variety of crops on more than 350 acres of land and in seventeen greenhouses. "We would not be able to farm without these guys," says Gary. He adds:

FIGURE 5.3 H-2A workers at Sam Mazza's farm. Many horticultural farms with high labor demand depend on H-2A workers, and the same men are known to return to some of these farms year after year.

It's pretty easy to get the crops in the ground, but then the hard work starts because there are only so many mechanical aids. You've got to have manual labor, especially to harvest. We do hire local people when they apply, but many don't show up on time, or at all. Those that do quickly develop a respect for the Jamaicans after working with them in the field, "How do those guys do it?" they ask. There's a lot of bending over, and long days. But it's more than just physical labor; back home the Jamaicans have to improvise a lot and they bring that skill and common sense here. For example, one of the men has become our irrigation expert. He knows how to put the pieces of the system together and fix problems to make it work; he doesn't need me to tell him what to do.

Hepburn puts it this way:

We understand what working is all about. But in Jamaica, even if you have a job you can't be sure if you'll have work or if you'll get paid. You go to work today and tomorrow there's no money there. Here, you come to work and you know what you're going to make, and you can plan what to put away. It's very good because it's helped me a lot, and many other people, too. I don't think I would live in a house the way I want to, or be able to send my kids to school. I have four children, and in Jamaica you have to pay for the government schools, not just the private schools, and it's very expensive.

It was hard at first to be away so much but you get used to it. Now, this is our home and we have another home in Jamaica. It's good to move around; we see and learn a lot of things in the U.S. The men come from all walks of life and all the parishes in Jamaica. You have to apply to the government to enter the program, pass a medical test, and be fit to work. Then you get an ID card. In the spring they call you and tell you when they will fly you from Kingston to Florida. From there we take a charter bus to New York, and men get off along the way to take other buses or vans that go to their farms. At first you don't know who is coming with you but then it is the same men coming back each year.

Gary explains, "We send in a list of names of the men that have already been here that we want to come back, which is usually all of them. Our guys are family men; they come here to work and send their money home. A private travel company in Florida takes our paperwork and makes the arrangements with the Jamaican government."

Laurie Mazza Bombard is the farm's co-owner and general manager, and is responsible for completing the paperwork necessary for the farm's participation in the H-2A program. This is how she describes the process:

> We depend on these workers every year, and every year I cross my fingers that I clear all the hurdles and our workers are here when we need them. The process begins two months ahead of the date workers are needed. We submit a job order with the Department of Labor and an application seeking temporary labor certification. Once this application is accepted for processing, the farm must begin the positive recruitment of local workers. We have very specific guidelines to follow for placing ads, contacting previous workers, and setting up interviews. We are also required to advertise in three additional states beyond Vermont. After submitting recruitment results, with luck, the farm will receive the certification for temporary employment, which is necessary before submitting an I-129 petition to Citizenship and Immigration Services.
>
> It seems that every year the requirements change to take part in the program, and a problem with any of the application steps can slow down or halt the process of receiving our workers so they may not get here when the harvest is beginning. Although this program is a necessary part of our labor force, every year is a new and tedious process. It would be great if our government representatives would recognize the importance of these farmworkers and make this process user-friendly.

Gary adds, "The H-2A program requires us to pay for transportation and to provide good housing, which gets inspected, and we pay a decent hourly wage that is set by the program. Overall the program is expensive for us but well worth it. These guys keep us in business, and we're a team. I would not ask Hepburn to do anything I wouldn't do, though granted he is going to do it faster. These guys are here every day, all day, in the growing season, willing to work. In America there are just too many easy paths to take besides hard work."

Undocumented Farmworkers

Many farms, including dairy farms, are not able to utilize H-2A because their labor needs are not seasonal; they operate year-round. The work is repetitive and difficult, and most farmers don't have time to integrate education

5.2 *Characteristics of Migrant Farmworkers*

- Most are younger than thirty-one years of age.
- 80% are male.
- Most have spouses or children who remain in their home countries.
- 75% were born in Mexico.
- 53% are undocumented, 25% are U.S. citizens, and 21% are legal permanent residents.
- Average annual income for a farmworker's family of four is about $16,000.
- 13% have completed high school, and the median highest grade completed is the sixth.

U.S. Department of Labor, *National Agriculural Workers Survey* (Washington, DC: U.S. Department of Labor, Employment and Training Administration, 2005).

programs, so interns are not an option. Farmers try to hire local workers, but even when decent hourly wages with benefits are offered, it's hard to find people who want to do the work and stay on the job over time. The people who are willing to do this type of work often come from other countries, primarily Mexico and Guatemala. They are typically undocumented due to the lack of applicable federal agricultural visa programs.

Across the country, farms employ hundreds of thousands, maybe millions, of undocumented immigrants—accurate data are hard to collect. Technically, these workers are illegal immigrants, without proper documentation to enter the United States to work. But in human terms they are simply people who want to make enough money to support their families, and the great majority of them are hardworking and honest (see box 5.2). They come here because they can't make a decent living in their home countries. There are no federal programs that allow agricultural workers to come to the United States for a few years and then go home, so both farmers and their workers are between a rock and a hard place in their pursuit of economic survival. When farmers can't hire workers in time to harvest their crops, the crops are left rotting in the fields, with losses estimated in the billions.[14]

Nationally, the share of hired crop farmworkers who are not legally authorized to work in the United States has fluctuated around 50 percent for the past decade, although some reports have it as high as 75 percent.[15] Since undocumented workers are in this country illegally, neither the farmers nor the workers have much incentive to provide accurate counts. However, the trend of increasing numbers of undocumented farmworkers is undisputed. According to the National Agricultural Workers Survey, only 7 percent of farmworkers were unauthorized in the late 1980s. Five years later, the proportion had risen to one-third. By 2000, it was more than half.[16] The majority of these workers are young males from Mexico.

In Vermont, it's estimated that there are fifteen hundred undocumented workers on farms, mostly dairies.[17] According to Erin Shea, coordinator of the University of Vermont Extension's Migrant Education Program, the primary reason that these workers come to the United States is to make money to send back home. According to Erin:

> Over half of the undocumented workers in Vermont come from Chiapas, one of the poorest regions of Mexico. Families there are suffering from extreme poverty, civil unrest, and loss of farmland. Even subsistence farming is difficult there and few jobs exist. Farmworkers don't want to leave their homelands and their families, but they come to the U.S. in search of a job so they can send money back to their families to meet basic needs like housing, food, medical care, and education.
>
> Undocumented farmworkers take major risks by coming to the U.S. The dangerous journey to the U.S. costs anywhere from $3,000 to $8,000; the money is paid to "coyotes," which is the term used for the people who bring undocumented immigrants across the border. Traveling illegally to the U.S. is risky, physically and financially. Some migrants don't survive the journey, and many others are forced to pay more than they bargained for.
>
> Anytime you suppress a community of individuals and force them to live underground, you get shady stuff going on. Illegal crossings and undocumented workers are easy targets for criminals seeking victims.

Erin has observed that, once in the United States, these workers receive about $8 per hour on average, plus housing in most cases. She says that the quality of the housing can be decent, but often it is substandard. "In total," she says, "workers typically make $15,000 to $20,000 per year working 70 hours per week in difficult conditions. They stay in this country for two to three years, just long enough to make enough money to help their families, then they go back home. Many farmworkers in Vermont express that they don't want to stay in the U.S. permanently; life is not easy for them while they are here. Due to the lack of a federal visa program, which supports the dairy labor force, most migrant workers come alone, without their families, and live incredibly isolated lives while here."

Communication between farmworkers and famers can be challenging, not only because of the language barrier but also because of cultural differences.

Erin explains, "If Mexican farmworkers come from extreme poverty and see green pastures and big barns and tractors, they think their boss is rich and powerful. They can't understand why their boss may not always meet payroll deadlines. Farmworkers from poor regions don't know about mortgages. They don't know about low federal milk prices. We educate the farmworkers to help them understand that the farmers may not be as wealthy as they appear. In the end, it turns out there may not be so many differences between the farmers and their laborers."

Interviews with Dairy Farmers and Their Undocumented Workers

The Golden Cage: Mexican Migrant Workers and Vermont Dairy Farmers is an interview-based exhibit project conducted by Chris Urban and coordinated by the Vermont Folklife Center.[18] The following excerpts are translated interviews with Mexican workers on Vermont dairy farms drawn from the exhibit website:

Well I walked; a lot of us came from my town, about twenty. We walked two days and two nights. And at the end, the third day, we were on the highway in Arizona. We were there all day, waiting to be picked up. It was really cold. I don't want to remember that. It's hard. Very, very nasty. It's not easy. You risk your life. You play with death. Yeah, because when I crossed in the desert I saw two, two bodies, two dead people. There are thousands that have stayed there. How do I tell you? They don't finish, they don't make their dream of arriving to the United States.

You know, you come with an illusion to do something, to have something . . . a business in Mexico that allows you to survive. I'm not rich because the rich are all connected; the rich are all hooked up. When you finally have something to survive on there, like a business so that you don't have to go back and cross the border . . . many people come and stay awhile but they do something, they save their money and they return and they get a business going so that they don't have to come back again.

Every day working, you just eat, rest, and the work waits for you. It's a little hard, it's not easy, but, well, our thought is that it's worth the pain to suffer a few years to have something.

The way that you live, the level of life, how do I tell you . . . is one thing, and the quality of life that you have is another because you are trapped and yeah you don't lack anything, that's for sure. You don't lack anything. Nothing, nothing, nothing. Only, just something very important, freedom. This is what you lack.

As challenging as the work environment is for undocumented workers, the farmers who hire them are in a difficult situation as well. The following are excerpts from interviews by the Folklife Center with dairy farmers who hire undocumented workers:

> I would definitely prefer something different than the scenario that is in place at this time. It's uncomfortable to me as an American citizen to have to feel that I'm doing something wrong.

> Farming is a business that needs to be run 365 days out of the year and Americans don't want to work Christmas, weekends, and I understand that. So we've gone to a workforce that we can depend on and rely on.

> If they left us tomorrow I'm not sure what we would do. You know, who would milk the cows? Who would do anything around here? You hear about it in other places where they've gone in and taken all the workers and you just wonder, are we going to be the next ones?

> They're scared just because there have been some deportations, arrests . . . But just to be afraid to go to the store that's two miles away? I mean, you're almost like a prisoner.

Life is difficult for undocumented farmworkers, and the farmers who hire them feel they have no other options. The labor situation is untenable. Immigration reforms and incentives that promote fair wages and decent work conditions are urgently needed. In ideal situations, where the farms provide decent pay, housing, and work conditions—and workers are not fearful of immigration officials just doing their job—the workers are self-replacing. That is, when one goes home, another family member comes along. This type of situation is beneficial for both the farmers and the laborers. The farmers have reliable, well-trained workers, and the workers have decent jobs with decent pay and accommodations. Everyone benefits, down to consumers who purchase a high-quality product made in a way they can feel good about.

Creating Win-Win Labor Conditions for Farmers and Workers

Simply put, our food systems would collapse without the farm labor provided by foreign workers, and we need to find ways to make it legal and safe for these people—documented or not—to contribute to our food security while maintaining their own safety and their dignity.

"Accountability is a critical incentive for farms to provide decent wages, safe working conditions, and healthy living quarters," according to Erin.

FIGURE 5.4 Food Justice Certification logo. The Agricultural Justice Project certifies farms that meet standards for fair treatment of workers, fair pricing for farmers, and fair business practices.

"Without accountability it's like the Wild West out there. Someone needs to start setting standards and taking action to protect undocumented workers."

That accountability can come from state programs, farmer co-operatives, and consumer support. States can ensure that farmworkers have access to basic services such as health care and education. North Carolina, for example, has the Migrant Housing Act, which specifies standards to be met and mandates housing inspections by the North Carolina Department of Labor and the local county health department. For farms that go above and beyond minimum standards, the North Carolina Department of Labor offers the Gold Star Grower Housing Program.[19] Since federal regulations do not address working conditions for undocumented farmworkers, each state must come up with its own standards and programs for ensuring those standards. The Gold Star Grower Housing Program lets farmworkers know who is meeting state standards.

Beyond influencing state policy, farmer cooperatives have opportunities to work closely with their farmer-members and promote reasonable standards for migrant labor working conditions, living conditions, and pay. Communities and individuals can also take steps to proactively support farmworkers. Community members living near farms can visit those farms and offer to help the farmers and their laborers meet some of their basic needs, by buying groceries for or with them or taking them to free medical clinics. Their needs may not be easy to meet; for example, in border communities, particularly in the North, where immigration authorities are relatively numerous, undocumented farmworkers may not want to leave the farm for fear of being detained and deported. Farmers then end up with the responsibility of taking their workers grocery shopping, or shopping for them, which is not something expected from a typical employer, let alone a busy farmer. Community members, especially those with some Spanish fluency, can also offer to visit with farmworkers who may feel isolated.

Consumers could also support farmworkers by purchasing farm products that were certified to meet high standards for work conditions — if such labels were widely available. They are not widely available yet, but some organizations are working on it. With the Fair Trade certification for workers outside the United States as a basis, four not-for-profits, including the Northeast Organic Farming Association (NOFA), the Farmworker Support Committee (CATA), Rural Advancement Foundation International (RAFI), and Florida Organic Growers (FOG), teamed up to develop standards for the fair and just treatment of farmworkers as well as fair pricing for farmers. Known as the Agricultural Justice Project, they created the Food Justice certification based on these standards, and they are collaborating with farmers, farmworkers, and other food system stakeholders to implement the certification program (fig. 5.4).[20]

In the absence of widespread labor certifications and labeling, consumers are on their own to figure out which farms provide their workers with decent wages and safe working conditions. Like most other aspects of local food systems, the best way for consumers to find out is to get to know their farmers, build some trust, and then inquire about their practices — not only production practices but farm labor practices as well. A well-trained, well-supported labor pool that meets the needs of both the workers and the farmers who employ them is a critical element of building sustainable food systems.

*Many modern agricultural practices
have unintended negative consequences,
or externalized costs of production, that
are largely unaccounted for in agricultural
productivity measurements.*

Committee on 21st Century
Systems Agriculture

6 ∾ *Farming and the Environment*

Farms by their very nature are disturbed ecosystems, sometimes referred to as agricultural ecosystems or agroecosystems. Farm soil is frequently worked in order to prepare a seedbed, natural vegetation is suppressed, and pests are controlled, with effects on non-target organisms. One could argue that even hunting and gathering alters the natural ecosystem, at least if done intensely over a long period of time. Thus human food systems have always had an environmental impact. A key question about that impact is: Are the natural resources upon which a food system depends being degraded to the extent that the system cannot be sustained? Since the damage may be incremental, it takes a long-term view to answer the question honestly.

History offers examples of food systems that did themselves in over time, like those in Mesopotamia and the Mayan Empire. One explanation is that as the complexity of a society and its food system increases, the result is "declining marginal returns."[1] In other words, once a society develops a productive food system, the population grows and consumption increases to a level that requires greater and greater resource use by the food system, with fewer and fewer additional returns over time. More land, water, fertility, and/or technologies are utilized to meet the demand for food, so local ecosystems are degraded and additional "external" inputs are substituted to compensate for that degradation. This leads to resource depletion (soil erosion, water shortages) and resource damage (low soil biological diversity, soil compaction, soil salinization, water pollution, etc.). If the climate also becomes less favorable for the established agricultural system, stress on the food system is exacerbated, and the stage may be set for collapse.

Ancient civilizations may not have understood the cause of their troubles or what they could do to sustain their food systems. But for at least a century, people have been articulating concerns about the environmental impacts of food production and describing ways to reduce them. Here is a small sampling of that thinking.

Liberty Hyde Bailey, after retiring in 1913 as dean of the New York State College of Agriculture, which he founded, wrote:

> The surface of the earth is particularly within the care of the farmer. He keeps it for his own sustenance but also for all the rest of us. . . . It is a public duty to train the farmer that he shall appreciate his guardianship. . . . It is recently proposed that Congress shall pass a law regulating the cropping scheme of the farmers for the protection of soil fertility. . . . We shall produce a much better and safer man when we make him self-controlling by developing his sense of responsibility than when we regulate him by exterior enactments.[2]

Sir Albert Howard was an English botanist working in India; he was one of the pioneers of composting and soil stewardship. The preface of his 1943 book, *An Agricultural Testament*, reads:

> Since the Industrial Revolution the processes of growth have been speeded up to produce the food and raw materials needed by the population and the factory. Nothing effective has been done to replace the loss of fertility involved in this vast increase in crop and animal production. The consequences have been disastrous. Agriculture has become unbalanced: the land is in revolt: diseases of all kinds are on the increase: in many parts of the world Nature is removing the worn-out soil by means of erosion. The purpose of this book is to draw attention to the destruction of the earth's capital—the soil; to indicate some of the consequences of this; and to suggest methods by which the lost fertility can be restored and maintained.[3]

Influenced by Sir Albert Howard's work on compost-based farming, Lady Eve Balfour conducted trials on her land in Suffolk, England, which are said to have been the first scientific, side-by-side comparisons of organic and conventional farming. In 1943 she published *The Living Soil*, in which she explained that the health of soil, plants, animals, and people was intertwined with food systems, though she didn't use that term.[4]

J. I. Rodale started *Organic Farming and Gardening* magazine in 1942, which widely shared the idea that better food could be produced by the cultivation of healthy soil using natural techniques. The magazine was one of the few sources of practical information for early adopters of sustainable and organic farming practices. Rodale is regarded by many as the father of the organic farming movement in the United States.

Over the past few decades, many scientists have described flaws in conventional thinking about modern agricultural production systems and offered insights into new approaches that would reduce negative impacts while sustaining production over time. These include Miguel Altieri, Stephen Gliessman, Fred Magdoff, and David Pimentel.[5] Such thought leaders have helped bring a more ecological perspective to agricultural research, though there is a still a long way to go.

Many, many innovative farmers have shared the knowledge they acquired while developing economically viable production systems that avoid dependence on external inputs and minimize environmental impacts. These farmers are key partners in research and education efforts that seek to improve agricultural sustainability.

Increasing Productivity, Inputs, and Impacts

As the United States grew in population and wealth, there was a growing demand for food. To meet this demand a combination of strategies were used, including mechanization to replace animal and human labor, increasing the amount of land used for agriculture, breeding to improve crops and livestock, expanding the use of irrigation and new techniques for irrigation, applying pesticides, and increasing fertilizer usage. Once domestic demands were met, food started to be exported; agricultural exports now amount to about 20 percent of agricultural production,[6] although the United States also imports a lot of food. The output of U.S. farms has increased steadily over time, but productivity increased most dramatically from the middle of the twentieth century to the present, as many new technologies were developed and implemented on farms.

Between 1950 and 1975, agricultural productivity practically tripled and farm output increased by more than half, while farm acreage dropped by 6 percent and the hours of farm laborers decreased by 60 percent. These dramatic changes resulted in part from the development of hybrid crops, intensive animal breeding, and a fourfold increase in the use of pesticides and fertilizers.[7]

The combination of mechanization, inexpensive chemical fertilizers and pesticides, increased irrigation, and advances in plant and animal breeding led to a growth in agricultural productivity that averaged 1.9 percent annually during the second half of the twentieth century. Some farmers were not able to adjust to the new technologies and the generally low prices for commodities, and as they sold their land to other farmers a rapid growth in average farm size occurred, accompanied by an equally rapid decline in the number of farms, farmers, and rural population. The intensive production of crops and livestock involving more purchased inputs and greater concentration on land that was easier to farm with large machinery also exacerbated environmental impacts.[8] These included degradation of soil, reduction of water and air quality, as well as negative effects on biodiversity and ecosystem health.

More than a billion pounds of pesticides are now used every year in the United States, at a cost of about $12 billion; agriculture accounts for 80 percent of this total.[9] So it should not be a big surprise that the majority of our produce has detectable pesticide residues.[10] About 20 million tons of fertilizers have been applied to U.S. farmland every year since the mid-1970s, despite a significant increase in cost over the past decade.[11] About 1.7 billion tons of soil erodes from U.S. cropland every year, though the loss is half of what it once was,[12] presumably due to the adoption of conservation tillage practices. Water pollution by nitrogen, phosphorus, and pesticides is widespread in agricultural regions.[13] Agriculture is a significant producer of some air pollutants, including ammonia, particulate matter, methane, and nitrous oxide.[14] The disconnect between livestock and crop production on farms and the increase in concentrated livestock feeding operations exacerbates the environmental risks posed by manure, especially the development of antibiotic-resistant diseases.[15]

Resource Conservation and Protection Programs

The number of agricultural conservation programs developed to address environmental concerns has steadily increased over the past sixty years. Early efforts focused on reducing soil erosion and providing water to increase farm production. Franklin D. Roosevelt established the Soil Erosion Service (SES) under the Department of the Interior in 1933, with the purpose of employing men on erosion control projects. The SES set up demonstrations in almost every state to show farmers how to conserve their soil. After the Dust Bowl storms the SES became the Soil Conservation Service in 1935, and moved to the USDA. As Congress put it: "The wastage of soil and moisture resources on farm, grazing, and forest lands . . . is a menace to the national welfare." Demonstrations were set up to teach farmers about practices like contour plowing, terracing, strip cropping, leaving residues on the soil surface, and planting windbreaks. In 1994 the agency's name changed to the Natural Resources Conservation Service (NRCS) to reflect a greater scope of environmental concerns.

Now more than twenty programs offered by the USDA provide about $6 billion annually to address natural resource concerns on private lands; many of these programs are aimed at agriculture.[16] Among the largest of these are the Conservation Stewardship Program and the Environmental Quality Incentives Program. They provide financial and technical assistance to farmers and landowners to plan and implement a wide range of practices that promote improved management of grassland, irrigation, manure, and pests; the maintenance of riparian buffers and wildlife habitats; and the adoption of cover crops, crop rotation, composting, and energy-efficient equipment.

The Environmental Protection Agency (EPA) is charged with protecting human health and the environment from pesticide risks. It administers pesticide programs that focus on ensuring the safety, certification, and training of farmworkers, preserving water quality, protecting endangered species, and promoting proper pesticide use. The EPA also develops risk assessment methods for evaluating new pesticides and reviewing older pesticides.

Environmental Concerns

Agriculture has an effect on water quality, soil health, air quality, biodiversity, and the genetics of crops and animals used for food. It also generates excess manure in some locations, while soil fertility depletion in other locations requires large applications of fertilizers, which poses a variety of environmental concerns.

WATER QUALITY. Water that is free of or extremely low in contaminants is essential for healthy people, farms, and the environment. Because of its widespread presence in the landscape, farming is a significant source of water contamination. Surface runoff from farms carries soil, manure, fertilizers, and pesticides into rivers and lakes. Water that percolates down below farm fields can move dissolved agrichemicals and nutrients into groundwater. Water quality is impaired in about 44 percent of U.S. rivers and streams and 64 percent of lakes, ponds, and reservoirs. Agriculture is the leading source of this impairment, affecting 39 percent of all impaired rivers and streams and 16 percent of impaired lakes and ponds.[17] The fertilizer nutrients of most concern are phosphorus and nitrogen. Phosphorus does not leach downward in soil as readily as nitrogen because it is more tightly bound to soil particles. However, it is often carried with surface runoff waters containing eroded soil particles into surface waters.

Agricultural pesticides are widely found in the nation's waters, especially in farming regions.[18] A ten-year study by the National Water-Quality Assessment program examined fifty-one major river basins and aquifers; pesticide compounds were detected in more than 90 percent of stream samples in watersheds dominated by agricultural, urban, or mixed land use. Organochlorine pesticides, which are no longer in use, were also found in fish and sediment from most streams in these watersheds. Pesticides were detected in more than 50 percent of shallow wells in agricultural and urban areas and in 33 percent of deeper wells that tap major aquifers. Annual concentrations of pesticides exceeded human health benchmarks in eight of eighty-three agricultural streams sampled; however, pesticides usually occurred as mixtures rather than individually, so their toxicity may be have been underestimated since analyses are usually based on single compounds. The negative economic impact of pesticide use has been estimated to amount to many billions of dollars annually.[19]

Water quality of the seas is also being affected by agriculture. The so-called dead zone in the Gulf of Mexico, one of many in the world, is a result of hypoxia, fueled by nutrient runoff from agricultural and other human activities in the watershed. Excess nutrients, primarily nitrogen and phosphorus, stimulate the growth of algae, which, when they decompose, consume most of the oxygen needed to support life. The size of the Gulf's dead zone varies from year to year but has been increasing over time. It now averages about 5,000 square miles, nearly the size of Connecticut. Hypoxic areas have increased in duration and frequency across the earth's oceans since first being noted in the 1970s.[20]

SOIL QUALITY. The terms "soil fertility" and "soil health" have been used to describe the attributes of soil that are desirable for farming (table 6.1). Healthy soil has the biological, chemical, and physical characteristics necessary to support the kind of agriculture that is suited to the climate and topography of a given location. Fertile soil is miraculous stuff—tens of thousands to millions of years old, chock full of minerals, able to retain as well as drain water, and home to millions if not billions of microorganisms in every spoonful. It's also resilient, so it can continue to support crop production even when abused—but not forever. Intensive agriculture harms soil health if erosion, compaction, salinization, pollution, and/or loss of organic matter are allowed to occur. The basic approach to stewardship of soil health is simple enough: avoid practices that cause harm, and utilize as many practices as possible that maintain or improve soil health.

Soil erosion is a big problem in crop production because whenever there is tillage the soil is exposed and thus vulnerable to the forces of water, wind, and gravity. Erosion not only affects soil quality and long-term crop productivity, but creates off-site impacts when eroded soil reduces water quality, air quality, and biological activity where sediments, and any agricultural chemicals adhered to them, are deposited. Eroded soil can harm habitats for fish and other aquatic life. Surface waters, including drinking supplies, may become

TABLE 6.1 *Indicators of Physical, Biological, and Chemical Health of Soil and Their Respective Soil Processes*

Soil Health Indicator	Soil Functional Processes Affected
Physical indicators	
Aggregate stability	Aeration, infiltration, shallow rooting, crusting
Available water capacity	Water retention
Surface hardness	Rooting, water transmission
Subsurface hardness	Rooting at depth
Biological indicators	
Organic matter content	Energy/carbon storage, water, and nutrient retention
Active carbon content	Organic material to support biological functions
Potentially mineralizable nitrogen	Nitrogen supply capacity, nitrogen leaching potential
Root health rating	Soilborne pest pressure
Chemical indicators	
pH	Toxicity, nutrient availability
Extractable phosphorus	Phosphorus availability, environmental loss potential
Extractable potassium	Potassium availability
Minor element contents	Micronutrient availability, element imbalances

Adapted from John Idowu, Harold van Es, Robert Schindelbeck, George Abawi, David Wolfe, Janice Thies, Bianca Moebius, Beth Gugino, and Dan Clune, "The New Cornell Soil Health Test: Protocols and Interpretations," *What's Cropping Up?* 17, no. 1 (2007): 6–7.

polluted directly, or they may be threatened by excessive plant growth from added nutrients. The amount of soil erosion depends on the intensity of rain and wind, soil type, slope, and farming practices (table 6.2). Erosion affects productivity because it removes the surface soils, which contain most of the organic matter and plant nutrients. Up to a point this can be compensated for by increased fertilization and irrigation, but ultimately short-term production must be balanced with practices that sustain soil health over the long term.

AIR QUALITY. Both livestock and crop production generate a variety of air pollutants that can affect human and environmental health. The six major types of such pollutants that can be generated by agricultural activities are particulate matter, ozone precursors such as nitrogen oxides and volatile organic compounds, greenhouse gases, ammonia, odors, and pesticide drift.[21]

TABLE 6.2 *Universal Soil Loss Equation*

Variable	Definition
A	Annual rate of soil erosion
R	Rainfall and runoff
K	Soil erodibility
L	Slope length
S	Slope steepness
C	Surface cover and management
P	Support practices that mitigate against runoff and erosion

A = R K L S C P. The universal soil loss equation is used around the world to estimate
the annual rate of soil erosion (*A*) and guide soil conservation planning.

In the United States, agriculture accounts for 90 percent of all ammonia emissions, 29 percent of methane, and 72 percent of nitrous oxide.[22] Suspended particulate matter emissions from agriculture are approximately 4,032,000 tons per year, or 18 percent of the U.S. total. These come mostly from crop tilling and livestock dust emissions. The emission of fine particulates (soot) comes mostly from tilling and harvesting; agriculture accounts for 16 percent of the U.S. total, or 946,000 tons per year. Increasing evidence also shows that the greater size and intensity of farms and concentrated animal feeding operations (CAFOs) increase the emissions of odor, greenhouse gases, and ammonia.

BIODIVERSITY. "Agricultural biodiversity" is the term used to describe the variety of plants, animals, and microbes found in farming systems. This variety exists at the genetic, species, and ecosystem levels, and is necessary to sustain key functions of agroecosystems structure and processes.[23] Biodiversity in agriculture includes domesticated species, wild plants and animals that are managed for food, and wild species that live in or pass through farms. Biodiversity can be found in a spoonful of soil in the form of microbial populations and across many square miles of mixed-use land that may comprise the territory of large animals.

Tillage, drainage, grazing, and the use of pesticides and fertilizers have significant implications for wild plants and animals that try to live in agricultural settings.[24] Even if they can adapt to an agricultural landscape, their survival may be limited by disturbance of soil, modification of water supply, reduction of food supply, operation of machinery, and/or toxicity of agricultural chemicals. Farming practices can cause fundamental habitat changes that lead to significant shifts in species composition both above- and belowground.

Given that agricultural systems are aimed primarily at creating habitats suitable for food crops and livestock, the challenge is to identify management practices in those systems that also maintain biodiversity. Such management can take place at the field, farm, and landscape levels.

Within fields, practices that promote biodiversity include using cover crops to keep living vegetation on the fields, adding animal manures, using complex crop rotations, timing certain disruptive activities such as grazing, haying, or tillage to minimize harm to wildlife, and limiting the use of biocides. Between fields, even those that are intensively cropped in a way that significantly reduces biodiversity, maintaining uncropped areas such as hedgerows and forests can promote biodiversity at the farm level by providing undisturbed areas that serve as wildlife habitats. At the landscape level, biodiversity can be promoted by the protection of essential nesting grounds, feeding areas, and reproduction sites for native or transitory species.

GENETICALLY MODIFIED ORGANISMS. Genetic engineering is the controlled manipulation of an organism's genes independent of natural reproduction and frequently involves inserting genes from other organisms into the target plant or animal. The result is a so-called genetically modified organism (GMO). The use of GMOs in agriculture and food production is highly controversial; some people believe it is primarily beneficial, while others see it as primarily harmful. The purported benefits include higher yields, reduced pesticide use, and more efficient use of fertilizers. The purported risks in-

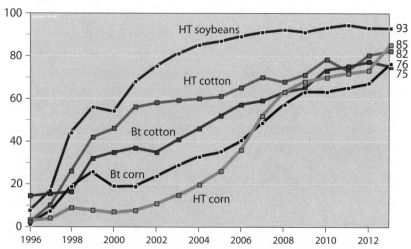

Percent of planted acres

FIGURE 6.1 Use of genetically engineered crops in the United States. The adoption of genetically engineered, or transgenic, crops has been rapid over the past two decades.

clude the production of allergens, harm to animals that consume them, the spread of traits to weeds and non–genetically engineered crops, and the overreliance on herbicides that has led to the development of herbicide-resistant "superweeds."

Genetic engineering in agriculture has focused on herbicide-tolerant (HT) crops and insect-resistant (Bt) crops that contain genes from the soil bacterium *Bacillus thuringiensis*. Herbicide-tolerant crops were developed to survive applications of herbicides that previously would have destroyed the crop along with the targeted weeds. About 90 percent of all corn, cotton, and soybeans in the United States are now HT, Bt, or both (fig. 6.1).[25]

Proponents of genetically engineered crops claim they offer numerous benefits beyond insect and weed management, including resistance to extreme weather and adverse climates as well as the production of abundant food at low cost to reduce world hunger. However, these claims have not been realized: crop losses to drought and rain continue, and the number of hungry people on the planet has not been reduced (box 6.1).

EXCESS MANURE. Livestock production in the United States results in 133 million tons of manure annually on a dry weight basis. Most animals for human consumption are now produced in concentrated animal feeding operations called CAFOs. The animals are held throughout their lives at high densities indoors until they are transported to processing plants for slaughter. Their feed may be produced locally, but commonly it is shipped in from regions concentrating on crop production. The nutrient content of the wastes can make them desirable as soil amendments and fertilizers for crops, but overapplication or spills can lead to water pollution and adverse health impacts on wildlife or humans. Animal wastes may also contain microbial pathogens that can cause human illness, as well as antibiotics that promote antibiotic resistance among the microbial populations present.[26]

In many watersheds, animal manures represent a significant portion of the total fertilizer nutrients added. In some counties with heavy concentrations of livestock and poultry, nutrients from confined animals exceed the uptake potential of non-legume harvested cropland and hayland. The USDA estimates that recoverable manure nitrogen exceeds crop system needs in 8 percent of all counties and recoverable manure phosphorus exceeds crop system needs in 15 percent of counties.[27]

Mitigating Environmental Impacts of Agriculture

Broadly speaking, there are two paradigms for the design of agricultural systems, and thus two approaches to reducing their impacts on the environment. One paradigm has been called industrial or conventional agriculture and the other ecological, or alternative, agriculture. These competing paradigms have six major dimensions: (1) centralization versus decentralization, (2) dependence versus independence, (3) competition versus community, (4) domination of nature versus harmony with nature, (5) specialization versus diversity, and (6) exploitation versus restraint.[28]

In general, mitigation of the impacts of industrial agriculture is aimed at an incremental reduction in the use of harmful inputs and practices, but not fundamental changes in the design of a farming system. In fact, mitigation is often initiated only in response to increased impacts; for example, regulations were adopted when large-scale animal operations were recognized to create unacceptable levels of nutrient runoff and odors. Ecological agriculture seeks to design farming systems that avoid environmental impacts in the first place. If agriculture is to become more sustainable in the face of environmental (and other) challenges, both incremental change and transformative change will have to occur.[29]

Among farmers there is a continuum of perspectives that span the extreme versions of the industrial and ecological paradigms; most farms are somewhere in the middle. For example, large-scale crop farms may depend on fertilizers and herbicides but also use cover crops and rotations. Confinement animal operations may capture and recycle wastes to protect water quality and generate energy. Alternative farming enterprises may use many ecologically oriented practices, yet fail to properly account for nutrient inputs and outputs over time, leading to water pollution; or they may consume significant fuel when processing and/or shipping their products to market. Few if any farms can be said to be ecologically perfect or completely imperfect.

A variety of actions have been implemented to reduce the impacts of farming on the environment. These include regulating the use of pesticides, plant nutrients, and manure; and promoting the adoption of integrated pest management, conservation tillage practices, and management intensive grazing.

PESTICIDE REGULATION. In 1947 the Federal Insecticide, Fungicide, and Rodenticide Act was passed by Congress. This act, amended several times since, covers all types of pesticides and requires product registration with the USDA, as well as pesticide labeling that lists ingredients, gives directions for use, and contains warning statements about effects on applicators and non-target plants and animals. In 1996 Congress passed the Food Quality Protection Act. It mandates that regulators consider the aggregate risk of pesticides, not just individual products, and that the greater risk for children be accounted for.

Several federal agencies as well as state agencies are involved in pesticide regulation. The USDA collects data on what kinds of pesticides are used on farms and how much is applied. Along with the Food and Drug Administration (FDA), the USDA also tests food for pesticide residues. The EPA decides which pesticides get approved and sets pesticide labeling requirements. It conducts dietary risk assessments and then sets the residue limits for pesticides on foods, which are called "tolerances" that are deemed to be safe. State agencies can further restrict which pesticides are allowed to be used. They license individual pesticide applicators and enforce pesticide laws in conjunction with federal agencies.

NUTRIENT MANAGEMENT. Nutrients can be managed by a set of best management practices aimed at reducing nutrient pollution by balancing nutrient inputs with crop nutrient requirements. This helps farmers estimate rates of nutrient applications for individual fields, account for available nutrients from all sources before making supplemental applications, time their nitrogen applications to align with crop needs, and reduce excessive soil phosphorus applications.[30]

Many states have enacted nutrient management regulations. These may mandate nutrient management plans for farms, limit the use of nitrogen- and phosphorus-based fertilizers and/or manure, specify that university soil test recommendations be followed, require certification of nutrient management consultants, and/or prohibit winter applications of fertilizer or manure. Some states have also regulated the non-agricultural use of fertilizer nutrients, especially for lawn care.

MANURE MANAGEMENT. States agencies and cooperative extension have been promoting voluntary manure management on farms of all sizes for many years. Manure management is also regulated to different degrees by the states, at a minimum to meet EPA requirements that large livestock farms develop and follow manure management plans. Key parts of a comprehensive manure management plan include a nutrient management plan that considers all sources of nutrients and crop needs, manure storage, handling and application methods, feed management to minimize excess nutrients in manure, and other manure utilization options such as composting, energy production, and off-site uses.

In 2003 the EPA revised Clean Water Act regulations to better protect surface waters from nutrients from CAFOS. When applying manure to crop- or pastureland, CAFOS must follow a nutrient management plan that specifies application rates and minimizes threats to water quality. However, livestock production can generate a variety of pollutants, including ammonia, nitrate, nitrous oxide, phosphorus, methane, carbon dioxide, pathogens, antibiotics, and hormones. Taking steps to reduce emissions that degrade water quality can lead to an increase of emissions to the air, and vice versa. Managing manure to protect both air and water quality can be complicated; it is most cost-effective if farmers simultaneously select and implement practices that address both goals.[31]

CONSERVATION TILLAGE. In recent years U.S. farmers have increasingly adopted reduced-tillage practices that leave crop residues on the soil surface. About a third of all crop fields are now managed using no-till, and this has greatly reduced the amount of soil lost annually from cropland. Residues on the surface are very effective at protecting soil from erosion by wind and water. One drawback to conservation tillage is that significant quantities of herbicide must be used to control cover crops and weeds in place of tillage.

INTEGRATED PEST MANAGEMENT. Integrated pest management (IPM) has been promoted as an approach that can save farmers money by reducing their need for pesticides while also protecting the environment and human health (fig. 6.2). Although there are many definitions of IPM, it is generally agreed that the approach has four main components: (1) establishing thresholds for taking action against a pest, based on its population level and the economic threat it poses; (2) preventing the pest population from building up in the first place, by using cultural practices like crop rotation and resistant

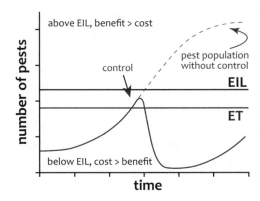

FIGURE 6.2 Pest populations and integrated pest management. Using IPM, the economic injury level (EIL) is the pest population level at which the cost of crop yield loss exceeds the cost of the control measures for the pest. The economic threshold (ET) is the pest population level that, if left untreated, is likely to exceed the EIL. Therefore, the ET is almost always lower than the EIL and is sometimes called an action threshold.

varieties; (3) monitoring (and properly identifying) the pest population; and (4) selecting the least toxic intervention(s) that will be effective if and when control is needed. The interventions may entail a pheromone to disrupt pest mating, a mechanical control such as trapping, a biological control such as a predator, or a synthetic pesticide.

In its most robust form, IPM uses a diverse set of tactics to optimize the control of all pests; this requires simultaneous monitoring and management of multiple pests and their natural enemies, as well as the use of multiple, suppressive tactics. However, there is little evidence that IPM is being intensively used in U.S. agriculture because it is time-consuming and complicated, farmers are busy, and pesticides can be a cheap insurance policy when there is a possibility of losing an entire crop. Thus a better name for IPM is "integrated pesticide management" since it tends to promote the judicious use of pesticides rather than a more holistic approach.[32]

MANAGEMENT-INTENSIVE GRAZING. Many farmers keep their livestock in confinement some or all of the time and deliver feed to them. That feed typically contains some mixture of grain like corn plus forages like alfalfa; these may be grown on the farm and/or purchased. Other farmers focus on grazing their livestock, so they grow forages, and the animals go to the fields to eat them. This may be supplemented with grains grown on the farm or bought in. Management-intensive grazing (MIG), also called rotational grazing, involves rotating animals through subdivided pastures for a relatively short stay in each pasture in order to provide them with high-quality nutrition while also optimizing the productivity of the pasture plants. Well-managed grazing systems provide many environmental benefits compared with poorly managed pastures that are over- or under-grazed or are located in environmentally sensitive areas such as riparian zones.

MIG has greater potential than confinement production to provide economic benefits to farmers, by reducing livestock production expenses for
growing or buying grains, operating equipment, and handling manure,
though production per animal is typically lower. It is not as easy to compare
the environmental impacts of MIG and confinement systems due to variability
among farms, their local conditions, and their management. However, soils
under well-managed pasture have been shown to have higher organic matter
content and biological activity, as well as better soil structure, which is associated with reduced runoff and erosion as compared with more intensively
cropped soils.[33]

Alternative Farming Systems

A variety of names have been given to farming systems that prohibit or
strive to limit the use of certain conventional inputs and practices. Some of
these systems, such as sustainable agriculture and agroecology, are conceptu-
ally based and have principles and goals but do not have standards. Others,
such as organic farming, have specific standards that a farm either does or
does not meet.

ORGANIC AGRICULTURE. Organic farming practices have been around for
a long time, since most predate the use of synthetic inputs. It was not until
there were concerns about conventional farming that some farmers and markets wanted to make the distinction. This was informal initially, first in Europe and then in the United States when in the 1970s grassroots organizations
such as California Certified Organic Farmers and the Northeast Organic
Farming Association (NOFA) began to more formally define which inputs and
practices were allowed on organic farms and to offer organic farm inspections
and certification. In 1990 Congress passed the Organic Foods Production Act,
creating national standards for the production and handling of organic food,
though it took another decade to work out the details and implement the law.
The National Organic Program was established at the USDA, which defines
organic agriculture as an ecological production management system that promotes and enhances biodiversity, biological cycles, and soil biological activity.
It is based on minimal use of off-farm inputs and on management practices
that restore, maintain, or enhance ecological harmony.

Organic farms and handling operations work with one of about fifty USDA-
approved organic certifying organizations to document their compliance with
the national organic standards. They keep records of all practices and materials used, and have an annual inspection. A three-year transition period
is required unless records prove that no prohibited substances were used in

or near the production area for that period. In general, synthetic inputs are prohibited and non-synthetic inputs are allowed, but there is a list of allowed synthetics deemed to be sufficiently non-toxic and a list of prohibited natural materials deemed to be too toxic for use in organic food production. Organic food accounts for about 4 percent of the $700 billion in U.S. annual food sales;[34] there are an estimated nine thousand certified organic farms with 3.6 million acres of land and $3.5 billion in annual farm-gate sales.[35]

In general, organic production systems typically yield about 8 or 9 percent less than conventional systems in developed countries, though this can vary widely.[36] Organic farms often have better soil health and smaller nutrient surpluses than conventional farms, which reduces the risk of water pollution. Organic crop production may also have lower greenhouse gas emissions than conventional production with full tillage, although it may not if compared with no-till. More life-cycle assessments are needed across different crops and production systems.

SUSTAINABLE AGRICULTURE. This term is defined in federal legislation as "an integrated system of plant and animal production practices having a site-specific application that will over the long-term: Satisfy human food and fiber needs; Enhance environmental quality and the natural resource base upon which the agriculture economy depends; Make the most efficient use of nonrenewable resources and on-farm resources and integrate, where appropriate, natural biological cycles and controls; Sustain the economic viability of farm operations, and; Enhance the quality of life for farmers and society as a whole."[37]

While some conventional farmers view sustainable agriculture as code for organic farming (which it is not), many others embrace the concept. Sustainable agriculture is a pursuit rather than a standard, and all farms can make improvements that render them more sustainable.

AGROECOLOGY. It could be said that agroecology is the science of agricultural sustainability. The goal of applied agroecology is to establish farming systems capable of providing their own soil fertility, crop protection, and yield stability by using ecological interactions and synergisms between biological components. The principles of agroecology are as follows:[38]

1 Enhance recycling of biomass, optimize nutrient availability, and balance nutrient flow.
2 Secure favorable soil conditions for plant growth, particularly by managing organic matter and enhancing soil biotic activity.
3 Minimize losses due to flows of solar radiation, air, and water by way of

microclimate management, water harvesting, and soil management through increased soil cover.

4 Diversify species and genetics of the agroecosystem in time and space.

5 Enhance beneficial biological interactions and synergisms among agrobiodiversity components, thus promoting key ecological processes and services.

Environmental Protection on a Large Dairy Farm: Evergreen Farms, Spruce Creek, Pennsylvania

The Harpster family owns and operates one of the largest dairy farms in Pennsylvania, with more than 4,500 acres of cropland that is used to grow feed for about 6,000 cows. Just over half the herd is young stock, and the other half produces milk, and lots of it: 220,000 pounds a day. The farm was started by R. Wayne Harpster in the early 1990s. He increased the herd size to about 1,800 cows and then transferred ownership to his three sons. The family has continued to expand the operation since then in order to produce income for all the partners and to improve efficiency.

The three sons and other family members divide up the complex management duties of running a large farm. Andy Harpster, who is responsible mainly for crop production, describes the farm's environmental philosophy this way: "It is in our best interest to do a good job caring for the environment. We have to comply with regulations, but we're also dedicated to stewardship because the land is ours and we value it; we don't want to hurt the ecosystem."

The farm is adjacent to Spruce Creek and to Little Juanita Creek, which are world-renowned for fly fishing. These creeks drain into the Chesapeake Bay, which has been the focus of water quality programs aimed at reducing runoff from nearby farms. As Harpster explains it:

> Given our location in such an environmentally sensitive area and the size of our farm, we are watched by local, regional, and federal regulators. We also have a personal economic stake in the health of our waterways. In addition to farming we operate several lucrative fly-fishing lodges. People come from all over the world to stay at our lodges and fish in the creeks.
>
> We're always trying to improve our practices to reduce their impact on the environment. That means we're always looking for new techniques as well as better equipment. Our farm has been 100 percent no-till since 1976, to reduce soil erosion. We started stream-bank fencing in 1980 to keep cows out of the creeks and we now have about 10 miles of fence. More recently, we started using cover crops very intensely to help mop up excess soil nutrients and add organic residues to our fields.

As a large farm we're required to have a comprehensive nutrient management plan, and we update it every three years. Manure is very valuable, but it needs to be managed properly and every year we try to do better at that. We separate the manure solids from the liquids so we can reuse most of the solids as bedding rather than spread them on fields. We soil-test all our fields every three years to determine their nutrient needs, and lately we have been ranking our fields to identify their relative risk for spreading manure in terms of slope and setbacks from wells and streams.

Having about 250 different fields, each with its own record, is a bit overwhelming. Given all the paperwork involved it adds up to a half-time position. That's a lot of time to spend to comply with regulations, but it does help us manage our land and crops better.

One challenge we face is that regulations aren't always practical when applied to a farm. What is done with calculations in an office may not make sense when it comes to implementation. For example, some northern states require farm manure to be stored all winter long, because the ground is usually frozen. They set a date when spreading is okay in the spring. That can have unintended consequences. Farmers store up millions of gallons of manure and then have to rush to apply it in a short window of time just before planting. You get a situation where every dairy farmer is spreading at once, and a big rain event can lead to a lot of runoff. It would make more sense to allow farmers to spread at times in the winter when conditions are appropriate.

We're not perfect but we are continuously improving our stewardship. Just over the last five years we've adopted a lot of new practices. It's something we will keep getting better at.

Transforming the Farming System at
Happy Cow Creamery, Pelzer, South Carolina

Tom Trantham started dairy farming in 1968, buying his current 100-acre farm ten years later (see fig. 6.3). It soon became one of the top-producing dairies in the state, and Tom was active in the agricultural community, serving as president of the Dairy Farmers Association. He recalls:

Everybody talked about production: how many cows do you have, how much milk do you make? I had blinders on, trying to make the most milk I could, using all the inputs I could. I bought in feed to supplement what I grew, and I was a big user of chemicals. I thought that's what farming was, using chemicals. I wasn't paying attention to the soil, the water, or the cows as well as I could.

I was very successful at making milk, but the input costs were so high that when

FIGURE 6.3 Cows on a large dairy farm. Farms with a lot of livestock produce a lot of food, and they also produce a lot of animal waste. Manure can be a valuable soil amendment if handled properly; otherwise it can pose a threat to environmental quality. On this farm, all the manure is mechanically scraped out of the barn and it then flows into an anaerobic digester.

the price of milk got low, eventually I couldn't borrow any more money. I already owed more than the farm was worth, so I told my son and daughter y'all got to leave because there is nothing I can do; I was on the verge of bankruptcy.

But then several things happened to make me realize I could farm differently, without all the inputs, and stay in business. First, the cows got out one day in April and fed themselves by grazing on the tops of plants in the field by the barn. I noticed that their production went up after that, so I let them out to graze again and watched their behavior. They were only eating the most nutritious parts of the plants, the tops, so I started thinking about designing a grazing system to meet their needs. I took pictures of the cows grazing, I sent in samples of the plants they were eating, and that's how I came up with my "twelve Aprils" approach, where I rotate pastures to try and maintain high-quality feed all year-round.

Then, I learned by accident that I could do no-till without herbicides. In the past we had always mowed a field and then sprayed it before planting, but my hired man had gone back in and mowed one field a second time, five days after the first mowing. The plants had used up most of their resources and didn't regrow much; so we no-tilled about a third extra seed than usual into that field and got a perfectly good stand.

I'm not organic but now I farm without chemicals while still maintaining high production. That's a huge cost to take off your farm bill. In addition, university tests show that my milk is of the highest quality and so is my soil. My cows are healthier and we have a product that people want. Eleven years ago we started selling milk direct to consumers at the farm and our farm store sales have been growing every year.

More farmers could do what I've done but most are afraid to take the chance. They have debts to pay, and the fear that a new farming system might not work keeps them locked into the old one. There's a lot of farmers been grazing forever, but this is not the way my grandfather did it; we have new plant varieties, improved equipment, and more information to help us. It's fun to be a dairy farmer again.

Transformational Change

There is an ongoing tension in modern agriculture. At the same time that it produces unprecedented quantities of food using ever-more sophisticated technologies, it continues to have significant and widespread negative impacts on the environment. Even as these impacts are incrementally ameliorated by improved management and the adoption of less damaging practices, their additive effects challenge the long-term sustainability of agriculture's natural resource base and "downstream" ecosystems. Increased regulation, IPM, nutrient management, and organic farming practices are desirable in terms of reducing reliance on agrichemicals and maintaining soil health and water quality. However, a more radical transformation of our approach to farming is needed to ensure its viability for centuries to come. The future of agriculture depends on the adoption of ecological principles in farming system design. That approach will avoid rather than reduce many environmental impacts, and it will also wean us from dependence on non-renewable inputs that are currently required to maintain high yields.

Miguel Altieri has written:

> The challenges to a transformational shift in farming practices are many, and they go far beyond the farm and farm policies to include the current economies of scale in agriculture and political power of global agribusiness corporations and current globalization trends. Ecological change in agriculture cannot be promoted without comparable changes in the social, political, cultural, and economic arenas that also constrain agriculture.[39]

Some of that change is taking place through social movements. These movements have many different but related foci, including childhood dietary wellness, farm-to-institution programs, GMO resistance, new farmers, urban agriculture, and watershed protection. If they continue to gain strength and are able to coalesce into a united voice for change, the seismic shift that is needed in our agricultural system can occur.

7 ∾ *Climate Change and Agriculture*

Agriculture is one of the most weather-dependent human enterprises. In recent years reports of extreme weather—heat waves, ice storms, floods, and hurricanes, for example—seem more frequent than in the past. However, recent weather events are not a good basis for assessing changes in the climate. The fact that it was hot one summer, or it hardly snowed one winter, or there was extensive flooding one spring should be viewed as individual pieces of data that in the aggregate, over time, describe climatic conditions. In other words, climate consists of weather patterns over many decades. There are ups and downs within seasons and over the years, but it's the long-term trends that are used to assess the climate. These trends include both temperature and precipitation patterns, which affect environmental conditions, in turn affecting plants, animals, and ecosystems.

Measures of Climate Change

The earth's climate is always changing, and patterns of change can be observed over different periods of time. Using ice cores, scientists have been able to estimate global carbon dioxide levels going back hundreds of thousands of years, and temperature has also been estimated for the areas where ice has collected over that period of time (fig. 7.1). These data show that when carbon dioxide levels rise, so too does the average air temperature.[1]

For 800,000 years, up until the industrial revolution of the 1800s, the concentration of carbon dioxide (CO_2) in the atmosphere fluctuated between about 180 and 280 parts per million (ppm). Over the past two centuries, that concentration has been steadily increasing, with a very rapid rise documented over the past half century, from slightly more than 300 ppm to almost 400 ppm (fig. 7.2).[2]

In the past century or so the earth's temperature has increased by 1.4°F.[3] That may not sound like much, but a small change in average annual temperature can make a big difference in weather events. The increase means

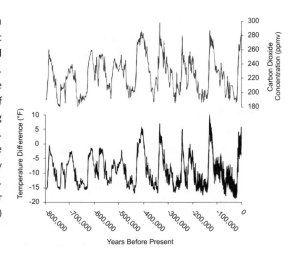

FIGURE 7.1

Estimates of atmospheric CO₂ concentration and Antarctic air temperature. These estimates are based on the analysis of ice core data extending back 800,000 years. Warmer periods coincide with periods of relatively high CO₂ concentrations. (ppmv denotes parts per million by volume.)

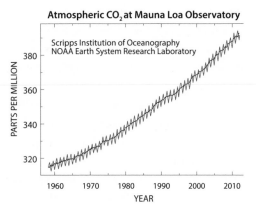

Atmospheric CO₂ at Mauna Loa Observatory

FIGURE 7.2 Measurements of CO₂ in the atmosphere. Data collected on Mauna Loa in Hawaii since 1958 provide the longest record of direct measurements of CO₂ in the atmosphere. The jagged line shows the seasonal fluctuation, and the smooth line represents the average annual data.

many more local and regional heat waves, bringing 100-degree days to places not well prepared to deal with extreme heat, like Buffalo and Seattle. As the planet heats up, water evaporates from the land, creating droughts in some places and the threat of wildfires. Warm air holds more moisture than cold air; it acts like a sponge and then dumps the water, causing flooding. The warmer atmosphere thus leads to heavier rainfalls and snowstorms. Warmer temperatures melt ice caps, and warm water expands, so the sea level is rising, and that threatens coastal cities.

Some areas of the planet are warming more than others. Temperature increases are most significant in the Arctic, where sea ice that stays year-round is shrinking and may soon vanish in summer. The change from a light-colored surface covered in ice to a dark-colored surface covered in ocean or tundra means that less heat is reflected, and thus more is absorbed by the earth. Warmer temperatures mean melting permafrost, which in turn threatens the native ecosystem and rural economies based on that ecosystem. It also disrupts transportation as roads become impassable, and it endangers people as buildings crack and buckle.

Across the contiguous forty-eight states, the temperature has risen at about the same rate as the average global temperature since 1901, increasing 1.4°F per century.[4] Average temperatures have risen more quickly since the late 1970s, and seven of the ten warmest years on record for the contiguous forty-eight states have occurred since 1998. Although most of the United States has been getting warmer, the trend is not uniform and a few areas have become slightly cooler.[5]

Precipitation patterns are also changing. Precipitation has increased by more than 2 percent per century over land areas worldwide and by nearly 6 percent in the forty-eight contiguous states in this country since 1901.[6] Certain areas, such as Hawaii and parts of the American Southwest have had less precipitation than usual. Recently, a high percentage of precipitation in the United States has come in the form of intense single-day events. Nationwide, eight of the top ten years on record for extreme one-day precipitation events have occurred since 1990.

In the northeastern United States, research conducted by the University of New Hampshire makes it clear that the climate is changing.[7] Scientists analyzed data collected by hundreds of weather stations and found that the Northeast's average annual temperature increased by 1.8°F from 1899 to 2000. Winters in particular have become warmer, with the average temperature from December through February warming by 2.8°F. These changes have already had significant effects on the environment, and therefore on agriculture.

For example, the Northeast frost-free growing season is eight days longer now than it was a hundred years ago. The number of extreme precipitation events, defined as more than 2 inches of rainfall over forty-eight hours, has increased from about three events to five events per year. There were, on average, sixteen fewer days with snow on the ground in 2001 than in 1970. Apple and grape bloom dates were about two days earlier per decade from 1965 through 2001. The maple sugaring begins eight days earlier and ends eleven days earlier than it did forty years ago.[8]

Implications for Agriculture

The United Nations Intergovernmental Panel on Climate Change (IPCC) concluded that the increased frequency of heat waves, droughts, and floods will negatively affect crop yields and livestock, especially for subsistence farmers at low latitudes.[9] In places like Bangladesh, rising sea level is the climate change effect that outweighs all others in importance, since it is a low-lying country.

It is one thing for farmers to cope with small changes in the climate and quite another to cope with significant shifts that are expected over the longer term if the rate of climate change continues unabated. A recent USDA report concludes:

> The U.S. agricultural system is expected to be fairly resilient to climate change in the short term due to the system's flexibility to engage in adaptive behaviors such as expansion of irrigated acreage, regional shifts in acreage for specific crops, crop rotations, changes to management decisions such as choice and timing of inputs and cultivation practices, and altered trade patterns compensating for yield changes caused by changing climate patterns. By midcentury, when temperature increases are expected to exceed 1°C to 3°C and precipitation extremes intensify, yields of major U.S. crops and farm returns are projected to decline.[10]

In the temperate United States, climate change has some positive as well as negative effects on farming.[11] For example, a longer frost-free growing season can help increase the production of annual crops. Milder autumns with later killing frosts allow pumpkin, squash, and other fall crops to grow longer and thus produce higher yields. Later frosts also allow fall raspberry growers to harvest fruit that would otherwise be lost. Milder winters may be beneficial for the winter survival of some grape vines that are sensitive to extremely cold temperatures. But there are serious downsides to climate change, too. For example, studies suggest that two very important crops in the Northeast—apples and maple syrup—may be negatively affected. Warmer winters could reduce apple fruit yields, and sugar maples over a large geographic area are likely to decline in health as the climate warms. The dairy industry will also face challenges, especially from an increase in summer temperatures, since milk production drops off when cows are exposed to hot, humid weather. Weather station data from the Northeast over the last half of the twentieth century show that occurrences of extreme precipitation events have increased significantly.[12]

Adaptation: Coping with a Changing Climate

There are two primary strategies for dealing with climate change, for farmers as well as society. One is called *adaptation*, which includes techniques for coping with current and predicted effects of climate change. The other is called *mitigation*, which focuses on slowing the rate of climate change by reducing greenhouse gas emissions.

The extent to which farmers will be able to adapt to climate change depends on what they produce, where they're located, and the climatic changes in their area. For example, it's likely that cool-season crops won't do as well in areas that warm up significantly, so farmers who grow such crops, like potatoes or crucifers, may need to switch to varieties that are more heat-tolerant, or if the temperatures rise dramatically they might have to change the species of annual crops they grow. Maintaining the comfort of heat-sensitive livestock such as cows might require dairy farmers to modify their barn designs to promote ventilation or, if temperature increases demand it, install misting systems or even air-conditioning to provide sufficient cooling. Other problems are harder to predict and likely more difficult to cope with, such as the gradual decline of some forest tree species or changes in the distribution and aggressiveness of weeds or insect pests.

Rising CO_2 levels is one climatic change that has special implications for agriculture. It may promote photosynthesis and thus increase the growth of crops, but some research suggests that biomass may increase without increasing harvests of desired plant parts — in other words, more bean plant growth, but fewer beans.[13] In addition, higher CO_2 levels will affect weed biology and management.[14] Some fast-growing weeds are especially well adapted to utilizing extra CO_2 because their photosynthetic system differs from that of most crops. These species may become harder to control in crops that can't use the extra CO_2 as well. Certain perennial weeds such as thistles and quack grass that can store extra energy underground may also become harder to control. Integrated weed management systems that combine tactics such as crop rotation, the use of cover crops, cultivation, no-till production, and mulching will become more important in the future.

Climate change will also alter insect pest populations, though exactly how is not well understood. As weather patterns change, new insects may arrive, some existing pests are likely to become more abundant, and others will decline.[15] For example, insect pests of crops that travel to northern areas on storm fronts from southern areas, such as several species of aphids and leafhoppers, corn earworms, and armyworms, could become more abundant as summer storm frequency increases. Other pests that overwinter in colder climates, such as the European corn borer, flea beetle, and tarnished plant bug, could become more abundant if milder winters encourage their survival, although reduced snow cover might lead to a reduction in overwintering populations.

Changes in rainfall patterns will affect crop diseases, since many plant dis-

FIGURE 7.3 Field erosion due to extreme rainfall and flooding. Extreme weather events associated with climate change can take a severe toll on agriculture. On this farm, unusually heavy rainfall led to unprecedented levels of flooding, causing the nearby river to carry away a large volume of valuable topsoil.

eases require moisture to proliferate. The likelihood of changes in pest pressure, plus the uncertainty about it, will make frequent monitoring for pests an even more important activity on farms than it already is. Farmers will want to avoid being taken by surprise.

Greater variability in precipitation patterns will have a big impact on agriculture, even if the total amount of average annual precipitation does not change. Farmers will need to take steps to deal with more intense rainfall events in order to avoid soil erosion (see fig. 7.3). This could include putting in soil drainage systems or establishing strips of permanent sod in or around fields. Dealing with longer periods of drought will call for more investment in irrigation systems and their water sources, like ponds and wells.

Drought, severe storms and flooding, pests, and greater unpredictability of the length of the growing season—as if farming weren't already challenging enough without adding climate change to the list of concerns! It's a good thing farmers are a resilient bunch, and many are already taking steps to adapt, whether they are in Vermont, Florida, California, or Wisconsin. Table 7.1 lists ways that farmers are adapting to the changing climate.

TABLE 7.1 *Typology of Climate Change Adaptation Strategies for Agriculture*

Key Adaptation Drivers	Farm Production Practices	Farm Financial Management	Farm Infrastructure	Technological Developments	Government Programs and Insurance
Increased variability in growing conditions (changes in seasonal temperature and precipitation patterns)	Change crop varieties and animal breeds, timing of farm operations; use season extension and irrigation; build soil health	Purchase crop insurance; participate in income stabilization programs; diversify household income	Install water management (catchments, tile drainage, swales), irrigation systems, weather prediction systems	Plant drought-/cold-/heat-tolerant crop varieties; install efficient irrigation systems; install weather and climate information systems; use decision support tools	Implement programs to influence farm-level risk management, technical support for risk management, policies to improve resilience
Increased soil degradation (increased erosion reduces soil quality)	Engage in soil conservation practices (no-till, mulch); build soil health	Participate in soil conservation cost share and easement programs	Install soil conservation structures, such as terraces, grass waterways, riparian areas	Soil conservation practices, soil building amendments (biochar, stabilizing agents)	Implement land and water management policies and programs to promote soil conservation and soil health management
Increased pest pressure, novel pests	Implement IPM practices; cultivate resistant crop varieties and livestock breeds, farmscaping	Participate in insurance programs	Purchase improved application technologies, pest protection structures	Pest resistant crop varieties, IPM options, early warning and decision support tools, pest suppression technologies	Participate in insurance programs, risk analysis, IPM and weather-based decision-making; obtain technical advice

Adapted from C. L. Walthall et al., *Climate Change and Agriculture in the United States: Effects and Adaptation*, Technical Bulletin 1935, U.S. Department of Agriculture, Agricultural Research Service, 2012.

Adapting to a Changing Climate at
Baldwin Dairy, Emerald, Wisconsin

Throughout the country, many farmers are taking note of changes in weather patterns over the years and adapting their management in response. John Vrieze, a dairy farmer in northwestern Wisconsin, explains how his farm is adapting:

We're changing the hybrids we're using to reflect a substantially longer growing season here. My father's generation would have planted eighty- to eighty-five-day corn hybrids and we're now using hundred-day hybrids. That is actually a positive change because with the longer growing season our yields are increasing. The downside is we're having to change practices related to weed and insect species and populations, and also more extremes in storm and rainfall events.

By far the biggest downside to climate change for me is heat mitigation for the cattle compared with fifteen to twenty years ago. When we first built our large dairy in 1997 we didn't even think about keeping the cows cool, as there was no reason to spend the extra capital for a couple of days of heat stress during the summer. As time has gone on we've had to first add a few fans, then lots of fans, then misters for evaporative cooling of the cows, and now that isn't even enough, so we're having to use soakers to try and control the internal temperature of the cows. If I was building a new barn today, climate control features would be first on my priority list in the design phase. This, of course, adds enormously to the capital outlay and also the ongoing energy and water usage.

Adapting to a Changing Climate:
Edgewater Farm, Plainfield, New Hampshire

Pooh Sprague has been a farmer all of his life. He grew up on a dairy farm in New Hampshire and has been growing vegetables, fruits, and flowers at Edgewater Farm for forty years with his wife, Anne (fig. 7.4). Having experienced the weather day in and day out on the farm, Pooh has no doubt that the climate is changing:

I'm a firm believer that something is going on. I don't know what it is and I don't know what to call it, but something is definitely going on with the weather.

Winters are a good indication of how something is changing. Growing up in central New Hampshire on a dairy farm, we skied all winter from Thanksgiving to the middle of April. In the mid-1970s there were all sorts of midsized ski areas in New Hampshire and they did just fine, plenty of natural snow. You can't count on snow anymore. The lack of natural snow and abbreviated ski seasons killed those small ski areas — they just couldn't count on Mother Nature to give them a good year.

FIGURE 7.4 Pooh Sprague in a field of tomatoes and cover crops at Edgewater Farm in Plainfield, New Hampshire. Pooh's family operates a diversified horticulture farm. He is concerned about changes in weather patterns and their impact on agriculture.

In the summers, the storms are more intense. They come with hail and electricity and are much more dangerous now. Twenty-five years ago, if there was a hail event, it was a big deal for the orchardists around here. Now the orchards are routinely getting hammered by hail. Those are indications that the weather is changing. All the farms around here think the weather is messed up. We see a lot more insects and disease. I don't know if that has to do with the weather or with globalization of trade, or both. There is no consistency in the weather, and we need to adapt how we grow crops.

We are growing more and more in greenhouses. We have added 30,000 square feet of poly greenhouses in which we grow bedding plants and greenhouse vegetables. We also have 45 acres of tillable land where we grow vegetables and small fruit, everything from arugula to zucchini and strawberries, raspberries, and blueberries. We use integrated pest management methods coupled with soil health management practices. This allows us to produce crops of the highest food value using the least amount of sprays and inputs.

Our produce is retailed directly at our greenhouses, our farmstand, and through our CSA. All sales are direct to consumers or through the nearby food co-op. People like to feel like they are a part of the farm, like it's their farm. Let me tell you a story about that. A while back, we decided to offer a CSA in the nearby town of Grantham because people don't want to drive to get to our farm. At the first meeting in Grantham, we explained how the CSA was going to work. One guy stood up to say that if the energy dries up or the climate changes and there's a food shortage, then we would be their farmer. That's a nice idea, but I had to be honest with them. If there really is a food shortage, our farm would be taking care of Plainfield, where our farm is. The lack of fossil fuels would reduce our farm's ability to produce food as well as travel because fossil fuels are needed for the production of fertilizers as well as operating tractors and field equipment. So we would have to downsize to a scale that would only serve a very local community. We wouldn't be able to drive to Grantham to drop off veggies. They would need their own farmer in Grantham.

Consumers have a hard time understanding farming and its relationship to the weather, so we try to do some education on the farm. Shoppers have been conditioned for twenty years to see strawberries from California and Florida from January to July, so people call me in early May asking to come berry picking. One year I took a visitor to where we could get a view of the riverbank. "That's ice," I explained. "You have to understand the seasons around here. We don't have berries yet."

We're changing the way we farm because of the changing climate, and we do what we can to reduce fossil fuel use. We plant some crops in far fields that don't need much day-to-day attention, like the pumpkins. Nobody has to drive there on a regular basis. The irrigation water pumps are egregious burners of fossil fuels in a dry year. I should turn on the pumps more for the crops but it costs a fortune to water them. So I pin my hopes on some rain possibly coming in this weekend and I try to limit the use of pumps.

We used to have a fleet of Toyota trucks. Now we have these little Kubota mini-trucks that are much more fuel-efficient. We are always watching our fuel costs, not only for climate change, but also for the day-to-day expenses. We are using biodiesel seasonally in our tractors and off-road vehicles at an increased cost to us. The benefit in terms of reduced emissions offsets this cost, although there are many questions regarding the sustainability of biofuel production.

Our practices are based not just on efficiency and profitability but also on long-term sustainability and compatibility with our environment. We believe that to be in business for the long haul we need to make the correct business as well as environmental decisions. Do we think we know everything and are a cutting-edge farming enterprise? Nope. Do we have a lot to learn? Absolutely. We are constantly trying to become better farmers and better stewards. In so doing we ultimately become better neighbors.

Mitigation: Reducing Greenhouse Gas Emissions

Besides planning for adaptation to climate change, farmers can help mitigate the problem by adopting practices that reduce their current GHG emissions. Although agriculture generates only a small part of the nation's GHG output (fig. 7.5),[16] farmers, like everyone else, can do their part to address the problem. The good news for farmers is that many agricultural actions that can reduce GHG emissions can also enhance profitability. For example, renewable energy systems can reduce fossil fuel use and CO_2 emissions while also lowering energy costs.

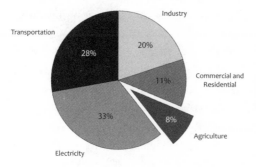

FIGURE 7.5 Greenhouse gas emissions in the United States by sector. Agriculture accounts for a relatively small portion of the nation's GHG emissions. Various estimates attribute 6 to 8 percent of all U.S. GHG emissions to agriculture.

Industry 20%

Transportation 28%

Commercial and Residential 11%

Electricity 33%

Agriculture 8%

In order to understand how farmers can help mitigate climate change, we need to understand something about the greenhouse gases involved. While much of the focus of GHG reduction strategies is on CO_2, nitrous oxide (N_2O) and methane (CH_4) are other gases that contribute to climate change. Although they are generated in smaller amounts by human activity than CO_2, they are far more potent in terms of their global warming effect. However, in comparison with most other industries, agriculture produces proportionally more N_2O and CH_4 than CO_2. In general, CH_4 from agriculture is released by livestock digestion and manure, and N_2O is released when excess nitrogen fertilizer is applied under certain soil conditions. Agricultural soil management is critical for mitigating climate change (fig. 7.6).

Considering this information, there are a several key steps that farmers can take to reduce GHG emissions:[17]

- Using nitrogen fertilizer more efficiently in order to avoid N_2O emissions. This involves proper timing, placement, and application rates.
- Improving manure management to decrease CH_4 emissions. This includes proper storage, timely application, and prompt incorporation into the soil.
- Taking CO_2 from the atmosphere and sequestering (storing) it in plant biomass and soils. This can be done through increased use of cover crops, permanent pastures, and reduced tillage systems that "tie up" atmospheric carbon while building soil organic matter.
- Increasing the efficiency of farm inputs such as fuel, fertilizers, and pesticides, thus reducing the consumption of fossil energy that is required to produce them.
- Increasing the production of biological-based energy to replace fossil energy. Farms across the nation already offer many examples of this, from the production of electricity from dairy manure by means of anaerobic digesters to the production of biodiesel using oil from canola, soybean, and sunflower crops.
- Utilizing non-carbon electrical energy sources such as wind and solar; as well as energy-efficient equipment for heating, cooling, and tillage.

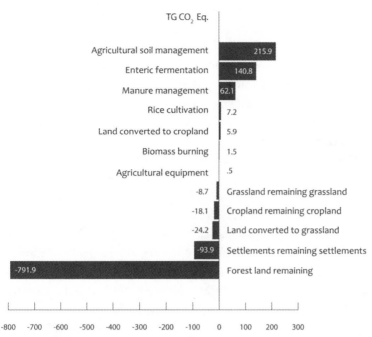

TG CO$_2$ Eq.

Agricultural soil management	215.9
Enteric fermentation	140.8
Manure management	62.1
Rice cultivation	7.2
Land converted to cropland	5.9
Biomass burning	1.5
Agricultural equipment	.5
Grassland remaining grassland	-8.7
Cropland remaining cropland	-18.1
Land converted to grassland	-24.2
Settlements remaining settlements	-93.9
Forest land remaining	-791.9

-800 -700 -600 -500 -400 -300 -200 -100 0 100 200 300

FIGURE 7.6 Agricultural sources and sinks of greenhouse gases. Management of agricultural soils is the largest source of carbon dioxide equivalents (CO$_2$ Eq) of all farming activities, followed by animal production, which includes enteric fermentation (emissions from livestock digestive processes) and manure management. Fossil fuel use for equipment is barely on the chart. The largest carbon sinks are undisturbed forestland and settled areas, followed by conversion of non-grassland to grassland.

The good news is that the application of these practices also provides many co-benefits for farms and society. For example, increasing organic matter and carbon in soils improves soil quality and productivity; more efficient use of nitrogen can reduce runoff and leaching and thus improve water quality; better management of manure also protects water quality and can reduce odors; and greater biofuel use in place of fossil fuels may enhance energy security, if such fuels are produced responsibly.[18] Whether a farmer is concerned about climate change or doesn't believe climate change is occurring, these practices make sense for long-term farm viability and the development of sustainable food systems. Of course, farming is not the only food system component that has to mitigate its contribution to GHG emissions and climate change.

What Can Consumers Do about Climate Change?

Every individual, household, and local community can take steps to reduce its fossil energy consumption, which will help reduce GHG emissions.

People can also plan to adapt to more extreme weather events with improvements to home and business designs aimed at avoiding damage from heavy rain, floods, and wind. They can conserve more water in drought-prone regions and avoid building where wildfires are becoming more common. The list goes on. But when it comes to food and climate change, there are some very specific actions that consumers can take.

Farmers respond to the marketplace, so consumers can support efforts to cope with and reduce the rate of climate change by buying less processed and less packaged food, by shifting to a lower-meat diet, and by patronizing farms that utilize renewable energy. Planning food purchases to minimize driving, buying only what will be consumed so as to avoid waste, and following energy-efficient practices in the preparation and storage of food at home are other ways that consumers can make a difference. Consumers can also support policies, from thoughtful land-use planning, to buy-local incentives, to grants for farmers and food enterprises aimed at energy efficiency, maintenance of carbon-sequestering land use, and access to fresher food choices that reduce packaging and waste.

A major obstacle to taking action, for farmers and consumers, is the politicized nature of the public conversation about climate change. Rather than addressing the scientific aspects or practical approaches to planning for a potential threat, the conversation has focused largely on the debate between climate change "believers" and skeptics. It turns out, as with many other contemporary political issues, that the views of most Americans are somewhere in between those at either extreme.

Beliefs about Climate Change

Americans have a range of views on climate change, from those who are concerned about it and believe action must be taken, to those who do not believe it is occurring and are against taking any action to deal with it. As shown in figure 7.7, research by the Yale Project on Climate Change Communication identifies six categories of American perspectives on climate change.[19] At one end of the spectrum, people in the "alarmed" category are convinced of the reality and seriousness of climate change and are already taking actions to address it. At the other end of the spectrum, people tin the "dismissive" category do not believe that the climate is changing and are actively involved in opposing efforts to address climate change. The "concerned" category is next to the "alarmed" category on the spectrum, and people in this group believe that global warming is happening but have not taken steps to personally respond to the issue. Just beyond the "concerned" is the "cautious" category, followed

| Alarmed | Concerned | Cautious | Disengaged | Doubtful | Dismissive |
| 13% | 26% | 29% | 6% | 15% | 10% |

Highest Belief in Global Warming   Lowest Belief in Global Warming
Most Concerned   Least Concerned
Most Motivated   Least Motivated

Proportion represented by area

FIGURE 7.7 Beliefs of the U.S. population about climate change. More than two-thirds of Americans believe that the climate is changing, a little more than 20 percent are not sure or not interested, and 10 percent dismiss the idea of climate change and oppose actions to address the issue.

by the "disengaged" and the "doubtful" categories. These categories represent people with different levels of belief in climate change. None are actively involved in taking steps to address climate change or in opposing efforts to do so.

The majority of Americans believe that the climate is changing. When combined, the alarmed, concerned, and cautious categories account for 68 percent of Americans. Although they share this belief, their behavioral responses to climate change vary. The alarmed, which account for 13 percent of Americans, are taking action and personal responsibility, while the concerned and cautious are not, though a majority of them support public policies that would address climate change and thus affect their behavior. Slightly more than 20 percent of Americans fall into the disengaged or doubtful category; they are either not sure what to believe about climate change or not interested in the issue. At the far end of the spectrum are those in the dismissive category, who account for 10 percent of the population and do not support personal or public actions to address climate change.[20]

The views of farmers in Iowa on climate change are similar to those of the general public, according to the Iowa Farm and Rural Life Poll (table 7.2).[21] An annual survey of farmers in that state indicated that 68 percent believe climate change is occurring, the same percentage of Americans according to the Yale study. Like the general population, some farmers are uncertain or skeptical about climate change. Twenty-eight percent of farmers in Iowa feel there is insufficient evidence to determine whether climate change is occurring; 21 percent of the U.S. population feels that way. Interestingly, fewer farmers are absolutely convinced that climate change is not occurring. Five percent of farmers do not believe that climate change is occurring, as compared with 10 percent of the general population.

TABLE 7.2 *Beliefs of Iowa Farmers about Climate Change*

Belief	Percent (%)
Climate change is occurring, and it is caused equally by natural changes in the environment and human activities.	35
There is not sufficient evidence to know with certainty whether climate change is occurring or not.	28
Climate change is occurring, and it is caused mostly by natural changes in the environment.	23
Climate change is occurring, and it is caused mostly by human activities.	10
Climate change is not occurring.	5

Gordon J. Arbuckle, Iowa Farm and Rural Life Poll: 2011 Summary Report, p. 2.
store.extension.iastate.edu/ItemDetail.aspx?ProductID=13717.

To summarize, more than two-thirds of the U.S. population, including farmers, believe that climate change is occurring. The remaining one-third is made up primarily of people who are not sure what to believe. A small part of the population, 5 percent of farmers and 10 percent of the general public, absolutely do not believe the climate is changing.

Vocal opponents on both sides of the spectrum are rallying advocates and arguing their points. The time has come to get beyond arguing and discuss ways to motivate and assist people to take action and adopt practices that will err on the side of caution—preparing for different weather patterns in the future while reducing the likelihood that they will be increasingly extreme. These steps make sense for our future, regardless of our beliefs about climate change.

8 ∾ *Energy, Food, and Farms*

Like the man behind the curtain in the *Wizard of Oz*, energy pulls the levers of food systems. But in this case, when you pull back the curtain, there isn't a single entity at work but rather a complicated set of connections between energy and food.

Food provides the energy our bodies need, but that energy comes from somewhere else before it gets stored in an apple, a slice of pizza, or a Happy Meal. For the most part, it comes from the sun. Solar energy drives the harvest of atmospheric CO_2 by plant leaves and its transformation into more complex carbon chains, like sugars and starches. Solar energy is thus turned into, and stored as, chemical energy. That energy is released when we consume and digest plants, or animals that were raised on plants, for food.

The sunlight-driven manufacture of living tissue by plants is called *primary production*. Just about every subsequent step in complex food systems relies on energy that comes from primary production, with the exception of non-carbon energy sources like hydro, solar, and wind power. The energy from primary production may be used in the short term, as when crops are grown and then fed to livestock, which are then consumed by people; or it may be used over a very long period of time, as when fossil fuels are formed and later collected and processed to make diesel fuel to power tillage and transportation.

In simple food systems, such as hunting and gathering, very little additional energy is needed to convert the sun's energy to food energy in one's stomach. In complex food systems, lots of energy is used in a large number of processes required to grow, harvest, process, package, and deliver the end product to consumers (fig. 8.1). As a result, energy use in the overall U.S. food system has been calculated to account for about 15 percent of the entire U.S. energy budget.[1]

To exemplify the use of energy in food systems, the USDA's Economic Research Service considered a hypothetical purchase of a fresh-cut salad mix by a consumer living on the East Coast:

> In this case, fresh vegetable farms in California harvest the produce to be used in the salad mix a few weeks prior to its purchase. The farms' fields are seeded months ear-

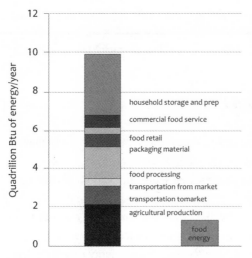

FIGURE 8.1 Total annual energy usage by sector of the U.S. food system. Most of the energy used in our food system does not actually end up in food. Life cycle analyses estimate that on average the U.S. food system requires between 7.3 and 10 calories of fossil fuel energy to produce 1 calorie of consumed food energy. The largest proportion, about one-third of the food system's energy use, is for home food preparation and storage, while only about one-fifth is for agricultural production. The remainder is for food processing, packaging, transportation, and marketing.

lier with a precision seed planter operating as an attachment to a gasoline-powered farm tractor. Between planting and harvest, a diesel-powered broadcast spreader applies nitrogen-based fertilizers, pesticides, and herbicides, all manufactured using differing amounts of natural gas and electricity and shipped in diesel-powered trucks to a nearby farm supply wholesaler. Local farmers travel to the wholesaler in gasoline-powered vehicles to purchase farm supplies. The farms use electric-powered irrigation equipment throughout much of the growing period. At harvest, field workers pack harvested vegetables in boxes produced at a paper mill and load them in gasoline-powered trucks for shipment to a regional processing plant, where specialized machinery cleans, cuts, mixes, and packages the salad mixes. Utility services at the paper mill, plastic packaging manufacturers, and salad mix plants use energy to produce the boxes used at harvest and the packaging used at the processing plant, and for processing and packaging the fresh produce. The packaged salad mix is shipped in refrigerated containers by a combination of rail and truck to an East Coast grocery store, where it is placed in market displays under constant refrigeration. To purchase this packaged salad mix, a consumer likely travels by car or public transportation to a nearby grocery store. For those traveling by car, a portion of the consumer's automobile operational costs, and his or her associated energy-use requirements, help facilitate this food-related travel. At home, the consumer refrigerates the salad mix for a time before eating it. Subsequently, dishes and utensils used to eat the salad may be placed in a dishwasher for cleaning and reuse—adding to the electricity use of the consumer's household. Leftover salad may be partly grinded in a garbage disposal and washed away to a wastewater treatment facility.[2]

Modern food systems have greatly increased the quantity of food produced per farmer, as well as its variety and availability. Over the past several centuries this has been accomplished by using energy to replace human labor, primarily with machinery and agricultural chemicals. Thus modern food systems represent a reversal of thousands of years of human history during which agriculture created more energy than it required. Humans without an excess energy supply would not have engaged in farming if it consumed more calories than it produced. But these early farmers, as well as hunter-gatherers, lived on relatively simple diets of what could be grown, caught, or collected in their local area. Their food was unprocessed, unpackaged, nutrient-dense, and probably pretty healthy. Adequate supplies were the main concern.

By comparison, today's supermarkets and restaurants offer an endless supply of a previously unimaginable variety of food products. These products come from all over the world, are processed in just about every manner conceivable, and are available at a relatively low cost. Ironically, this food abundance comes with a wide range of concerns about its impact on people's health, the environment, and culture.[3] Some of these concerns relate specifically to contemporary food systems' reliance on fossil energy, such as a vulnerability to interruptions or price hikes in energy supplies and the impact of GHG emissions.

At least since the first "energy crisis" of the 1970s, people have been thinking about how to reduce both overall energy use and dependence on fossil fuels, and studies have concluded that significant improvements are possible.[4] These can be achieved by adopting practices that increase energy conservation and efficiency, shifting to a diet that is less energy-intensive, and adopting renewable energy sources in place of fossil fuels. The three approaches are complimentary, and their combination is essential for making meaningful progress in reducing both dependency on fossil fuels and GHG emissions generated by food systems.

Local Food and Energy Use

At first glance, greater reliance on local foods seems to be a logical way to reduce energy use. After all, if food travels a shorter distance, less energy is consumed, right? That's a key reason that the concept of "food-miles" has been used to promote local foods. One challenge to this reasoning is that energy used for transportation is only a small portion of overall food system energy use, although transportation energy becomes more significant if one does not include energy used for household food storage and preparation in the calculations. Another challenge is that some forms of long-distance transport, such as trains and ships, are relatively efficient in terms of energy used per unit of food moved per mile, compared with trucks, which are commonly used to transport food locally.[5]

The lack of an efficient local transportation infrastructure suggests that local foods use a relatively large amount of transportation energy per unit of food compared with the commodity food system. In other words, a fully loaded tractor-trailer with tens of thousands of produce items has a much lower energy cost per box of vegetables per mile than a pickup truck full of fresh vegetables going to a farmers' market. Further, since the production, transportation, and consumption of local foods are just as reliant on unsustainable fossil fuels as are long-distance foods, some have questioned why local foods should be thought of as part of the solution to food systems' energy problems.[6]

Comparing the energy consumption of local and long-distance forms of food transportation turns out to be more complicated than just counting food-miles. For example, although ship transport and rail transport have a low energy cost per unit of food per mile, long-distance air transport has a very high cost, and trucking is in the middle of the pack. Further, without knowing the actual distances traveled, the method of transport, and the total quantity of food on board, it is impossible to calculate the specific amount of energy used to move an individual item of food from one location to another. Adding to the complexity is the fact that when food travels long distances, the energy used is well beyond that of the primary shipment method. There may be associated transportation before and after the long-distance transport, as when a train is loaded and then unloaded to trucks that drive to and from warehouses. Once inside the warehouse the food is moved around again, only to be loaded back onto trucks that deliver it to retail food outlets or other end users. Long-distance transport is also likely to depend on energy for controlling the climate in storage facilities at each end of the trip and to require energy to manufacture and dispose of containers for both wholesale and retail trade. Local foods that are sold more directly from farms to consumers avoid some of this energy use.

To the extent that local food systems promote dietary shifts to less processed and packaged food, they may lower energy use. Local foods may also lower energy use to the extent that they lower the consumption of commodity animal products, which tend to be energy-intensive to produce. Thus greater reliance on local foods can reduce energy usage in ways not directly related to the impact of food-miles.

Reducing food transportation and the energy it uses is still a worthy goal, but it makes more sense for some foods than others. In other words, some foods are transported a long way when they could easily be produced in greater volume closer to home, like apples in the Northeast, while other foods must come from places far away with different growing conditions, like bananas and chocolate.

From an energy-use perspective, long-distance transportation of food is generally best suited to high-value, non-perishable products, while it makes sense to produce food with lower value and/or shorter shelf life closer to its markets.[7] This idea is supported by the historical record; for example, spices were moved around the world, even during the Middle Ages, because they were high-value, lightweight, and non-perishable.

Reducing energy use to move, store, and package food is just part of the motivation for shifting to more local food systems. If local food systems are also integrated with local, renewable energy generation, they offer greater food supply resilience in the face of fossil energy shortages. Local food systems can also increase people's awareness of what they are eating and thus have a positive effect on dietary behavior and human health. It's the powerful combination of these multiple benefits, not just the need to reduce energy consumption, that has driven many state and local entities to institute public policies and marketing campaigns to increase the production and consumption of local food.

Renewable Energy on Farms

Farmers are innovators; they have mechanical and technical skills, they're good at keeping down costs in a business with tight margins, their energy use is higher than it is in many other professions, and they have access to the land needed to produce some types of renewable energy, especially biomass. In other words, they are ideally suited to taking a leadership role in the adoption of renewable energy, and that's what they have been doing all across the country.

A wide range of renewable energy systems is being used on farms, and it includes many different energy sources as well as many different technologies for using those sources. The energy sources include biomass, solar, and wind. The technologies include anaerobic digestion or combustion of biomass, and photovoltaic or thermal capture of solar energy, to name a few.

The type of energy system that a farmer may be interested in depends on the energy needs of the farm (heat, liquid fuel, or electricity), the availability and cost of energy feedstocks on or near the farm (grass, manure, oilseeds, shell corn, solar, wind, wood), and the incentives or disincentives in the form of grants, tax policy, public opinion, and technical support. Clearly, when it comes to renewable energy and agriculture, a one-size-fits-all approach does not make sense. The options farmers seek are highly site- and commodity-specific.

While there are many reasons for exploring renewable energy systems, including environmental and geopolitical concerns, farmers, like the rest of us, want to understand the economic implications before they take action. A standard calculation for evaluating the economics of a new energy system is the payback period. That is, at a given fuel price and annual consumption rate, how long will it be until the investment is paid back through lower consumption and/or cost of energy? The payback period is based on a predicted market price for energy and must account for depreciation and maintenance of the energy system. Clearly, an energy system that is not expected to last longer than its payback period is not an attractive investment. For some farmers, the potential environmental and social benefits are also part of their calculations, even if these are hard to quantify economically. For example, there is value from a renewable energy system that reduces GHG emissions or increases sales to ecologically minded customers.

A payback more rapid than that achieved with any renewable energy system used to replace fossil energy is one that comes from increasing energy conservation and/or energy efficiency. Conservation means reducing total energy usage (e.g., using fewer gallons of fuel), while efficiency means increasing the work or yield per unit of energy consumed (e.g., getting more miles per gallon from a fuel). Like most businesses and residences, farms can usually improve the efficiency of the lighting, heating, and cooling systems in their buildings. In addition, they can address the efficiency of unique farm activities, such as grain drying, irrigation water pumping, milk cooling, tractor driving, and vegetable refrigeration. These efficiency improvements represent investment opportunities, where farmers with the knowledge and capital to make them can reap higher profits in the future.

Energy Quality

The quality of energy affects its value to an end user, and this plays a critical role in the selection of a renewable energy system. Although different forms of energy can be compared in terms of their energy content (as in British thermal units, or Btus, per gallon of oil, or cord of wood, or therm of natural gas), each form of energy has specific uses and a set of quality requirements for those uses (see fig. 8.2).

Solid fuels combusted for heating energy must be of the right size and

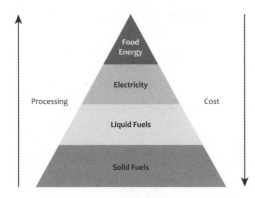

FIGURE 8.2 Value of different forms of energy. Highly processed forms of energy are typically higher in value or cost per unit of energy, though there is a great deal of variation.

shape, with an optimal moisture and ash content for the furnace they'll be put in. Liquid fuels for transportation energy must also conform to their intended distribution and equipment systems and meet specific purity standards. Electricity, too, has stringent quality requirements; it must be suitable for transmission lines and specialized equipment. And, of course, food energy has very stringent quality requirements: it must come in a form that is digestible, nutritious, non-toxic, and preferably palatable. All of these energy forms require some processing to ensure that they meet the appropriate standards. While it's a little like comparing apples and oranges, in general the more processing that's needed, the higher the quality and the value of the energy.

Not only does the processing of an energy form add to its value for end users, but external energy inputs are required to conduct the processing, and these two factors tend to increase its cost. Food is a very expensive form of energy to produce, while electricity and liquid fuels are in the middle of the pack, compared with solid fuels, which are relatively easy to produce and thus lower in cost.

For example, a 1-pound loaf of white bread typically contains 1,400 calories; 1 food calorie is equivalent to 4 Btus of energy. If a loaf costs $3, then $1 buys 467 Btus of food energy. When the bakery turns on its electric oven, a typical cost is about 12 cents per kilowatt hour (kWh), equivalent to 3,414 Btus, so $1 buys more than 28,000 Btus of electricity. Fueling up the bakery's delivery truck with diesel costs $4 per gallon, and each gallon contains about 128,000, Btus, so $1 buys 32,000 Btus of liquid fuel energy. Having a piece of toast in a house heated with wood pellets at $280 per ton burned in a stove that's 80 percent efficient costs about $22 per million Btus, so $1 buys 45,000 Btus of solid fuel energy. The point of all this is to illuminate the fact that sometimes it doesn't make sense to compare very different forms of energy. You can't eat wood pellets and you wouldn't try to heat your house with bread! However, it does make sense to compare energy forms when they can be interchanged, and this is often the case when it comes to producing and processing food. For example, a farm could heat a greenhouse full of tomatoes with electricity, heating oil, natural gas, or wood; these fuels will have different costs per Btu, as well as different GHG emissions, equipment needs, materials handling, and labor requirements to consider.

Energy Return on Investment

Another way to compare forms of energy is to calculate the amount of energy it takes to make a fuel relative to the final amount of usable energy obtained from it. This ratio is called the *energy return on investment*, or EROI. Since getting all fuels to the point of utilization requires some energy input, all fuels have an EROI. For example, trees growing in a forest may not require any energy input (other than the sun, which doesn't count), but to process them for cordwood fuel to heat a building requires gasoline for chain saws, diesel for logging and delivery trucks, and maybe electricity to run the blower in a wood furnace. These energy inputs are calculated and totaled, then compared with the usable energy obtained from combustion of cordwood in the furnace to determine the EROI.

Although in theory EROI is a valuable concept, it's not that easy to use, for two reasons. First, the same kind of energy can be produced in different ways, with different amounts of fossil energy inputs. For example, electricity can be made with solar panels, with hydropower, or by burning coal to drive a turbine; thus the EROI of electricity is dependent on the processes used to generate it. Second, assumptions vary with different EROI analyses. For example, when calculating the EROI for a fuel like biodiesel, one has to assume a certain yield of oilseed crop (like soybeans) per acre, decide whether to count indirect energy inputs such as transportation of supplies and fertilizer to the farm, and determine if the energy contained in by-products after the biodiesel is made (like soybean meal) will be considered. As a result, published estimates of biodiesel's EROI range widely from about 1:1 to 8.7:1. Even a consistent analytical approach will produce different results when individual production conditions are accounted for. A study of five Vermont farms and one used-vegetable oil processor found the EROI for the production of biodiesel to range from a 2.6:1 to 5.9:1.[8]

Overview of On-Farm Biofuels

On-farm sources of energy may be carbon-based (biofuels) or non-carbon-based (geothermal, hydro, solar, or wind-generated). Biofuels include very dif-

FIGURE 8.3 Anaerobic digester on a dairy farm. The manure from a thousand cows flows into this 600,000-gallon insulated concrete tank, where it "ferments" for several weeks, producing methane that powers generators in a nearby building. The solids from the digested manure are used as bedding for the cows, and the liquid is applied to fields. The system provides enough electricity for about four hundred homes annually, and it helps the farm with nutrient management.

ferent kinds of fuel that are derived from biomass. Solid biomass fuels include grasses, shell corn, and wood; liquid biomass fuels include biodiesel, ethanol, and vegetable oils. Biogas is fuel produced by the bacterial decomposition of organic material. In general, but with many exceptions, solid biomass is used to provide heat, liquid biofuels are used in place of diesel or gasoline, and biogas is used to generate electricity. Producing and/or using these fuels on farms requires the appropriate natural resources, equipment, and technical know-how.

Anaerobic digestion is most commonly used on large dairy and hog farms, where there is often more manure than is needed to maintain soil fertility. At the heart of the system is the digester, a giant tank that is sealed from outside air to keep out oxygen (fig. 8.3). It's filled with manure that bacteria feed on, releasing biogas, which is mostly methane (the main component of natural gas). The biogas can be combusted to make heat, but more often it's used to run generators that make electricity for sale to the grid.

The price farmers get for electricity they sell varies widely, but generally it is not enough to justify the cost of a digester. However, digesters provide other value to livestock farmers. They assist with the management of manure, which is important since most states require nutrient management plans. Waste heat from electric generators can produce hot water, which is used in large quantities, especially on dairy farms. Digested dairy manure solids may either be used for animal bedding in place of a purchased input like sawdust or sold as soil amendment, generating revenue. This list of potential benefits makes digesters sound like a no-brainer, but they typically cost more than a million dollars to install and require ongoing maintenance. They make the most economic sense on farms with about a thousand animals or more. Grants, "green energy" utility rates, and/or tax incentives also help pay for these systems.

Biomass combustion is simply fire, which occurs when some low-moisture biomass (like wood) and oxygen are combined at high temperatures, forming CO_2, water vapor, and heat. That heat can be used to keep barns or greenhouses warm, make hot water, or dry crops such as grains. While wood is commonly used for combustion, any dry plant material can serve as a combustion feedstock. In fact, all plants provide about the same amount of energy per unit of dry weight—but there are significant differences in what is required to grow a unit of dry weight, how much dry weight can be produced per acre, what processing is needed to get it ready for utilization, and what equipment is needed to burn it. For example, trees have a lot more biomass per acre than a field of grass, but it's produced over a different amount of time; wood can be easily cut into logs or chips, but more processing is required to form it into pellets.

Wood energy has been used on farms for thousands of years. Many contemporary farms contain woodlots, and firewood collection can be a management tool for removing undesirable species and improving the woodlot's long-term value for timber. A variety of modern wood-burning systems are available that combust wood more efficiently than older systems, reducing emissions of particulates, which is a serious health concern.

Fast-growing trees such as willow can be grown in rotation with other crops on farms, providing combustion feedstock, usually in the form of wood chips. The fields can go back to row crop production in several years if the farmer so chooses. Grasses, especially those that produce a lot of biomass quickly, such as switchgrass and *Miscanthus*, have potential for on-farm combustion. However, the equipment for making grass pellets and burning them is not as well developed as the equipment involved in wood combustion. Grasses also have higher ash content than wood, so a grass-burning furnace must be designed for that characteristic.

Shell corn has a high energy content, and corn production and handling equipment is widely available. However, corn combustion can be tricky; corn is harder to ignite than some other fuels, and when combusted it leaves behind a solid form of ash called a clinker. Corn furnaces must be designed to deal with these attributes. The value of corn for food and livestock feed makes its use as a fuel controversial. Shell corn may have multiple benefits for some diversified farms, since it provides a beneficial rotation crop for vegetable by reducing disease pressure and adding back a lot of plant residue, in the form of corn stalks, to the soil.

Biodiesel is a diesel fuel substitute that can be made from a variety of vegetable oils or fats. It can be made from virgin oils or from waste oil that has already been used for deep frying. The highest-quality biodiesel is made from virgin vegetable oils that are extracted from canola, soybean, sunflower, and some other seeds. After the oil is extracted, the remaining seed meal has value as a livestock feed ingredient, because it's high in protein. Biodiesel is not the same as straight vegetable oil, which can also be used as a liquid fuel but requires diesel equipment modification and poses a challenge to cold-weather operation since it will congeal.

Biodiesel is made by the reaction of vegetable oil and an alcohol like methanol, and the use of a catalyst to remove glycerin from the vegetable oil. The resulting products are biodiesel, which is thinner than vegetable oil and thus similar to regular diesel, and glycerin, which can be used for making soap and other products — if the processing equipment keeps it pure. In order to make high-quality fuel safely, biodiesel producers must have a good understanding of the underlying chemistry of the biodiesel process. It's far simpler to just sell oilseeds to large biodiesel processors as a commodity than to take the time and effort to process the seeds and manufacture biodiesel on the farm. A few farmers have pooled their efforts and built mobile processing units that can be shared among farms. Most small-scale biodiesel producers do not make or test their fuel to meet stringent federal standards for commercial sale, so their biodiesel is appropriate only for on-farm use.

Ethanol is grain alcohol that's commonly made from corn. Since it combusts easily and cleanly, U.S. ethanol production has been targeted by government policies and subsidies for supplementing gasoline supplies. Production rarely takes place on farms; it is centralized in large-scale plants in the Midwest near areas where corn is widely grown. Most ethanol plants are dry mills that ferment corn flour into ethanol, leaving behind distiller's grains, a by-product that is fed to livestock. Wet-mill plants primarily produce corn sweeteners, along with ethanol.

Making cellulosic ethanol from grasses, wood, and crop residues is more challenging than using starch-based crops like corn to make ethanol, in part because the optimal enzymes for breaking down the residues are not yet available. This technique could ultimately be more efficient in terms of EROI and less costly than current ethanol production, though that is not currently the case. It could also alleviate concerns about industrial ethanol's demand for corn, which promotes environmental damage when fragile land is used for production. And it could avoid competing demands for corn, which increases the cost of many food ingredients and livestock feed, leading to higher food prices.

Small-scale on-farm ethanol production is possible and may make economic sense, especially if waste products rather than crops are fermented; however, ethanol is highly regulated and on-farm production is not exempt.

While biomass energy can significantly contribute to efforts to reduce the food system's dependence on fossil fuels, it cannot meet all its energy needs. There simply is not enough land, and that land is also needed to grow food, livestock feed, and soil-improving cover crops. In the case of woody biomass, excessive removal of trees can disrupt ecosystem stability and wildlife habitats. Thus there is ongoing debate about what level of biomass production is sustainable, and some suggest that agricultural land should not be used to grow crops for fuel until after a satisfactory diet is made available to every person in the world.[9]

Renewable Energy at Cider Hill Farm, Amesbury, Massachusetts

Glenn and Karen Cook own Cider Hill Farm in northeastern Massachusetts (fig. 8.4). For three decades they've been improving production and marketing at this diversified farm with 145 acres of orchards, vegetables, and woodlots, eleven greenhouses, retail facilities, and four homes for family and workers.

Glenn had several motivations for using renewable energy on the farm:

The farm uses a lot of energy and I wanted to control that as much as possible. There's a lot we can't control, like the weather, but I thought if we could produce our own energy we could have some insurance against rate increases, and that would help keep our food prices competitive. I'm also kind of green and liked the idea of not burning oil. Plus, our electric bill was about thirty grand a year, so when renewable energy grants started to come along, it was time to get a program going.

We first thought that wind would be the way to go. We have a big hill, and we're not far from the Atlantic Ocean. An online wind database suggested we had a good

FIGURE 8.4 Wind turbines at Cider Hill Farm. Three relatively small wind turbines on the farm generate electricity that is net-metered. Net metering allows consumers to generate electricity on-site and deliver it back to the local distribution grid, offsetting what they would otherwise pay for electric energy provided by their utility. More than forty states allow net metering but their policies vary significantly.

wind location. So five years ago we installed three 10-kilowatt (kW) turbines, saving the best spot for a larger turbine if it worked out. But the small turbines have each produced only 3,000 kWh/year, far less than the projected 9,000 kW. Plus, there are a lot of moving parts that I think will limit the life span of the systems to about ten years, so we are not so enthusiastic about wind power.

Four years ago we put in a 10-kW solar PV system to compare with wind. In the first year it exceeded the projected production of 11,000 kWh/year by making 13,000 kWh. Soon the price of solar panels came down a lot, so over the next three years we put in another 120 kW of solar capacity, using three different systems, all on land not very useful for agriculture. They have worked very well. Our first system was just a single-row low-profile field mount, which has to be cleared off in big snowstorms. Next was a 25-kW ballasted system, like a weighted billboard frame of panels in between two greenhouses, with good clearance off the ground. Then we did another 10-kW system, on the roof of our chicken barn, right in our public access area so it's good PR. The last system was an 80-kW ballasted frame on a field edge.

Payback varies greatly since every system was done uniquely. Grants and rebates helped with the smaller solar systems. We paid for all of the largest systems ourselves, but we take advantage of solar renewable energy credits where utilities pay a premium for renewable power. The payback for that was expected to be four years, but now there are so many commercial solar systems going in that the credit values are going down. On average, our entire solar system will pay back in five years. Then we'll make free power for twenty-five to thirty years, with very little maintenance.

We took control of our farm's electricity needs, but we also wanted to get away from oil heat, and I thought biomass would be great. We started with two large outdoor wood boilers and tried to heat all eleven greenhouses with them. The boilers were incredibly hungry. We used a hundred cords of wood the first winter, and the smoke they produced was not good. We took them out and went with a couple of smaller outdoor wood gasifiers that could heat just a couple of greenhouses and our workers' housing. There is a big efficiency savings with gasification versus straight combustion because you lose much less heat up the stack, and the exhaust is cleaner with a lot less particulates. Now we use thirty to forty cords of wood, which is what we can produce on a renewable basis from our forest so the system is sustainable. We switched the remaining greenhouses to natural gas since it's a lot less expensive than oil and burns cleaner.

I get dozens of phone calls about our energy systems, and that's great. Before you install an alternative energy system it's important to learn from others. There are lots of great energy ideas and a huge number of ways to combine systems. You need to mix and match for your own farm. I am not sure what our next direction will be for energy conservation and production, but I will be certainly keeping my eyes and ears open.

The Role of Consumers

While farmers are reducing their energy usage, consumers can do their part as well. The role of consumers in reducing energy use in food systems turns out to be rather large. For starters, the eating public can support lower fossil-energy consumption through their purchasing behaviors, such as buying grass-fed beef and organic foods grown without synthetic nitrogen fertilizer and by avoiding air-freighted products and those with excessive packaging. By supporting farms like Cider Hill, consumers support renewable energy use by food producers.

People can also reduce the amount of energy used to produce their food by changing what they eat. That means stepping back and considering the energy implications of their diets. Some of us could start by eating less food in general, and many others could eat less highly processed food, since processing requires energy inputs but often doesn't add to the dietary value of food.

Shifting some caloric intake from animal products to plant products is another way to reduce the energy used to produce food, since it is typically less energy-efficient to use crops to feed livestock than it is to use crops to make food for direct consumption by humans.

In the home, where fully a third of food system energy is consumed, there are significant energy savings to be had by switching to energy-efficient refrigerators, dishwashers, and hot water heaters and by minimizing how much of the diet requires cooking and refrigeration. Minimizing food waste avoids the loss of energy that was used to produce the spoiled or unused food. Composting food that does go to waste can eliminate the additional energy expenditure needed for trucking to and managing sanitary landfills. Combining their efforts, it is clear that farmers and consumers can significantly reduce the amount of energy needed to fuel food systems.

We can't expand healthy food access if
we limit ourselves to one or two strategies;
it's about using every tool in the toolbox
to create community-specific solutions.
Kathleen Merrigan, former
U.S. Deputy Secretary of Agriculture

9 ⌇ Access to Healthy Food

The cost of food for the average U.S. household has been steadily declining for the past fifty years and is now below 10 percent of disposable income,[1] yet 15 percent of households do not have enough food to eat.[2] At the same time, more than one-third of Americans are obese (box 9.1).[3] There is no question that the United States has an obesity epidemic. Every state is affected to various degrees, with higher rates of obesity in the South and slightly lower rates in the Northeast and West.

Food is cheap, but a lot of people are hungry, and many more are overweight. What is going on?

The Conundrum of Cheap Food: Hunger and Obesity

It may seem paradoxical, but obesity and hunger go hand in hand; they are both outcomes of food insecurity (box 9.2; fig. 9.1).[4] That's because both stem from limited access to healthy, affordable foods.[5]

Hunger and obesity are serious problems that need to be addressed throughout the country, especially in low-income communities. Local agriculture is often a source of fresh healthy food, and many farms would benefit from additional markets. Can the creation of connections between local farms and low-income communities help address these issues?

Programs aimed at feeding the hungry don't necessarily make the connection between local farms and local communities, and there are good arguments why they don't need to. The goal of most food programs is to relieve food insecurity, and these programs attempt to make as much food available as possible and keep costs as low as possible. It doesn't matter where the food comes from, and fresh unprocessed products can be harder for philanthropic food programs with limited infrastructure to store and distribute, since they spoil more easily than processed products.

Programs that provide increased food security attempt to address three elements of food insecurity:

9.1 *Overview of Obesity in the United States*

- During the past twenty years, there has been a dramatic increase in obesity in the United States, where obesity is defined as being more than 30 pounds overweight.
- More than one-third of U.S. adults (36%) and approximately 17% (or 13 million) of children and adolescents aged two to nineteen years are obese.
- The South has the highest prevalence of obesity (30%) followed by the Midwest (29%), the Northeast (25%), and the West (24%).
- By state, obesity prevalence ranges from 21% in Colorado to 34% in Mississippi. No state had a prevalence of obesity that was less than 20 percent. Thirty-six states had a prevalence of 25% or more.

U.S. Centers for Disease Control and Prevention, *Overweight and Obesity: Data and Statistics*, 2011. www.cdc.gov/obesity/data/facts.html.

1 Food access: how people get their food. In the United States, we buy most of our food from retail markets, primarily supermarkets. But food access also includes growing food at home or in community gardens, buying it direct from farmers, and getting it from a soup kitchen or food bank. Access is affected by the locations of food that can be bought, grown, or obtained through a food shelf. Access also is affected by the resources an individual has to put toward food.

2 Food availability: how easy it is to find different types of foods at different times of the year, whether food is grown where we live or transported there. California's "salad bowl" provides fresh lettuce, strawberries, and other fruits and vegetables many months of the year.[6] In the Northeast, zucchini are more than plentiful in August and gardeners gladly give them away. In January, they can still be found at the supermarket but they cost more than in summer, when they're local. Supermarket zucchini in winter may come from Mexico.

3 Food utilization: how people use food, including storage, preparation, and cooking methods. Fresh foods can be difficult for low-income families to deal with if they don't have access to kitchen facilities and cooking equipment or if they lack the skills or energy to prepare meals from scratch. Knowledge about nutrition and the preparation of foods can greatly expand food utilization.[7]

These three types of programs are supported by federal, state, and local governments in collaboration with nonprofit organizations. Partnerships between federally funded programs and efforts at the state and local levels are critical for successfully addressing food insecurity throughout the United States.

9.2 *Overview of Food Insecurity in the United States*

- The World Food Summit defines food security as existing "when all people at all times have access to sufficient, safe, nutritious food to maintain a healthy and active life" (World Health Organization).
- The USDA measures three different levels of food security, with very low food security meaning that "food intake of one or more household members is reduced and their eating patterns are disrupted at times during the year because the household lacks money and other resources for food" (Coleman-Jensen et al. 2011). In other words, people are hungry.
- Estimates of food insecurity range from 7% in North Dakota to 19% in Mississippi. The U.S. average is 15 percent.

Alisha Coleman-Jensen, Mark Nord, Margaret Andrews, and Steven Carlson, *Household Food Security in the United States in 2010 (ERR-125)*, Economic Research Report, Economic Research Service (Washington, DC: United States Department of Agriculture, 2011); World Heath Organization, *Food Security*. n.d. www.who.int/trade/glossary/story028/en/.

Some of the earliest organized efforts to feed the hungry in our nation began during the Great Depression. Soup kitchens and breadlines were set up by churches and community centers in cities and towns starting in 1929, shortly after the stock market crash. They were aptly named, since the main menu items were soup and bread. Soup was an inexpensive meal that could be made with whatever ingredients were available, and more water could be added to the soup to feed more people. Although soup kitchens were originally established through religious and private charity, government support increasingly contributed to their operation as part of the federally led effort to address poverty during the Great Depression. With the unemployment rate as high as 25 percent in the 1930s, criticism was leveled at the government that subsidizing soup kitchens wasn't enough. Feeding people was important, but more had to be done to address the root causes of unemployment and poverty.[8] The same concern exists today.[9]

Over the decades, soup kitchens and breadlines have transitioned to food shelves and food banks that offer much more than soup and bread. The first food bank was established in the late 1960s in Phoenix, Arizona, when a soup kitchen volunteer asked local grocery stores for donations. More food was offered than what the kitchen could dish out, so the extra food was sent to a warehouse, which served as a "bank" for storing food donations until they were needed and distributed to soup kitchens around the city. In the 1970s the

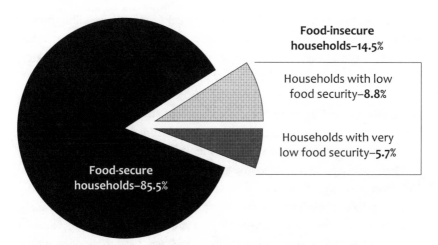

Food-insecure households–14.5%

Households with low food security–**8.8%**

Households with very low food security–**5.7%**

Food-secure households–**85.5%**

FIGURE 9.1 Food security status of U.S. households. Approximately 85 percent of U.S. households are food-secure. The remaining 15 percent (more than 17 million households) are food-insecure, meaning they have difficulty at some time during the year providing enough food for all their members. Almost 6 percent of U.S. households (about 7 million) have very low food security, meaning people are going hungry as a result of limited resources.

food bank concept spread to other cities with the help of the federal government.[10] Today, more than two hundred food banks and 61,000 agencies (e.g., food shelves) serve more than 37 million Americans every year, including 14 million children and 3 million seniors. Food banks are increasingly involved in more than emergency food relief; they advocate for policies that help reduce hunger, teach classes on nutrition, and work with local farms to "glean" excess fresh produce from the fields for families in need.[11]

Throughout the country, and especially in rural areas where agricultural land is abundant, farmers are doing their part to help fight hunger. More than likely, they are helping to combat obesity at the same time by providing healthy, fresh food. Through gleaning programs, donations to food banks, low-income and senior discounts on CSA farm shares, and programs that sell seconds and excess products at below-market prices, farmers, usually teamed up with community organizations, are making local food more accessible to families of all income levels.

Affordable Local Food

The local food movement has grown rapidly in recent years. With this growth has come the perception that local food costs more, that the movement is elitist — not for the average U.S. family.[12]

It is true that consumers who seek out local food and are willing to pay higher prices for it place importance on product quality, nutritional value, methods of production, impact on the environment, and/or support for local farmers.[13] Low-income families are less likely to pay a premium for these attributes.[14] But the perception that local food costs more is not always accurate: studies show that depending on the product and the location, local food may be priced the same or even lower than food from farther away.

At the same time that sales of local food have increased, more and more families have come to rely on food assistance, in the form of the Supplemental Nutrition Assistance Program, or SNAP, food shelves, and food banks. More than 17 million households in the United States are food-insecure, meaning that at some point during the year they do not have enough food.[15] Several states have developed programs to help make fresh, local food more affordable for everyone, especially low-income families.

Local food is often associated with direct sales from farms to consumers, since these sales tend to take place on farms or not far away from them. Thus growth in direct sales can be used as an indication of increased interest in local foods. During the past ten years, direct-to-consumer food sales doubled in the United States, while total agricultural sales increased by less than 50 percent.[16] Direct sales primarily take place at farmstands, farmers' markets, and CSAs.

Local food is also increasingly available "one step removed" from the farmer—at restaurants, food co-ops, general stores, supermarkets, and institutions such as schools and hospitals that buy from local producers. While retail sales from farm to customer are generally considered to be driving the growth of local food systems, the use of local foods is increasing among retailers and institutions. Purchasing locally produced and procured foods is on the rise among schools, hospitals, and supermarket chains, though this increase may have lagged behind the growth of direct markets, and fewer data are available about local purchasing by some of these sectors, especially supermarkets.

Although many types of local foods are available in most locations, fresh produce appears to be at the core of local food system growth, since sales of fruits and vegetables make up a large portion of all direct market food sales. According to the USDA, vegetable, fruit, and nut farms represent about 6 percent of all U.S. farms, yet they generate 65 percent of total sales of locally grown food.[17] Research has consistently shown that the consumption of fruits and vegetable is positively correlated with weight management and lowered risk for chronic diseases such as diabetes.[18] Perhaps that is one reason many people associate local food with healthy dietary options. When it comes to increasing access to local food, many efforts have focused on local fruits and vegetables — at farmers' markets, though urban agriculture, and in farm-to-school programs.

Yet most Americans do not meet the dietary guidelines of the U.S. Department of Health and Human Services, especially in the area of fruit and vegetable consumption.[19] One challenge to increasing access to local foods among low-income households is that poorer people tend to eat fewer fruits and vegetables.[20] Families with household incomes of less than $15,000 per year spend just 60 percent of the national average of annual household expenditures on fresh produce, while families earning $100,000 or more per year spend 160 percent of the national average. The primary reasons that low-income families eat fewer fruits and vegetables have to do with cost and convenience.[21] How can we reconcile efforts to strengthen local food systems with the fact that for many people, fresh, healthy food appears to be a luxury they can't afford?

Does Local Food Cost More?

In addition to the idea that it costs more, some common assumptions about local food are that a lot of it is organic, and organic food is especially expensive. Direct markets are the primary source of local food, and they can be perceived as expensive, too. To answer the question of whether local food costs more than "regular" food, we have to compare apples with apples. Wholesale, retail, organic, conventional, and different commodities shouldn't be lumped together in the analysis.

Some types of food will inevitably cost more from local producers, due to the comparative advantage of farmers in locations with more ideal growing conditions, where it will be less expensive to produce a given crop or animal. For example, Idaho averages 383 hundredweight of potatoes per acre, while Alabama averages 170 hundredweight per acre for the same crop.[22] Since the cost of fuel and road use is relatively low in this country, making transportation relatively inexpensive, there is no way Alabama — or Michigan or Vermont or just about any other state in this country — can produce cheaper potatoes than Idaho. That's why a bag of Idaho potatoes almost always costs less than locally grown potatoes, either in a supermarket or at a farmers' market. In places like Washington State, with an abundance of apples, local apples have the comparative advantage over apple-challenged locations and a relatively level playing field with apple-growing regions elsewhere in the country and the world.

A different kind of comparison has to be made between fresh local food and processed food from farther away. Thanks to subsidies, tax breaks, and the economic "efficiency" of industrial processes versus the production of more "natural" products, processed food is often cheaper than similar food with more "raw" ingredients—the ingredients associated with a healthy diet. For example, a large soda from a convenience store costs less per unit of volume than real apple cider, in part because industrial corn sweetener is subsidized by U.S. farm and food policies while apples from a local or regional orchard are not, at least not much.[23] The same is true for the cost per pound of cheeselike products made with milk powder and by-products like whey versus cheese made with real milk, or for a chopped and formed turkey breast diluted with low-cost added ingredients versus a real turkey breast. These differences in cost have more to do with policy-driven economic advantages of making processed food over making less processed food than they do with the "localness" of food, yet they are often attributed to local food since it tends to be less processed.

Organic food is also often associated with local food, and again the higher cost of organic food than conventional food is sometimes attributed to local foods. When studies have compared the cost of local foods, especially fresh produce sold at direct markets, with that of their equivalent counterparts sold in a supermarket or chain store, there is often no significant difference.[24] In some cases, as with CSAs, the local food may be less costly,[25]—which is not to say that local food without a comparative advantage won't cost more (e.g., meat in New England), or that fresh healthy food isn't more expensive than processed food (remember that soda), or that gourmet artisan cheeses don't cost more than run-of-the-mill cheddars, wherever they come from.

Wholesome Wave: Connecting
Needy Families to Local Food

Wholesome Wave is a nonprofit organization that builds connections between local food systems and low-income families. Their goal is a "more vibrant and equitable food system for all people."[26] They run three programs that simultaneously address food insecurity and support farm viability:

1 The Double Value Coupon Program is Wholesome Wave's longest-running program. The program matches SNAP benefits used for fresh, local produce at farmers' markets, effectively doubling the value of the benefits. This means the consumer gets twice as many carrots and the farmer receives twice as much money from that consumer than would otherwise be the case. More than three

hundred farmers' markets and farmstands in twenty-five states participate in the program each year, providing additional income for 2,500 farmers.

2 The Fruit and Vegetable Prescription Program targets overweight and obese children and pregnant women. Community health care providers write prescriptions for fresh fruits and vegetables, and the prescriptions can be redeemed at farmers' markets. The program takes place at twelve sites in seven states.

3 The Healthy Food Commerce Initiative was launched with the goal of directing capital and business development assistance to "healthy food hubs," which are organizations with facilities that aggregate, store, process, distribute, and market locally produced food products.

Wholesome Wave programming works in twenty-eight states and the District of Columbia with sixty partners to implement the three programs in more than three hundred farm-to-retail venues such as farmers' markets and farmstands. In addition to farm-to-retail venues, Wholesome Wave's partners include community leaders, health care providers, nonprofits, and government agencies. They recognize that a vast network of collaborators is needed to help make fresh, local food affordable for all families while also providing income opportunities for farmers.

Post Oil Solutions: Direct Markets for All Income Levels

Post Oil Solutions (POS) works in Brattleboro and other communities in southeastern Vermont. Richard Berkfield is the executive director of the nonprofit, which was started by local citizens less than a decade ago. He describes the organization's work as "building sustainable communities and a big part of that is bringing people together and re-learning how to work with our neighbors. Food is one of the best ways that we've found to bring people together. Food is an environmental issue, a health issue, an economic issue, and a social justice issue. We use food to celebrate. It's part of our culture. When you take a food systems approach, you see how all the issues come together."

POS is working to address access to farmers' markets for low-income people (fig. 9.2). "Often, a farmers' market is an upper-middle-class scene," says Richard, "and it's not just prices that are a problem, but also the culture. Even with programs that let people use federal food assistance at farmers' markets, there is the stigma of using a different system of payment; people have to go to the market table and use their Electronic Benefits Transfer (EBT) card to get tokens and then face the vendors, who know that those are the low-income tokens."

FIGURE 9.2 Farmers' market. The experience of shopping at a farmers' market is attractive to many people, though not to all. For people with limited incomes, these markets may seem too "upscale" and the food prices may be higher than those of other local sources. Some farmers' markets accept SNAP benefits, which can improve access to fresh local food for limited-income households.

The Brattleboro farmers' market, like many, can be especially off-putting for low-income people because it sells not just fresh food, but many "luxury" items as well. Ceramics, jewelry, clothing, expensive baked goods, and other prepared foods are abundant. The farmers' market is also a major tourist attraction—that's great for the farmers and other vendors, but maybe not so great for a low-income family that might just want to buy a head of lettuce and some cucumbers.

Transportation can also be a major problem for families without cars; many farmers' markets are located outside of town, and the bus route may not be convenient for getting there.

To address these issues, POS started farmers' markets in low-income neighborhoods and recruited farmers who were willing to keep their prices relatively low. In Brattleboro, POS set up its first neighborhood market at an affordable housing complex, working with Amy Frost from nearby Circle Mountain Farm. Amy sells at several "regular" farmers' markets, and she was enthusiastic about the chance to connect with a wider range of neighbors and give back to her community.

"As a farmer, I am low-income too," she explains. "To be able to make a living and still serve my low-income neighbors is refreshing. I'm honored to be able to grow food that is affordable for people who don't fit into the traditional market model of retail prices. It's a mutually beneficial relationship."[27] To maintain her business while meeting the needs of her neighbors, Amy uses price differentiation. Her "standard" prices at other farmers' markets and for her CSA shares allow her to charge reduced prices at the low-income community farmers' market. Other farmers have since become vendors as part of this program and use similar tactics to grow their businesses while still serving lower-income customers. Richard explains, "There are a lot of young farmers in Vermont who are fantastically optimistic and idealistic and want to grow good food for their neighbors."

A second such farmers' market was started at a low-income senior housing project, and after several years the lessons learned from running these markets helped shape changes in the program. It became apparent that customers might not be familiar with the products or how to cook them, so POS started to educate customers about the preparation of meals with fresh food products. The market managers also make sure unusual produce comes with identification and recipes that clearly explain what to do with the food and how to store it. Frequent food-cooking demonstrations, recipe handouts, taste tests, and even farm visits help to reconnect them with local food.

POS does more than start farmers' markets in low-income neighborhoods. It works with the statewide food bank to organize gleaning programs in the Brattleboro area and is working to start more gardens in public schools. POS also helps run workshops on topics ranging from home gardening to backyard poultry. These efforts are aimed at building sustainable communities as part of a sustainable local food system.

Increasing Access to Local, Healthy Food

Local food was for the poor not that long ago. Growing your own food, preserving it, trading with neighbors, and buying as little as possible from stores—that was what low-income families did. Food was grown without chemicals for the most part because pesticides and herbicides were expensive, and alternative systems had been developed to cope with insects and weeds. Rich people were the ones who bought processed food from far away in stores. This was true throughout the United States less than a hundred years ago, and it was still true in rural areas less than fifty years ago. How quickly and dramatically things have changed. Now low-income families lack access to local food, and a bag of potato chips is cheaper than a bag of locally grown potatoes.

Local food has been accused of being elitist.[28] And the truth is that local food can cost more, especially when the price has to bear the full cost of production. A local vegetable is on its own. There are no price supports like those for large-scale agricultural commodities such as corn and soybeans and wheat. No subsidized transportation system is needed to truck it across the country. Crop insurance programs are not as applicable, or not well utilized, for losses to drought or flood.

Even if local food costs more, if consuming it helps improve people's diets, then it may be a bargain for society, since that could lead to reduced health care costs and to longer productive lives. More data are needed to make that case, but recent research has found positive relationships between lower obesity rates and direct sales of local foods, including sales through CSAs and farmers' markets.[29] Increasing access to and consumption of local foods can also contribute to a vibrant working landscape, and all the hard-to-measure benefits it provides, from ecosystem services to tourism revenue.

There are many ways that access to local food for people of all income levels can be increased, and a few of them have been highlighted here. Soup kitchens, food banks, and gleaning programs are part of charitable efforts to share the benefits of local foods. Gardeners can share extra veggies with neighbors in need or plant an extra row to give to a local food pantry. Community gardens can help families without their own land to grow their own vegetables. Cities and towns are passing ordinances that allow small flocks of hens (no roosters, please!) to produce backyard eggs. Youth agriculture programs are putting kids to work where they can produce food for their neighbors and learn to appreciate where it comes from. Food hubs are being organized to aggregate and distribute low-cost local wholesale food to people who could otherwise not afford to pay full retail prices at retail stores.

Local food consumption is bound to increase further as larger institutions, including colleges and universities, hospitals and prisons, public and private schools, senior housing, and day care centers, engage in more local food buying as part of their wellness programs. These efforts will help make healthy food accessible and affordable for all.

10 ∾ *Farm to School*

The growing interest in local food systems has led to "farm-to-school" programs, which aim to improve child nutrition while simultaneously enhancing local markets for farmers. These programs generally work on two levels: (1) increasing the use of healthy, locally sourced food in school cafeterias and (2) adopting educational programs that help kids understand and connect to where their food comes from as part of the effort to promote good eating habits.

While it is obvious that many factors beyond the school affect both child nutrition and local food purchasing, schools can have a significant influence on both. The USDA reports that almost 32 million kids consume more than 5 billion lunches during the nine-month school year as part of the national school lunch program, and nearly 13 million kids consume more than 2 billion breakfasts at school. More than two-thirds of these lunches and more than 80 percent of these breakfasts are provided for free or at a reduced price. All this costs the federal government almost $15 billion annually.[1]

The importance of providing healthy food to schoolchildren is one reason school food programs have been targeted for improvement. Specifically, these programs can use more local foods, including fresh, whole, unprocessed ingredients that have the potential to improve children's dietary behavior by reducing their consumption of highly processed foods, which are often offered as part of school meals and snacks. Offering healthy food from any location is a good thing; adding the "local" component can facilitate behavior change so that healthy food is actually consumed. "Local" may mean food from as close to the students as their own school garden, or it may come from nearby farms that students have some direct knowledge of or real connections with.

Sources of food that kids can see—their gardens, the farms in their town or state, farmers who come to their classroom—create a platform for learning about agriculture and human nutrition as well as economics, environmental science, marketing, and much more. That learning may take place in the

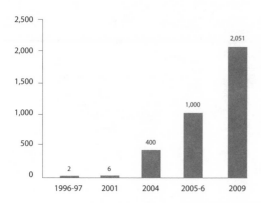

FIGURE 10.1 Growth in the number of U.S. farm-to-school programs. The number of these programs increased dramatically in a relatively short period of time.

classroom, with a formal curriculum or through ad hoc lessons. It may also happen during field trips or in a hands-on school setting, which can be a garden but might also be a greenhouse, a "grow lab" of lettuce under lights, or a cafeteria that features informational labels and posters, or perhaps a project to measure the volume of food waste that is diverted for composting. Farm-to-school programs are expanding (fig. 10.1), and they are introducing innovations, from "harvest of the month" menu offerings, to videos on the history of farming in town, to "healthy harvest" programs that get kids picking local fruits that will be frozen and later served by their school food service companies. To be most effective, these programs combine a variety of approaches aimed at building food system understanding and helping children develop healthy eating habits that will last a lifetime. To be successful, farm-to-school programs also engage a range of partners—in the cafeteria, the classroom, and the community.

The fact that people are drawn to farm-to-school programs for different reasons is at the core of their growing popularity. Child wellness, specifically diet-related health, is a powerful motivator. Agricultural economic development, specifically the creation of new markets for local food producers, is another. Educational performance and the potential to improve it through better student nutrition is yet another. In the aggregate, these goals attract a broad and motivated constituency for farm-to-school programs. Further, the expected outcomes of healthier children, more local food sales, and better performance if kids eat well are intuitively understood to be valid and achievable, so there is little "prove-it-to-me" pushback against farm-to-school programs, though there may be resistance to additional costs for purchasing local food or for food education programs.

The alarming trends in childhood "diabesity" are often cited as justification for farm-to-school programs. Obesity may be the most widespread medical problem affecting children and adolescents in the United States, where one in six children is obese.[2] During the past thirty years, the rate of obesity among children has tripled,[3] with obesity quickly transitioning from a rare occurrence to a national epidemic. In a relatively short period, the average weight of American children has ballooned and is now recognized as a major public health concern.[4] Associated diseases, especially type 2 diabetes, are on the rise as well. If trends continue, the present generation of children will have a shorter life span than their parents' generation.[5]

Why the rapid increase in overweight and obese children? Simply put, more calories are being consumed than are used, leading to excessive weight gain over time (box 10.1). This is also happening to many adults in the United States, but it is more worrisome in children, since they face the possibility of suffering from diet-related illness throughout their lives rather than just in their later years. There are several things that children and adults can do to avoid excess weight gain. These boil down to limiting caloric intake, eating healthy food, and getting regular exercise. Farm-to-school programs are a piece of the larger effort to get kids to take these actions.

Parental obesity is positively correlated with childhood obesity, suggesting that both genetics and family lifestyles play a role. The importance of the home environment for promoting healthy eating and lifestyle patterns can't be overstated. However, external environments also have a strong influence, especially for school-age children and teens. Television ads promote junk food, fast food restaurants and vending machines serve it, and some school cafeterias don't do much better. School-sponsored events and fund-raisers that sell high-calorie foods are also a part of the problem. Efforts are under way to improve the role that schools play in determining children's diets; this entails not just influencing what food is served, but also making available the knowledge needed to make healthy food choices.

The U.S. Centers for Disease Control and Prevention found that one of the main ways to reduce obesity is to eat more fruits and vegetables, and farm-to-school programs tend to focus on local fruits and vegetables.[6] Born of the local food movement, farm-to-school programs are part of a broader cultural shift, an attempt to move away from the fast food nation that defines much of the United States and toward a nation that is connected to the land and promotes healthy lifestyles.

Evolution of Farm-to-School Programs

Educational programs that help children learn where their food comes from have been around for almost a century. One of the earliest that is still active today is the Mobile Dairy Classroom run by the Dairy Council of California. Beginning in the 1930s, a mobile classroom, including a truck with a live cow, traveled to schools to teach children about dairy cows and how milk is produced and processed into a variety of dairy products. The program originally served urban students in Los Angeles, but as California became more urbanized, the program expanded to serve urban areas throughout the state.[7]

As the United States has urbanized and suburbanized over the past century, fewer children have made connections with agriculture and food production through their families and communities. These lost connections contribute in some way to poor food choices, because a highly processed, sugar-saturated, multicolored plastic-packaged diet seems normal if you have little exposure to fresher and more natural food options. This is one reason that some people began to perceive a need for school-based education about nutrition and farming: to increase kids' awareness of alternatives to the food choices they see on television, in vending machines, and at fast food restaurants. Thus school field trips to farms became popular class outings, while at the same time parents and activists were paying more attention to the food served in school cafeterias and putting pressure on schools to make their menus healthier and, in some cases, to remove low-quality foods from school vending machines. All this aligns with providing fresher, and often more local, food in schools when possible.

A variety of efforts aimed at improving school food and connecting it to local agriculture were scattered across the country by the 1990s. These came together in 2000 under the National Farm to School Program with support from the USDA's Small Farms/School Meals Initiative. Groundbreaking meetings were organized that brought farmers and school food services together for the first time in Kentucky, Iowa, and Oregon, where approximately six pilot programs were running at the time.[8] Over the next fifteen years, parents, educators, administrators, and health professionals all over the country jumped on the bandwagon. Farm-to-school programs are now operating in more than ten thousand schools spanning all fifty states. The National Farm to School Network "envisions a nation in which Farm to School programs are an essential component of strong and just local and regional food systems, ensuring the health of all school children, farms, the environment, economy and communities." The network does this by providing resources, education, and training for schools, parents, and organizations.[9]

Farm-to-School Efforts in Vermont

Farm-to-school programs come in various shapes and sizes. The programs are developed or adapted to meet the needs and resources of a given state, school district, town, or school. Today, most states have an umbrella organization and/or leading state agency that provides support for regional and local efforts that actually establish and operate farm-to-school programs.

In Vermont, a statewide project called Vermont FEED (Food Education Every Day) has worked since 2000 with more than one-third of the schools in Vermont to help them make greater use of local food in their cafeterias, offer expanded education about farming and nutrition in their classrooms, and forge connections with their communities to build and sustain these efforts (see fig. 10.2).[10] Vermont FEED is a collaborative project of three nonprofits with related educational and agricultural missions: the Northeast Organic Farming Association of Vermont, Food Works at Two Rivers Center, and

FIGURE 10.2 Canned food in an elementary school kitchen. Many farm-to-school programs seek to improve the dietary behavior of children by increasing their consumption of fresh fruits and vegetables. Sometimes this also requires changing the cooking practices of school food service personnel, who may not be accustomed to preparing and serving fresh foods or equipped to do so.

Shelburne Farms. It works with local and regional partners to advocate for farm-to-school policy, to provide school communities with farm-to-school program development, and professional development for teachers and school nutrition staff. In 2007 Vermont was the first state to pass legislation for farm-to-school funding, including training and grants for schools. The grant program is in its seventh year and has benefited more than sixty-five schools so far. According to Abbie Nelson, Vermont FEED director, "Farm to school in Vermont is not a fad—aspects of it are being incorporated in schools and changing school food culture. Students and school communities are valuing food and the land and the people who grow food."[11]

While it is important that statewide organizations support farm-to-school programs, smaller, more regionally focused efforts are a critical part of this movement, too. Examples can be found in all parts of Vermont, with most regional efforts focused on a county or two. In the northeastern part of the state, Green Mountain Farm-to-School (GMFTS) is a nonprofit organization that "promotes the health and wellbeing of Vermont's children, farms and communities by providing programs to connect schools and farms through food and education. Since 2005, GMFTS has grown from a single school garden program to a nonprofit organization serving twenty-four school communities in the Northeast Kingdom with school gardens, educational programs and fresh local foods from Vermont farms."[12]

In northwestern Vermont, the Burlington School Food Project is working to connect farms and schools (box 10.2). It is "a community based Farm to School initiative working to transform school food culture in Burlington and beyond. The mission is to connect students and their families with whole, fresh and local foods to improve their health and the health of our community."[13]

According to the Project's website:

In Burlington, Farm to School is much more than putting local veggies on the lunch tray. It's about fostering a culture that respects the land and people that produce the food we eat. It is also more about community development (with school food on the center of the plate) and Burlington is just about the best place to try and make this happen. Not only are we surrounded by a vibrant rural farming community, we also have our own agricultural gem within city limits, the Intervale, where a handful of organic farms produce an abundance of food and provide space for city residents to connect to the land. Students take field trips to the local farms, and farmers visit their classrooms. We now see this influence coming full circle, as Intervale farmers begin to send their own children to school."[14]

Thomas Case of Arethusa Farm is one of those farmers at the Intervale who sends his children to school in Burlington. Arethusa Farm was one of the first farms that started working with the Burlington School District. Thomas recalls the early stages of working with the Burlington School District:

At that point my oldest daughter was not in the school system yet but I knew she was going to be. I didn't know what school lunches were like, but I assumed they were not very good. Improving school food is important to all the children in the community, so I'm willing to contribute a certain amount of time and energy towards that goal. I sort of raised my hand, I guess, and went to a meeting with the local school food service director, the coordinator of Vermont FEED, and a parent of one of the school students who is a community activist and one of the main forces behind the effort. We met to try to figure out where we could come together on price and product. I'll be honest, it was difficult at first. I'd say, "Everyone loves carrots." The food service director would say, "We can't get carrots from you because we can get them from the government at a super cheap price. Kids only eat baby carrots anyway." I was surprised to hear kids only eat baby carrots. My kids eat regular carrots. You know what baby carrots are? They are regular carrots that are chiseled to make them small and then slightly cooked to make them tender.

Then the parents and teachers organization at my daughter's elementary school set up a salad bar, working with the school food service, and they bought fifty pounds of carrots from me. Carrot sticks were out on the table. The kids were picking them up and eating them and came back for more. Since then they have bought a fair bit of carrots from me.

So I asked about winter squash; we grow a lot of winter squash here. And the answer was, "Kids don't eat winter squash." I couldn't believe that. Kids don't eat winter squash? So I asked about zucchini. And the answer was, "Well, maybe. We can put it in soups." Then we talked about the price. "Well, we can't buy zucchini at the price you sell it for because of our budget." So I said, "What about big zucchinis?" We agreed on the seconds, those zucchini that get left on the vine an extra couple of days. The school is going to grate them up anyway. And that's where we broke through. The agreement was five hundred pounds per season of zucchini. We would sell them seconds at half of our regular price, so they were getting a good deal and we were selling seconds that are hard to wholesale.

Eventually the food service director became a real supporter of buying from local farms. One day he came down to our farm, and the crew was on the ground weeding onions. I think it was eye-opening. He saw what it takes to grow organic vegetables. You can tell people we hand-weed, but it's not the same thing as seeing it. With onions we're actually crawling around on the ground on our hands and knees. We're dirty, and we're working in the hot sun. That's why our organic onions cost a little more.

The local schools are totally on our side now. There are a lot of limitations of where they can spend money but the food service director is trying to do it in a way that benefits the children and the farmers. It's very exciting to be part of the farm-to-school program and know that our city is a national leader.

Farm-to-School Efforts in Windham County, Vermont

In southeastern Vermont, the Windham County farm-to-school program manager finds inspiration and practical information from the many efforts throughout the state and the region. Katherine Gillespie explains how the program started: "In 2007 Vermont passed legislation that established a statewide grant program to help schools develop and strengthen farm-to-school programs. The three elementary schools came together as the Brattleboro Farm to School Program and received one of these grants, which helped support teacher training, farm field trips, taste tests, and the purchase of a commercial food processor to enable the inclusion of more fresh produce in school meals." The Brattleboro Farm to School Program has grown, and in 2009 Katherine was hired through AmeriCorps to coordinate its efforts full time. Then Katherine helped found Food Connects, a nonprofit that now runs the Brattleboro program and has expanded support to more schools in the county. This support is for educators, food service directors, farmers, and community members, and it includes professional development for teachers, taste tests of local produce, school gardens, farm field trips, and mobile classroom cooking carts.[15]

The goals of the Food Connects' Farm to School Program are broader than putting local food on cafeteria trays. Katherine explains:

In some ways I think farm to school is a bit of a misnomer because it's not just about bringing the farm to the school. We're also bringing the students to the farms, engaging parents in growing and cooking with local foods, connecting neighbors with school gardens, and coordinating community events that strengthen our understanding of local food systems.

We have adopted Vermont FEED's comprehensive approach, which includes the three C's: classrooms, cafeterias, and communities. With this approach, teachers, parents, and food service directors feel more support, are less likely to burn out, and are able to make sustainable changes. Weaving farm-to-school programs into the fabric of the community is what strengthens and sustains programs and their communities over the long-term.

There are many community partners eager to support and connect with farm-to-school programs. For example, our strong relationships with the Brattleboro Food Co-op and the University of Vermont Extension 4-H Youth Agriculture Project have brought tremendous resources and support to our school communities, including garden support, hands-on classroom cooking lessons, the high school harvest program, and farm field trips, to name just a few.

We work with school communities to build capacity and provide program and event support. For example, we help initiate and organize farm-to-school committees, we organize professional development opportunities, we support school wellness policies, and we help identify and secure program material needs such as cooking carts and grow labs. Additionally, we work with school-based committees to coordinate and market a variety of farm to school activities, such as monthly taste tests, the Vermont Harvest of the Month campaign, farm field trips, school gardens, community celebrations, and curriculum connections. We meet with food service directors regularly to let them know which local foods are available, or should be available in coming weeks as they plan their menus in advance, and we share tips for buying and processing local foods that help them continue to meet their budgets. We have found that most food service companies want to use local food but face many barriers, including labor costs, appropriate kitchen equipment, and of course local food prices. For example, we are fortunate to have a great supply of salad greens in our region, but are there salad spinners in the school kitchens to wash and dry the greens? If food service professionals don't have large salad spinners in their kitchens, it's very difficult for them to consider buying local greens. It's much easier and more affordable to open a bag of pre-washed, pre-chopped greens. But local greens are healthier and taste better. To make it work, we all need to understand the challenges and work cooperatively to support one another.

My favorite part of this work is pulling together different groups of people and making new connections between classrooms, cafeterias, and communities. An example of this is our 5th Grade Garlic Project. We were approached by a private school that already had a large school garden and incorporated a lot of school-grown and local produce into their school snacks, but they wanted to do more for their school community and reach out to other schools in the area. So they offered land to use for a fund-raiser for Brattleboro Farm to School. A group of partners decided to grow garlic on that land, as its growing season aligns nicely with the school calendar.

We developed this concept into the 5th Grade Garlic Project. Fifth grade students from three public elementary schools and the private school learned about growing garlic, how to use it in food, its nutritional value, and its cultural significance. The students, with the support of teachers and many community partners, came together to plant garlic in the late fall. In the spring, the students came back for a weeding session and to check on the progress of the garlic. In June, the students harvested garlic scapes. In the summer, the private and public school families had a local wood-fired pizza dinner together and harvested the garlic. We then worked with the local food co-op to sell the garlic, specially labeled and at slightly higher prices, with all the proceeds going to future farm-to-school projects. We'd love to develop more grade-specific projects like this that really integrate the 3-cs in a meaningful way.

We recognize teachers have limited time and, therefore, it is essential that we integrate farm to school into the school curriculum. Curriculum-based projects strengthen student ties to the land, local food, and their community—and that's the beauty of farm to school.

We now work in fifteen schools throughout the county. Funding is a challenge, but we've found that the most sustainable model is to have a farm-to-school program manager, me, who supports committees at each of the schools. I do not provide much direct service to students, but rather work with school staff and food service professionals to build their capacity at the school level and connect the school with relevant community resources that can assist in program delivery. In this model the school sets the direction of their farm-to-school project, deciding their own priorities. As the program manager, I support their efforts by sharing best practices and resources. Once that framework is developed it can withstand changes over time. We're still working on how best to sustain our existing programs and expand to meet the growing demand for farm-to-school support. We have been fortunate to have the great support of superintendents and administrators,

FIGURE 10.3 Elementary school cafeteria. Farm-to-school programs aim to improve children's diets, in part by ensuring that more healthy, local food is served in school cafeterias. Documenting that kids actually change what they eat can be a challenge.

which has encouraged financial support from school boards, food service companies, foundations, and donations from the communities. Despite the challenges it is an exciting time as our community increasingly recognizes the importance of farm to school and its positive impacts on children, farms, and communities.

Challenges for Farm-to-School Programs

A major challenge for farm-to-school programs is documenting their impacts. Has the diet of children, or their health, improved? Has more food been purchased from local farms, and have they profited from this? Do healthier food offerings in schools improve educational performance or related test scores? These are not easy questions to answer and many groups are working to do so (fig. 10.3).

A meta-analysis of evaluations of farm-to-school programs examined fifteen programs in several states, including California, Illinois, Pennsylvania, Michigan, Oregon, Washington, and Vermont.[16] The meta-analysis focused on several outcomes, including

1 Student dietary behaviors
2 Student knowledge and attitudes
3 Overweight and obesity measures
4 Parent behaviors
5 Farmer benefits

STUDENT DIETARY BEHAVIORS. How have the food choices of students changed as a result of farm-to-school programs? Fruit and vegetable consumption is a particularly telling indicator, as many farm-to-school programs focus on fruits and vegetables. Of the fifteen studies reviewed in the meta-analysis, eleven examined student dietary behavior changes. Of those eleven studies, ten concluded that "positive dietary behaviors result when students are served more fruits and vegetables, especially when the product is fresh, locally grown, picked at the peak of their flavor, and supplemented by educational activities."[17] Only one study reported no changes in student dietary behaviors as a result of the farm-to-school program. Five of the eleven programs also looked at student dietary behaviors outside of the school, with four out of five reporting increases in fruit and vegetable consumption outside of school as well as in school. This suggests that farm-to-school programs influence the food choices of students in school and outside of school.

STUDENT KNOWLEDGE AND ATTITUDES. How do farm-to-school programs affect students' knowledge of and attitudes toward nutrition, health, local foods, and agriculture? Four of the fifteen studies looked at the impacts of farm-to-school educational activities conducted in the classroom and outside of the classroom. Generally speaking, the studies showed an increase in student knowledge about healthy foods, sustainable agriculture, local foods, and gardening skills. All four studies described outcomes related to increases in student knowledge, including the following:

– Data from one study found an 8% increase in correct student responses regarding seasonality of foods and the ability to identify foods grown in the region after the educational program was implemented.
– Before a farm trip, 33% of students responded correctly about where food comes from, and 88% responded correctly to the question afterwards.
– During an activity aimed at sequencing cards in the order food travels from farm to table, 12% of students responded correctly on the pretest, compared to 52% of students on the posttest.
– Only 50% of the students were aware of the daily fruit and vegetable consumption recommendation before the program; 80% of students were aware of this afterwards.
– Students participating in the program could correctly identify healthier options to buy in a supermarket (62% pre-program as compared to 90% post-program).[18]

OVERWEIGHT AND OBESITY MEASURES. Students may gain knowledge and make better food choices as a result of farm-to-school programs, but are they actually healthier? Only one study evaluated body mass index (BMI) as an indicator of farm-to-school success in improving children's health. In that study, researchers did not find significant decreases in BMI for students in the schools with farm-to-school programs during one school year. Longer-term evaluations are needed to assess changes in overweight and obesity measures.

PARENT BEHAVIORS. While students' food choices appear to be positively affected, what about those of other family members? Three of the fifteen studies reported on parent education components of farm-to-school programs. All three reported positive changes in parental behaviors including the following:

- 90% of parents self-reported positive changes in grocery shopping patterns, cooking at home, and conversations with their children about food choices.
- 32% of parent respondents believed that their family diet had improved due to their child's participation in the farm to school program.
- 32% reported buying more local foods.
- 45% were willing to pay more for the school's hot lunch if it contained food from local farms.
- 90% believed that lessons on food, farms, and nutrition would affect children's long-term food choices.[19]

FARMER BENEFITS. Four of the fifteen studies included data about farmers' participation and sales from farm-to-school programs. Annual sales for farmers to farm-to-school programs ranged from $8,000 to $55,000. Farm-to-school programs varied greatly in their expenditures on local food and the number of farms they purchased from. Not surprisingly, sales per farmer were higher in programs where only a few farmers were involved. For most farmers, income from farm-to-school programs was less than 5 percent of their farm income. Still, farmers were enthusiastic about being involved. Clearly they were not participating in farm-to-school programs just for the money. Several farms were involved in multiple ways, providing food for school lunches and hosting farm tours or educational activities in the classroom. The meta-analysis concluded that farmers "tended to see these efforts as a way to create synergy between the educational institutions, agriculture, and community, with the added potential benefit of additional sales through other venues."[20] In other words, farmers are building social and community capital through their participation in farm-to-school programs.

To summarize the meta-analysis, farm-to-school programs do seem to have positive impacts on the food choices of students and their families. The report found that "evaluation study designs vary greatly, though findings consistently indicate that the farm-to-school approach results in students eating more fruits and vegetables per day in the cafeteria, classroom, or at home, making positive lifestyle changes, as well as improving knowledge and attitudes about healthy eating and sustainable agriculture."[21] On the negative side, sufficient evidence is not yet available to show direct impacts of changes in food choices on the health of children and their families. Several years of systematic data collection will be necessary to show changes of this sort. For farmers, the monetary benefits appear to be limited. Although revenues for farms are modest to negligible, farmers are still willing to participate because farm-to-school programs build social and community capital.

A recent study by the University of Wisconsin's Department of Family Medicine corroborates these findings for the statewide Wisconsin Ameri-Corps Farm to School Program.[22] The study looked at twelve schools that served as program sites. An advantage of this evaluation is the ability to compare farm-to-school programs that have been in place for different periods of time. Of the twelve schools, two were new to the program, two had participated for one year, four had participated for two years, and four had participated for three years. The study examined three outcome measures also mentioned in the meta-analysis: student dietary behaviors, student knowledge and attitudes, and overweight and obesity measures.

To assess student dietary behaviors, lunch tray photo observations were used. The study found that the largest number of fruits and vegetables were observed on trays at schools with more than one year of farm-to-school programming. Regarding students' knowledge and attitudes on food, nutrition, and agriculture, it was found that knowledge generally increased over the year. As with dietary behavioral changes, schools with previous farm-to-school programs showed higher scores on knowledge and attitude scales than did schools new to farm to school. As in the case of the meta-analysis, sufficient data were not available to measure changes in overweight and obesity. For this evaluation, baseline data were recorded, indicating that 39.1 percent of students were overweight or obese, which is 4 percent higher than the national average for children that age. Future evaluations are needed to make comparisons with baseline data regarding overweight and obesity changes.

The results described in the report suggest that the Wisconsin farm-to-school programs improve student dietary behaviors and increase knowledge of and attitudes toward food, nutrition, and agriculture. An important finding is that improvements in student food choices tended to increase with more years of farm-to-school programming. The study concludes that farm-to-school programs may have "gradual, yet sustaining positive impacts on student health behaviors."[23]

Further evidence of the value of farm-to-school programs can be found in the USDA's first report on farm-to-school initiatives. The report highlights positive impacts, as well as barriers to implementation.[24] During the course of a year, fifteen school districts across the country were visited by a team of government representatives who evaluated their farm-to-school programs.

Strong partnerships were found to have formed between school administrators and farmers with the shared goal of providing fresh, local produce and meats. However, several challenges were identified that must be addressed for farm-to-school programs to be successful in the future (box 10.3).

Despite these challenges, the report indicated that school administrators and farmers were committed to overcoming the obstacles and continuing to improve farm-to-school programs. They have the backing of the USDA in their efforts. According to former Agriculture Deputy Secretary Kathleen Merrigan, "There are a lot of barriers, but none of them are insurmountable. What this shows me is that there really is a pathway forward to expand farm to school in a big way."[25]

Strengthening Farm to School in Your Town

Parents who want to see fresh, local food in their children's school lunch have two options: pack the lunch or work with schools as an advocate for healthy lunches with local ingredients. Motivated parents, innovative food service personnel, flexible farmers, and supportive administrators and policy makers are all critical to the success of farm-to-school programs. They each have unique yet interconnected roles, and their engagement can become synergetic as it leads to win-win-win results: kids eating food that supports their well-being; schools buying food that supports viable farms; communities connecting with each other to take control of an issue that indirectly affects a host of important issues, from student performance to land use to health care costs.

Whatever role one plays in providing healthy school food, and whether a school is just getting started with a farm-to-school program or already has a lot going on and wants to expand its offerings, the National Farm to School Network is an excellent resource. It offers Web-based case studies, lists farm-to-school organizations in each state, and provides planning tools and contacts that can assist individuals, schools, food service companies, and communities in their efforts to take on what kids take in.

Agritourism used to be something for kindergarteners. Now, with the local food movement, college kids think farmers are cool.

Beth Kennett, Liberty Hill Farm,
Rochester, Vermont

11 ∾ *Agritourism and On-Farm Marketing*

As the economic and social fabric of rural communities has undergone changes in the past century, many communities have experienced a transition from economic dependence on natural resource extraction (e.g., agriculture, timber) to service-based economies, particularly tourism. Population shifts transforming rural areas into suburban sprawl have made it increasingly difficult for some small and midsize farms to remain viable. In response, entrepreneurial farmers and ranchers have merged farming, ranching, and tourism into the alternative agricultural enterprise known as *agritourism*. The growing interest in local food systems has provided new economic opportunities for small and medium-sized farms throughout the country.[1]

In the United States, where produce typically travels 1,500 miles from point of production to point of consumption,[2] one motivation for local food systems is to bring farmers and consumers closer together, literally. Selling agricultural products and experiences directly to consumers is one of the most effective ways for farms to increase their share of the food dollar and receive more value for products sold. Direct marketing can take a variety of forms on and off the farm. Farmers markets, catalogs, and e-commerce are frequently used to sell products directly to consumers off the farm. Community-supported agriculture uses both on-farm and off-farm direct sales models, as consumers may pick up their shares on the farm or at central delivery locations off the farm. On-farm sales derive from roadside stands, pick-your-own operations, and several forms of agritourism and culinary tourism.

Agritourism can be defined as "a commercial enterprise on a working farm or ranch conducted for the enjoyment, education, and/or active involvement of the visitor, generating supplemental income for the farm or ranch."[3] A farm engaged in agritourism has been defined as one "combining primary elements and characteristics of agriculture and tourism and providing members of the general public a place to purchase farm products and/or enjoy a recreational, entertaining or educational experience."[4]

FIGURE 11.1 Pick-your-own strawberries. Pick-your-own or U-pick enterprises exemplify the overlap between the marketing of farm products and the marketing of a farm experience. Some customers may be motivated primarily by the opportunity to purchase super-fresh fruit, while others are more attracted by the chance to spend time outdoors in a farm field.

Agritourism includes many kinds of activities, such as overnight farm stays, hayrides, corn mazes, and the use of farmland for bird watching, bike riding, hiking, horseback riding, hunting, snowmobiling, and other recreational activities. Some farms may charge for these activities or use them as a way to promote retail sales. Agritourism also includes educational programs for the public, schoolchildren, seniors, and all types of visitors, often involving exhibits, demonstrations, and workshops around specific topics and skills. At on-farm classes, visitors are taught how to milk cows, make cheese, prune raspberry bushes, and bake apple pies, for example.

On-farm retail sales offer a unique "shopping experience" that helps farms compete with traditional retail stores. The experience of visiting a farm, seeing its environs, and talking with the farmers and their employees as one shops can be of value by itself; in many cases that value to the consumer is enhanced by educational activities on the farm. These can include observing or petting animals, picking one's own produce, and touring the farm or its facilities (fig. 11.1).

Farmstands, community-supported agriculture, value-added processing, and other commercial food enterprises on the farm often overlap with, and are complemented by, agritourism. The scope of agritourism on any given farm usually goes beyond food; it may also be about cultural heritage, family entertainment, and the enjoyment of natural resources. In other words, it's a multifaceted experience that is connected to, and takes place on, a farm. During that experience, farm visitors may learn basic information about food production. They also take in the sights, sounds, smells, and tastes of a farm, and along the way they may develop an appreciation for the hard work involved in producing food.

Agritourism may or may not be closely connected to the marketing of agricultural products. Farms that produce wholesale commodity products, like fluid milk, may offer tours, accommodations, or recreation, but they usually don't, or can't, sell their primary product directly to their visitors. When schoolchildren take a field trip to a farm to learn how fruits and vegetables are grown or how cows are milked, the focus is education, not marketing. Offering a tangible product, perhaps an apple, a carrot, or some cheese, may be part of the experience. The goal of this kind of visit is to help children understand where food comes from.

For other farms, the visitor experience is the marketing strategy for their products. Pick-your-own apple orchards do more than sell fruit; they sell an experience that goes with it. The experience may include a beautiful setting for a family excursion, an apple cider–making demonstration, samples of hot cider, or the chance to see the farm's horses or tractors at work.

Contrast this to the consumer experience of buying apples in the supermarket, where it's all about the product and its attributes, from appearance to price. When a consumer purchases fruit at the supermarket to bring home and eat, the value lies solely in the product, not in the experience of shopping. Buying at a farmers' market is an intermediate experience between a supermarket visit with no connection to the farm and purchasing directly from a farm. For most consumers, there is value in the farmers' market shopping experience akin to that of on-farm agritourism; the farmers' market is a place to chat with farmers and neighbors, perhaps sample different kinds of apples or tomatoes, and enjoy the outdoors. Farmers' markets have some of the characteristics of agritourism, where consumers get value from an experience associated with food or a farm — not just the product. The same is true for CSAs, particularly when consumers go to a farm to pick up vegetables and other products on a regular basis. Many CSA members appreciate the experience, which includes interacting with "their" farmer and building a sense of community and social connections derived from belonging to a group with a common purpose.

In some cases, agritourism may not involve a farm product, but there may still be indirect market benefits to the farmer. For example, after touring a

FIGURE 11.2 Spectrum of farm products and experiences. Farms offer a variety of products, experiences, and combinations of the two. Most farms sell their products wholesale to distributors or retailers; however, an increasing number of farms provide a product combined with an experience and education by selling direct to consumers. Some farms focus on providing experiences that enhance product sales and promote education about agriculture.

vineyard, some visitors will purchase a bottle of wine, but others may not—although their experience may lead them to buy wine from that vineyard at a later date. Visitors to a dairy farm, who can't purchase the milk directly, might be more inclined to buy locally produced cheese that was made with that farm's milk.

Direct sales and agritourism include a range of experiences; some are directly connected to the marketing of a farm's product and some are not. In essence, they provide authentic experiences related to agriculture that enhance the marketing of farm products, educate the public about farming, and improve public support for agriculture (fig. 11.2).

Evolution of Agritourism

Although the term "agritourism" is relatively new, the concept of traveling to celebrate and learn about agriculture has existed for centuries. Native

FIGURE 11.3 Maple syrup sign on a dairy farm. In the Northeast, maple syrup production allows some dairy farms to sell products directly to consumers, which can enhance other on-farm enterprises such as retail stores, recreation, or accommodations. Their primary product, fluid milk, is sold in bulk to processors, not directly to consumers.

American tribes traveled long distances to participate in planting and harvesting feasts and ceremonies. Maple syrup production in the late winter was a time of reunion and renewal for tribes such as the Ojibwe and Abenaki. Family groups, reunited with their bands toward the end of winter, would gather for the ritualized work of collecting sap and boiling it into maple syrup. European settlers in rural America learned about maple syrup from Native Americans and created their own cultural traditions and sugaring celebrations. Today, sugarmakers attract visitors with on-farm breakfasts and accommodations, sugarhouse tours, and direct sales of maple syrup, maple candy, and other maple products (fig. 11.3). This combination of activities is a major source of farm income in areas where sugar maples are abundant.

Throughout the nineteenth century, many large farmhouses also served as country inns. Immigrants traveling westward would spend their nights at these farms along their route, paying or working for room and board. In the late 1800s, as the United States became increasingly urbanized, families living in cities would visit farms or ranches for a few weeks or months in the summer to escape the heat and hectic pace of city life, and learn about farming and rural life during their stay. Some urban families would visit the same farm or ranch year after year, developing close relationships as their children grew up together.

A typical farm stay in the Northeast in the late 1800s is described by the Adams Farm in Wilmington, Vermont: "Walter and Ada Adams opened the Adams Farm homestead to the public during the late 1890s, for summer guests to get away and beat the heat of the city. Families would bring their children and spend a week or two enjoying Vermont's beauty, swimming in the Deerfield River and Lake Raponda, gathering eggs, playing with lambs, and eating fresh delicious home baked foods from the farm kitchen."[5]

The Adams family continued to offer summer farm stays into the next century, and they also opened up their farmhouse to winter visitors who traveled to Vermont. Many came for the sport of skiing starting in the 1950s. The Adams family took a brief break from agritourism in 1969, when they expanded their dairy herd and shifted their primary focus to dairying. A decade later, milk prices fell and the family invited guests back to the farm, this time for winter sleigh rides. Nearby ski areas provided the Adams Farm with a steady stream of visitors, who bought maple syrup produced on the farm. Run by the fifth generation of the Adams family today, the farm continues to offer horse-drawn sleigh rides and direct sales of maple syrup. For more than a century, agritourism in a variety of forms has provided supplemental income for the Adams family, helping them keep their land in farming even when commodity prices dropped and other farming ventures became unprofitable.

While farm stays were becoming popular in the Northeast in the late 1800s, dude ranches in the West were beginning to attract wealthy easterners and Europeans to hunting trips and sightseeing excursions. To supplement their income, western ranchers began taking in paying guests, or "dudes," who would share their homes and learn about the ranching lifestyle, horseback riding, herding cattle, hunting, and fishing. Famous dudes such as Theodore Roosevelt helped popularize dude ranches in the early 1900s, and railroads made travel to dude ranches feasible. Tourists arrived on trains with their steamer trunks and often stayed for the entire summer, as dude ranches became the main tourist attraction in the Rocky Mountain area during the 1920s and 1930s.

Today, farm and ranch stays continue to be a major component of agritourism in rural America, and they dominate the agritourism market in many European countries where agricultural and culinary tourism complement each other. Culinary tourism, travelers' pursuit of unique and memorable dining experiences, emphasizes fresh foods creatively prepared and is a hot trend in tourism throughout the world.[6] Growth in culinary travel brings external resources into local food systems, as farmers earn revenues by selling experiences and products to people from other areas. For example, California's success in attracting tourists to wine tastings at vineyards by marketing the Napa Valley Wine Train has been extended to other specialty food products, including those featured in the Wisconsin Cheese Tour and the Oregon Beer Trail.

Food festivals are another part of culinary agritourism, where crops and foods with special significance to an area are celebrated and promoted. Some of these festivals have been around for a long time, while many are relative newcomers. The Apple Blossom Festival was started by the first apple shipper in Wenatchee, Washington, in 1919. The Florida Strawberry Festival was established in 1930 in Plant City, Florida, where 10,000 acres of the fruit are grown nearby. In 1967 the Morton Pumpkin Festival began in the Illinois town where most of the world's canning pumpkins are processed. In California, the Gilroy Garlic Festival started in 1979 and the Stockton Asparagus Festival in 1986. The Chatsworth, New Jersey, Cranberry Festival began in 1983 to celebrate one of the state's most valuable fruit crops. West Stockbridge, Massachusetts, kicked off its Zucchini Festival in 2003. While some of these festivals attract tens of thousands of people, there are hundreds if not thousands of small-town events celebrating crops and foods in their own unique ways.

Some food celebrations are less festival and more feast. They may be more exclusive, perhaps requiring reservations and fetching a high price. For example, "feasts in the field" are dinners that take place in farmers' fields or barns. Some are gourmet affairs, where accomplished chefs create multiple-course meals made with locally sourced products and served with local wines. Others may be family-style meals made with the farm's products, perhaps ground beef and sweet corn. From festivals to feasts and everything in between, recent studies of consumers and tourists indicate that demand is increasing for agricultural products and experiences, especially those focused on local foods and authentic experiences.[7]

Agritourism Impacts and Trends

According to the U.S. Census of Agriculture, 23,350 farms provide agritourism and recreation services valued at $566 million.[8] This vastly underestimates the actual value because the census survey asks about "agritourism and recreation services, such as farm or winery tours, hayrides, hunting, fishing, etc." Direct market sales are inquired about separately, and other agritourism activities such as farm stays, educational events, and weddings are not covered by the survey. Research using a broader definition of agritourism estimates that $800 million to $3 billion a year is generated for U.S. farm income from agritourism activities.[9]

Agritourism takes places throughout the United States (map 11.1). In western states and the Southeast, recreation on farms and ranches, such as hunting and fishing, is popular. In the Northeast and on the West Coast, farm tours and hayrides are included in census calculations, although direct sales through farmstands, U-pick, and CSAs are not. Such retail activities can be an important part of agritourism along with farm stays and school field trips.

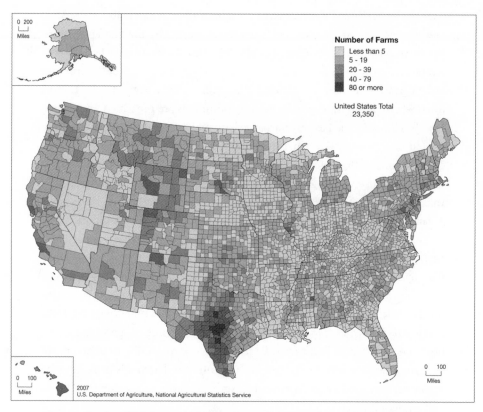

MAP 11.1 Number of U.S. farms with income from agritourism and recreational services. As evidenced by this map, agritourism is important throughout the country, with concentrations of farms in the Northeast and West. Texas farms are especially popular for recreational services such as hunting.

According to the National Agricultural Statistics Service, agritourism includes "agritourism and recreation services, such as farm or winery tours, hayrides, hunting, fishing, etc."[10]

Nationwide, more than 62 million adults visit farms each year, and agritourism is on an upward trajectory, having increased substantially during the past few decades.[11] Primary reasons for visiting farms include learning where food comes from, participating in farm activities, purchasing agricultural products, and enjoying rural scenery. Entrepreneurial farms throughout the United States are diversifying and expanding to keep pace with the growing demand for on-farm experiences and products.

Long-term agritourism trends are difficult to track due to a lack of longitudinal data; however, studies conducted in Hawaii and Vermont indicate significant growth in agritourism over a short period of time. The value of Hawaii's agritourism activities increased 30 percent over a three-year period. Revenues generated from agritourism were led by on-farm sales accounting for 40 percent of total revenues, followed by retail sales of products from other farms and souvenir items, outdoor recreation, and accommodations.[12]

Research conducted by the National Agricultural Statistics Service indicated that the value of agritourism increased substantially in Vermont, with an 86 percent jump in only two years. As in other states around the country, small farms were more likely to be involved in agritourism than large farms. Agritourism income was most commonly derived from products produced and sold on the farm site, including maple syrup and maple products, fruits, vegetables, Christmas trees, cut flowers, nursery products, and cheese.[13] Over a five-year period, the number of farms involved in direct sales increased 27 percent and the number of farms involved in agritourism increased 91 percent.[14]

As in Hawaii and Vermont, agritourism revenues in New York and Maine are led by direct sales of products produced and sold on farms. According to a survey in Maine, roadside stands were the most popular agritourism enterprise, with an economic impact of $40.8 million, including indirect and direct contributions. Farmers reported that major obstacles to the start-up or expansion of agritourism activities included dealing with insurance issues, formulating business plans, recruiting and training qualified personnel, paying taxes, providing customer service, and coming up with promotional ideas and advertising techniques. Forty-six percent of respondents to the survey indicated that they intend to embark on enterprise start-up or expansion in the next twelve months.[15]

According to New York State statistics, agritourism components of farm businesses brought in $211 million in statewide income, and almost two-thirds of the New York State agritourism businesses surveyed indicated that they planned on expanding or diversifying their business or product lines during the next five years.[16] In New Jersey, 21 percent of all farms were found to be engaged in some form of agritourism, and 43 percent of New Jersey's total farmland base is associated with farm operations engaged in agritourism. Agritourism generated $57 million in farm-gate revenues and had a statewide economic impact estimated to be $90 million. In addition, agritourism activity raised an estimated $8 million in local and state taxes.

A recent study in Tennessee found that the most common types of agritourism businesses were on-farm retail markets, school field trips/tours, event hosting, pick-your-own operations, hayride or wagon rides, farm tours other than school field trips, on-farm gift shops, weddings, other family fun activities, and pumpkin patches.[17] The 110 agritourism operators who reported visitor numbers estimated that they hosted more than 1.75 million people on their farms in one year. Visitor expenditures at these agritourism attractions were estimated to be more than $34 million, and the statewide economic impact, with multiplier effects, more than $54 million.

Western and southeastern parts of rural America rely on hunting, fishing, and wildlife watching activities for much of their agritourism income. A study in Colorado reported that agritourism contributes more than $10 million to the economy annually, accounting for 13 percent of total farm income. Hunting and fishing on private agricultural lands generated much of the income. However, farms and ranches are increasingly diversifying and including educational experiences such as farm tours, entertainment such as corn mazes, and direct sales of farm and ranch products.[18] In Mississippi, the direct economic impact of the agritourism industry on farms is $3.5 million annually; when one factors in recreational activities such as hunting, angling, wildlife watching, and horse trail riding on Mississippi farms, the annual economic impact is nearly $2.7 billion.[19]

A California study found that 2.4 million visitors participated in agritourism at farms and ranches.[20] They experienced a wide range of activities, such as staying at guest ranches, picking peaches, playing in corn mazes, attending weddings in fields and vineyards, and shopping at on-farm produce stands. The USDA estimated that 685 California farms earned a total of $35 million in revenue related to agritourism, but the study found that three-quarters of those who entered the agritourism sector for financial or employment reasons also did so because they "wanted to educate visitors," "enjoyed working with people," or wanted to provide "outreach to the community."

Not included in these numbers is California's most well-known form of agritourism: visiting vineyards in Napa Valley. The total annual economic impact of the Napa Valley wine industry is $11 billion, which includes direct and secondary impacts that account for re-spending of the money brought into the economy by wine tourism. It has been estimated that the wine and vineyard industry in Napa Valley attracts 3.5 million visitors annually, who spend $714 million on wine-related tourism.[21] This information has been used to encourage public and private investment in California's wine tourism industry.

Food travel is growing in importance, and new studies are validating investment in farms and food. A recent study of traveler behavior indicates that more than half of U.S. tourists travel to learn about or enjoy unique forms of eating and drinking.[22] In particular, travelers are interested in local and authentic foods and experiences. Festivals motivate travel, as do educational opportunities. The World Food Travel Association projects tremendous growth for the culinary traveler market, as nearly two-thirds of U.S. leisure travelers say they are interested in culinary travel during the next year. All of this bodes well for the future of agritourism, as long as the supply side can keep up with the demand side. The projected growth in culinary travel and agritourism brings opportunities for economic development, along with challenges for farmers, ranchers, and communities seeking to maintain their agrarian authenticity.

The Evolution of Agritourism at Liberty Hill Farm in Rochester, Vermont

Beth Kennett of Liberty Hill Farm talks about "plastic pumpkin farms" when she expresses her concern about the authenticity of on-farm experiences for visitors. She advocates applying quality standards to farms engaged in agritourism. A ninth-generation farmer, Beth believes that agritourism is an important tool for educating a public that is increasingly removed from farming and food production.

Beth and her husband, Bob, were running a dairy operation when milk prices plummeted in the late 1970s and early 1980s. They knew they needed to do something differently to keep the farm operating. At the same time, business was booming at a nearby ski area. Their farm is located just off Route 100, which was becoming known as the Skiers Highway. A parade of cars would drive up from the cities in New York, New Jersey, Connecticut, and Massachusetts every weekend.

Interest in skiing was growing faster than accommodations for skiers. Some skiers ended up sleeping in their cars, and local radio stations were begging Vermonters to open their homes and take in skiers. Two of Beth's neighbors were doing just that, and benefiting from the ski traffic, but they couldn't always keep up with demand. Beth, Bob, and their two young sons lived in a large farmhouse with several extra bedrooms, and they were toying with the idea of renting rooms to skiers. They took the leap in the winter of 1984, when a neighbor already renting out rooms to skiers called to ask if the Kennetts could help out a family from New Jersey. That first experience went so well that Beth and Bob decided to open their home to guests—and the family from New Jersey has come back every year since.

This was a time when the bed-and-breakfast craze was taking off in Vermont, partially inspired by the TV sitcom *Newhart*. In that popular show, Bob Newhart played an innkeeper who runs a Vermont bed-and-breakfast with ruffled pillowcases, Victorian lace curtains, and antique furniture; children are not allowed. That may have been the norm at the time, but it wasn't what Beth was looking to create. She decided to learn more about her options and went to a workshop on how to start a bed-and-breakfast. A successful innkeeper at the workshop gave critical advice. He emphasized that everyone has pillows and beds, but each innkeeper needs to find a unique way to market his or her inn. In a room of two hundred aspiring innkeepers, he pointed to Beth and said, "You've got the cows. That's your niche." Beth was stunned. Growing up on a farm, she hadn't considered that visitors would be interested in the cows and learning about life on a farm. She came away from the meeting thinking that cows, kids, and her home cooking could be Liberty Hill Farm's niche.

The next step was to borrow money from the bank for paint and wallpaper to fix up the 1820 Greek revival farmhouse. Beth still bristles when she remembers her meeting with the local banker. His response to her request for a loan was "Why would anyone want to stay on a farm — and does your husband know what you're up to?" The bank wouldn't help. To pay for the renovations, Beth and Bob had to fall behind on their payments to the grain company.

There were no dinner restaurants in town at the time, so breakfast and dinner were part of the package for an overnight stay. Beth learned she had to get a restaurant license to offer meals to paying customers. Dinners at the Kennetts' have always been family-style, with guests and family members sitting around the large dining room table eating hearty meals made from scratch. Beth grew up helping her grandmother can and freeze everything from the garden and had always used local food in cooking without thinking much about it. Eating local and using the freshest ingredients were just what they did. When *Gourmet* magazine did a story on Beth's cooking, she realized that meals made with fresh, local food had become a large part of the attraction of her farm stay. It wasn't anything new for her, but it was exceptional for her guests.

The interest in local foods and farms has grown exponentially during the past decade or so. Beth explains, "Agritourism used to be something for kindergarteners. Families with young children were my niche. It's no longer just about school tours. Now, with the local food movement, college kids think farmers are cool. It's the college kids who are so excited about coming to the farm, and the twenty-somethings and thirty-somethings want to learn about growing and storing food. We went from the Newhart B&B syndrome to being part of the innovative local food movement. Everyone is becoming more aware of where their food comes from."

For thirty years, guests from all fifty states and from around the world have visited Liberty Hill Farm to experience life on a dairy farm and to savor Beth's home-cooked meals. As a testament to the success of Beth's crazy idea to invite guests to her farm, Liberty Hill Farm has been written up not only in *Gourmet*, but also in *Travel & Leisure*, *Yankee*, *Family Fun*, and *Vermont Life* magazines as well as the *New York Times* and the *Boston Globe*. It has also been featured on *Good Morning America*.

Beth played a leading role in helping agritourism spread throughout the region. A few years after her successful farm stay business was up and running, a University of Vermont Extension specialist in community and economic development knocked on Beth's door. He said that she was on the leading edge of a national movement called agritourism and that he wanted to work with her to help other farms get in on it. Over the next several years, the two traveled around Vermont explaining agritourism to farmers and ultimately helping create a nonprofit organization dedicated to supporting agritourism called Vermont Farms! Association. The organization was established to provide opportunities for educating the public about agriculture. One of the major goals is to sustain and further develop the working landscape that characterizes Vermont. Today, the association offers technical assistance and inspiration for farmers looking to diversify, not just in Vermont but in other states as well.[23]

Benefits and Challenges of Agritourism and On-Farm Experiences

The blending of agriculture, marketing, and tourism poses both challenges and opportunities (table 11.1). Farmers taking on more interactions with the public have to deal with interruptions in daily operations and public scrutiny of farming practices. On-farm marketing and agritourism require different skills than other aspects of farming. These are areas in which many farmers do not have training. They also require different or expanded uses of land on farms, such as parking areas, housing, and trails. They may require additional signage and restrooms. An agritourism enterprise that is not a farm's main marketing method may be viewed as an additional business, on top of the farming business. It can require additional investment, human capital, and cash flow to generate additional returns.

The rapid growth of agritourism has some farmers concerned, especially when the diversification and expansion move beyond "authentic" agriculture, which has different meanings to different people. There are two concerns about agritourism's public image; both are related to the idea of an

TABLE 11.1 *Benefits and Costs of an Agritourism Business*

Benefits	Costs
Provides potential additional income.	Provides a low financial return, at least at first.
Creates a physical operation that appreciates in value.	Interferes with farming or ranching operations.
Efficiently uses underutilized facilities, equipment, land, and talents.	Requires hard work! Adds workload to family members.
Allows you to be your own boss.	Demands your full and constant attention, interfering with family time and activities.
Allows you to work your own hours.	
Allows you to express yourself creatively.	
Allows you to live your own creation.	Steals your privacy — people are always around.
Is personally rewarding.	
Generates new opportunities for spouse and children.	Requires you always to be "on" — upbeat, available, and attentive.
Maintains family attention on and interest in the farm or ranch.	
Provides the opportunity to meet people — visitors as well as agritourism and nature tourism professionals.	Involves risk and liability.
	Can create staffing problems.
	Generates excessive paperwork.
Provides the chance to play a significant role in community activities.	
Provides the chance to educate people about rural living, nature, and the agriculture industry, which in turn can lead to improved local policies.	
Provides the chance to learn about outside perspectives, which in turn can lead to better-educated rural residents and improved local policies.	
Promotes the agriculture industry.	
Models sustainable local industries.	

Adapted from E. Rilla and H. George, *Agritourism and Nature Tourism in California*, 2d ed.,"
University of California Division of Agriculture & Natural Resources, Publication 3484 (2011).
Copyright 2011 by Regents of the University of California. Used by permission.

"authentic" farm. The first concern is that "agri-tainment" on a working farm will take away from the core business of food and fiber production on the farm. But this doesn't have to be the case. Agritourism in Europe is typically far-removed from the corn mazes, hayrides, and other forms of entertainment often found on U.S. farms that host visitors. Rather, European farm visitors stay overnight and immerse themselves in a true farm experience; they don't visit just to play for a few hours. There is no rush to install catapults for smashing pumpkins, or apple cider doughnut machines, on European farms. Like American fast food, agri-tainment can provide a fast farm experience. It may seem satisfying in the short term and it can fit our fast-paced schedules, but like fast food it doesn't nourish us over the long term. A fast farm agri-tainment visit often lacks substance and authenticity; it's a distraction, not a true educational experience.

The second concern about agritourism is that a tourist attraction may pose as a farm in order to draw visitors. For example, a bed-and-breakfast owner with a few acres of land may plant a vegetable garden and put up some pickles and jams. Does that make it an authentic farm experience? A roadside stand may have an apple press and offer fresh-squeezed cider. Does that help people understand what fruit growing is all about? Or is the public's knowledge of and respect for food production actually diminished by hobby farms posing as real farms for the purpose of engaging in agritourism? Such concerns lead some farmers to avoid the term "agritourism" even while welcoming visitors to their farms for educational and enriching agrarian experiences.

Despite the challenges, the benefits of agritourism for farmers and their communities are numerous, from increased economic activity to the preservation of rural lifestyles and landscapes. Interactions with consumers build new connections that give farmers and their work visibility and public support that they might not have otherwise. Agritourism can provide opportunities for income generation beyond the growing season, creating potential to hire year-round rather than seasonal employees. By adding agritourism to their farm enterprise, farmers may be able to include additional family members in the business, enhancing the likelihood that farms will be passed on to the next generation.

The La Mota Ranch just outside of Hebbronville, Texas, is a prime example of an enterprise that has reaped the benefits of agritourism for multiple generations. The cattle ranch was founded in the 1890s and is still owned and managed by descendants of the original owners. La Mota's primary business is its purebred and commercial cattle herds. Being amateur historians, La Mota's owners, the Hellen family, saw the value of promoting the unique mixture of

Mexican and Texan ranching history along the south Texas border. They were further encouraged by the state legislature's recognition of the area's historical significance, so they capitalized on their natural amenities, historic buildings, and local color to create ranch tours. The added income from running tours has allowed the Hellen family to keep the ranch working, and the involvement of the entire family in the tourist enterprise has made the business strong. The La Mota Ranch is an agritourism leader in their region and has helped other businesses with similar goals through a regional agritourism collaboration known as the Llanos Mesteños South Texas Heritage Trail.[24]

On the other side of the country, Karen Fortin of Carman Brook Maple & Dairy Farm in the remote northwest corner of Vermont credits direct sales of maple syrup on the farm for broadening her children's cultural awareness and sensitivity. While Karen educates visitors from around the world about traditional Native American methods of making maple syrup, she and her family learn about the traditions and lifestyles of visitors who come from Canada, Europe, and Asia. According to Karen, "Inviting visitors to our farm has opened up new worlds to us. Living in this rural part of Vermont, my kids would have only known our neighbors, who are a lot like us. Now we have friends from around the world."

Strengthening Farmer–Consumer Connections

Engaging with the public on farms is not for all farms, or even most farms. Throughout the country, regions with the strongest record of direct sales and agritourism account for only about 20 percent of farms selling direct to the public; and those tend to be small farms for the most part. In one-third of the states, fewer than 5 percent of farms engage with the public.[25] The challenges are many for those farmers who do decide to open their farms to visitors. They need to develop new skills for marketing and hospitality, expand infrastructure on the farm to accommodate visitors, and deal with zoning and liability issues, all in addition to the primary function of producing food, fiber, or fuel.

For those farms that do engage with the public, the rewards can be great — for the farmers, for consumers, and for the broader community. Direct sales and agritourism enterprises allow farmers to diversify their core operations and add jobs, often keeping family members employed on the farm. By adding new revenues, these additional enterprises help keep farmland in production, preserving scenic vistas and maintaining rural traditions. At the same time, the public is educated about the importance of agriculture for our economy, quality of life, and culture. This creates greater public support for agriculture, which is critical now that 98 percent of the U.S. population does not have a connection to farming.

With direct sales and agritourism on the rise, every year more farms, along with their barns, pastures, fields, and forests, open their doors to visitors. Consumers have an increasing array of options for on-farm experiences. Going to a farmers' market is a good way get to know your farmers and learn about their production practices. Visiting their farms is an even better way. Farms offer myriad opportunities to learn about agriculture and enjoy fresh, local fare right where it's produced. From farm stays to pick-your-own to feasts in the field to CSAs, the farmer–consumer connection is a key contributor to sustainable food systems that produce healthy, affordable, and safe food.

12 ◌ *Food Safety from Farm to Fork*

Remember when kids would lick the batter off a spatula when their mom was making a cake? Not anymore. Many parents today recognize that the raw eggs in the batter can potentially contain *Salmonella*, which could make their kids sick. Concern about food safety has increased in recent years, especially in response to news of significant contamination in the food system. Half a billion eggs were recalled in 2010 after nearly 2,000 people became ill throughout the United States. In 2011, cantaloupes grown in Colorado sickened at least 147 people in twenty-eight states. Thirty-three people died.

Public concern about food safety is not unjustified. The U.S. Centers for Disease Control and Prevention (CDC) estimate that one in six Americans gets sick every year from foodborne diseases; 128,000 are hospitalized; and 3,000 die.[1] Table 12.1 lists eight known pathogens that account for the vast majority of food safety problems in this country. These pathogens contribute to domestically acquired foodborne illness, hospitalization, and death. The victims of foodborne illness are disproportionately young because children, especially those under the age of five, have not fully developed their immune systems.

The CDC estimates are a broad-brush summary of food safety risks. It is very difficult to provide separate data on how many people become ill as a result of improper food-handling practices in their own homes, at restaurants, on farms, or by food processors. And the estimates are just that, not hard and fast numbers. That's partly because measuring foodborne illness is tricky: many people don't realize when they have it, and even if they do, they may fail to report it, since for the majority of people it amounts to a stomachache or flulike symptoms for a few days.

Although the true extent of foodborne illness may be fuzzy, one trend is clear: when an outbreak occurs today, it has the potential to affect many more people and cover a wider geographic region than in the past.[2] This is because much of our food comes from sources that are unknown to the consumer and is prepared in facilities that mix raw ingredients from many locations. Then,

TABLE 12.1 *Pathogens Most Associated with Food Safety Problems*

Pathogen	Cause of Illness (%)	Cause of Hospitalization (%)	Cause of Death (%)
Norovirus	58	26	11
Salmonella, non-typhoidal	11	35	28
Clostridium perfringens	10	—	—
Campylobacter spp.	9	15	6
Staphylococcus aureus	3	—	
Toxoplasma gondii	—	8	24
E. coli (STEC) O157	—	4	—
Listeria monocytogenes	—	—	19

Adapted from Centers for Disease Control and Prevention (CDC), "CDC Estimates of Foodborne Illness in the United States," February 2011. www.cdc.gov/foodborneburden/2011-foodborne-estimates.html.

the final products are placed in a variety of packages, sold under different brands, and shipped all over the continent. If someone gets sick from eating the product, there may be a recall, legal fees, and corporate fines, but no single person is usually held responsible and often no single source of contamination can be identified.

The USDA and the FDA are responsible for developing a variety of food safety regulations and guidelines — and our food is safer for it. But the continued occurrence of foodborne illnesses, whether the source of contamination is in the home or in the factory, attests to the challenge of developing appropriate food safety plans and implementing best practices for a wide range of activities conducted by farmers, food processors, food handlers, and food retailers. The challenge is made greater by the range in scale of food-related enterprises, given that we have local, regional, national, and international food systems.

The Evolution of Food Safety Regulations

For thousands of years, people had three tools for ensuring the safety of their food: cultural norms, common sense, and direct relationships with food producers. Without the knowledge of science, let alone microbiology, they relied on culturally embedded safe food-handling practices that had developed over time, presumably through trial and error. They coupled these practices with commonsense behaviors for avoiding filth when producing and handling food and with personal trust when obtaining food from neighbors or local farmers.

But frankly, until recent times, people relied a lot on luck to keep their food safe. To the extent that they had bad luck, natural selection was aided in endowing modern-day humans with the ability, albeit limited, to withstand a variety of undesirable elements in their diet.

More than 150 years ago, a new approach to food safety began to unfold in the United States. In 1862 Abraham Lincoln established the USDA, which included a division of chemistry that eventually became the FDA. Since Lincoln's time, the federal government has become increasingly involved in the regulation of food in order to promote its safety, starting in the late 1800s with laws that prohibited the sale of tainted meats.

The modern era of food safety regulation arguably started in 1906 with passage of the Pure Food and Drug Act and the Federal Meat Inspection Act. The former prohibited the manufacture or sale of adulterated or misbranded foods, drugs, medicines, and liquors, while the latter prohibited the sale of adulterated or misbranded meat and required slaughtering and processing to maintain sanitary conditions. In 1938 Congress passed the federal Food, Drug, and Cosmetic Act, which allowed the FDA to issue specific food safety standards. Over the years, a variety of regulations were promulgated, such as those that prevented the addition of harmful ingredients to foods and those that provided for the oversight of poultry and egg processing similar to what was required for meat.

The 1990s ushered in key changes to food safety regulations. In 1993 an outbreak of *E. coli* 0157:H7 occurred in ground beef, causing hundreds of people to fall ill and four to die. In response, a new approach to food safety regulation, Hazard Analysis and Critical Control Points (HACCP), was implemented. This focused on the prevention and reduction of microbial pathogens on products, rather than testing after the fact (box 12.1). The government set safety standards, and food producers were responsible for developing plans to meet them. By 2000 HACCP was implemented in all federal- and state-inspected meat and poultry slaughter and processing facilities. Dairy producers and processors have come under similarly intense regulation by federal and state authorities in recent decades.

Also in the 1990s, significant media attention was devoted to several food safety incidents associated with fresh produce. Prior to that time, producers of fresh fruits and vegetables had been pretty much left to follow commonsense approaches to minimizing food safety risks, since the risk to public health from contaminated produce was perceived to be relatively small. There was some risk, however, as CDC records show. There had been dozens of incidents over several decades in which contaminated produce made hundreds of

12.1 The Seven Principles of Hazard Analysis and Critical Control Points

1 Conduct a food safety hazard analysis and identify preventive measures to control these hazards.
2 Identify critical control points or places in a food process at which control can be applied to prevent, eliminate, or reduce food safety hazards.
3 Establish critical limits for each critical control point.
4 Establish critical control point monitoring requirements.
5 Establish corrective actions for cases when monitoring indicates a deviation from an established critical limit.
6 Establish recordkeeping procedures.
7 Establish procedures for verifying that the HACCP system is working as intended.

U.S. Department of Agriculture, *Key Facts: The Seven HACCP Principles* (Washington, DC: U.S. Department of Agriculture, Food Safety and Inspection Service, 1998).

people ill, but in fact very few people died. Most of these incidents were limited to a relatively small geographic area. Complex food systems have become more "industrial" in that they increasingly rely on the large-scale aggregation and distribution of fresh produce, so the impact of a single contamination incident has become more likely to affect people in a wide geographic area — typically dozens of states. This increase in geographic scope has led to more media attention, and that in turn has increased the perception of risk associated with fresh produce, even though the vast majority of the produce we consume is safe.

From fresh produce to ground beef, when raw products from many different farms are aggregated, processed, and/or packaged, then widely distributed under different brands to a variety of retailers, the risk posed by contamination on a single farm is considerably amplified. The number of consumers potentially exposed to the contamination, and thus the potential harm, is much greater than when smaller batches of food are produced and less widely distributed.

The more complicated the flow of food, the more places where problems can occur. The possibility of contamination exists at every step, from seed planting, to crop harvesting, to washing and packaging, to shipping, to wholesale distribution to retail sales, to food preparation, and finally to consumption. The average piece of produce travels 1,500 miles before it is consumed,[3] giving microorganisms time to grow and multiply with each passing day, especially if highly perishable food is held at a temperature above 40°F for more than two hours at a time during shipping or storage. With warm temperatures, microorganisms such as bacteria, viruses, and parasites can flourish.

A contamination event in an industrial food system elevates risk not only for a large number of consumers but also for many producers that are not directly involved with the event. During and after a food safety outbreak, and the media coverage associated with it, farmers and processors who grow and handle the crop under scrutiny typically lose tens of millions of dollars as sales plummet until the public no longer perceives that crop to be dangerous to eat.

In 1998, in response to elevated concerns about the safety of fresh produce, the government developed Good Agricultural Practices (GAPs), a voluntary set of guidelines for growers to follow to reduce the risk of contamination from a variety of sources (box 12.2). GAPs address a wide range of management activities, including training employees how to wash their hands, tracking the temperature of refrigerators, checking fields daily for the presence of wildlife, and instituting trace-back procedures so specific products can be quickly identified and recalled if necessary. GAPs also limit how and when manure can be applied to fields, much like organic farming rules do. GAPs did not get a lot of attention until large commercial buyers, such as supermarket chains, began to require their vendors to pass a GAPs audit.

In 2011 the Food Safety Modernization Act (FSMA) was signed into law. It has been called the most sweeping reform of food safety laws in more than seventy years. It is the first food safety law to directly regulate fresh-produce farms. Like the voluntary GAPs, FSMA focuses on preventing contamination. FSMA also put the FDA in charge of regulating food safety on produce farms, rather than the USDA, which has typically regulated farm practices.

To comply with FSMA (which has yet to be fully implemented at this writing) or to pass a GAPs audit can be time-consuming and expensive. Either involves extensive recordkeeping and may necessitate significant investment in new infrastructure on the farm. Such rigorous food safety efforts make sense for large farms that sell a lot of produce to places far away on a commodity basis. But for small farms that market modest quantities of food much closer to home, a less stringent system could be used to address food safety concerns. Small and midsize produce farmers are worried about the impact of the growing pressure to implement food safety rules on all farms. It's not just regulations that cause concerns; it's public perception as well. As more supermarket chains require all farms they buy from, large or small, to pass a

12.2 *Key Elements of a Good Agricultural Practices Farm Audit*

- General questions (food safety plan, traceability, recall program, worker health and hygiene, pesticide/chemical use)
- Farm review (water use, soil amendments, animals/wildlife/livestock, land use and land use history)
- Field harvest and field packing activities (pre-harvest assessment, field sanitation units, harvesting containers and equipment, water use, transportation of produce, emergency cleanup procedures)
- House packing facility (water use in packing facility, treatment of processing water, sanitation program/general housekeeping, worker health and hygiene, containers, pest control)
- Storage and transportation (mechanical equipment, ice and refrigeration, transportation and loading)
- Wholesale distribution center/terminal warehouse (receiving, sanitation program/ general housekeeping, water use in packing facility, treatment of processing water, storage facility/temperature control, containers, mechanical equipment)
- Preventive food defense procedures (food defense plan, personnel, facility procedures, key/entrance accountability, deliveries, separation of products, allergens)

U.S. Department of Agriculture, *Good Handling Practices Audit Verification Checklist* (Washington, DC: U.S. Department of Agriculture, Agricultural Marketing Service, 2012).

GAPs audit or similar certification, more markets will likely follow to cover themselves against risk, real or perceived, including liability concerns. These markets may start using food safety as a marketing tool, saying, "All of our produce comes from farms certified in food safety procedures." Where will that leave small farmers who can't afford the time or money to implement GAPs or who are not required to comply with FSMA? What will they tell consumers who ask about food safety?

To meet the needs of small-scale producers and the smaller markets they typically supply, Cooperative Extension, commercial grower associations, and state agencies of agriculture offer practical food safety training and in some cases a certification program that covers the core principles of GAPs but without all the detailed procedures that create a need for expensive recordkeeping. Taking reasonable steps to reduce risk—steps that fit the potential risk—is important for small and midsize farms that have been engaged in the boom in local food sales in recent years. It wouldn't take too many media stories covering food contamination by small-scale local producers to put a damper on the local food market.

There is much uncertainty about how food safety regulations will affect small farms and local food in the future. FSMA expands the FDA's authority to require food producers to evaluate hazards and prepare food safety plans. It also authorizes the agency to establish standards for the harvesting and handling of raw fruits and vegetables. The Act does exempt small farms (based on their annual gross revenue and geographic range of sales) and some processors from federal regulations, but not from state food safety regulations. Implementation of these regulations will have to strike a balance between reducing risk and avoiding an excessive economic burden on farmers. Asking small farm and food businesses to implement an industrial approach designed for large commodity farms and processing facilities could drive many of them out of business. It makes more sense to have scale-appropriate regulations to minimize the risk posed by products from small farms with local markets. That approach, combined with farmers putting their name on every product they sell, is a rational and cost-effective path to promoting food safety and local food systems. And it's one that small farms are increasingly, and voluntarily, adopting.

A Practical, Small-Scale Approach to Food Safety: Cedar Circle Farm, East Thetford, Vermont

Cedar Circle Farm produces 35 acres of diversified organic vegetables, fruits, and flowers. The owners took the initiative early and created their own food safety plan long before any buyers or food safety regulations required them to (see fig. 12.1). Megan Baxter, the production manager, explains:

> Food safety concerns were starting to ramp up about three or four years ago, after the big spinach and peanut butter scares. We were concerned that our practices were not as effective as they could be and that we would have to play catch-up if new legislation came along. We would rather be on top of it than scramble to get things done.
>
> There are multiple benefits from our approach to food safety, and one of them is quality. We want our produce to last longer. We don't want to throw things away after they have been harvested. If crops are harvested and processed and stored correctly, their shelf life is much longer. We bring a better and cleaner product to market which people are impressed by. Other farmers say, "Wow, your carrots are really clean. How did you get them like that?" We triple-wash just about everything that goes to market. That washes off potential pathogens, reducing food safety risks and it also increases product quality.[4]

FIGURE 12.1 Small-scale vegetable washing system. Cedar Circle Farm was an early adopter of practical measures to reduce the risk of foodborne illness from fresh produce. A series of stainless steel sinks were installed to facilitate multiple washes of vegetables prior to sale, a practice that helps remove harmful bacteria that may be present.

Cedar Circle Farm markets through a farmstand and a CSA program where members pick up produce at the farm or have it delivered to a nearby central location once a week. Pick-your-own strawberries and blueberries are available to the public. Cedar Circle also delivers vegetables to local schools and restaurants, but most of the produce is sold directly to consumers at the farm.

These direct markets mean that Cedar Circle has a steady stream of visitors coming and going. Add to that an on-farm café serving prepared foods cooked in the farm's commercial kitchen and several food festivals each year and you have just about every food safety concern a small farm can have. A few years ago, Megan created a food safety manual for farm employees. That took care of procedures aimed at the farmstand, farmers' markets, café, and wholesale operations. However, the U-pick operations, where consumers harvest berries directly, were another concern.

U-pick is a great way for the public to connect to the farm, and Cedar Circle emphasizes on-farm experiences as part of its educational mission, but U-pick presents a challenge to the farm's food safety plan. According to Megan:

> It's the one thing we can't control. It was the one hole in our system for keeping food clean before it went to a customer. That is the reason we implemented specific U-pick policies, to make sure we had a safety net to cover that gap in what we were doing.
>
> We realized the importance of washing your hands—for our employees and our U-pick customers. It's the stuff that your mother tells you. We ask visitors to wash their hands before picking berries, and we provide outdoor wash stations to make it easy. We also prohibit pets from the U-pick areas. People think of farms as being public spaces where they can walk their animals at leisure. But you don't bring dogs everywhere you go, and you can't bring them to our U-pick. This is the number one thing that people get upset about. Nobody complains about hand

washing. I think, maybe thirty or forty years ago they would have, but now we live in a germ-phobic culture and people are used to washing their hands.

Transparency and education are key elements of Cedar Circle's food safety plan. To prevent contamination of fresh produce, staff members are trained to follow specific procedures, and educating consumers about sanitation is a high priority, especially those consumers who visit the farm for U-pick. Problems could still happen if farmworkers or consumers didn't comply with best practices. Workers might fail to clean out harvest containers before reuse, spreading bacteria from one crop to another. Visitors might ignore the hand-washing signs and inadvertently contaminate berries after going to the bathroom or touching the chickens elsewhere on the farm. A clear and consistent set of procedures for both groups is key to keeping the risk of foodborne illness low.

With the help of Extension food safety specialists, private consultants, and other farmers, small farms around the United States are developing practical food safety plans and adopting best practices specific to their situations. In doing so, they are usually educating their customers at the same time. Whether they're handling U-pick berries, leafy greens, or ground beef, consumers have to be aware that they also play a key role in food safety by following basic sanitary practices. What Cedar Circle Farm is doing sets a good example of both on-farm risk reduction and consumer education, and this contributes to a culture where people take responsibility for food safety at all food system levels.

Some risk will always remain, however, and in fact most people are exposed to potentially harmful microorganisms on a regular basis. As we noted earlier, no one seemed concerned about *Salmonella* being in the raw eggs of mom's cake batter a few decades ago. What has changed over time? Are eggs more dangerous, or are consumers more concerned?

When Things Go Wrong with Food Safety

The risk of an egg being internally contaminated with *Salmonella* serotype Enteritidis (SE) is extremely low, at 1 egg in 20,000.[5] Even when exposed to a few cells of *Salmonella*, many people will not have any symptoms. Those who do may experience nausea, vomiting, stomachache, fever, and diarrhea for a few days. Most cases resolve on their own. *Salmonella* is normally not life-threatening, but it can cause more severe symptoms, as well as death, particularly among the elderly, infants, and people who are already sick. In general, the odds are good that the raw eggs in the cake batter won't make you sick, or at least not extremely sick, but there is still some risk that they will.

So what happened when half a billion eggs were recalled because a couple of thousand people were sickened by eggs over the course of seven months? It's a textbook case of what can go wrong when food safety best practices are not followed in large production facilities.

The egg industry has undergone major consolidation during the past thirty years, with fewer than two hundred large companies owning 95 percent of the laying hens in the United States, down from 2,500 companies in 1987.[6] This trend in ownership was accompanied by an increase in vertical integration, where one owner (e.g., processor/distributor) controls several links along the supply chain. In the case of eggs, one owner could produce the chicks that become laying hens, grow the crops and formulate the feed mix for the layers, as well as produce, package, and distribute the eggs themselves. Throughout the handful of major egg-producing states (Iowa, Ohio, Pennsylvania, Indiana, and California) the vertically integrated egg production model is common. So it takes mistakes by only one owner with facilities in several locations to create an enormous food safety problem. Prior to the major egg recall, it turns out that one egg company in particular was well known for repeatedly being fined by state and federal officials for violating workplace and environmental regulations in several states, stretching from Maine to Iowa. In Iowa, the attorney general labeled this company a "habitual offender" of water quality laws. The company appeared to prefer paying millions of dollar in fines to cleaning up its facilities. All this happened before a food contamination event made the egg recall necessary.

When reports of *Salmonella* cases first spiked, the CDC responded by using high-tech methods to identify the food responsible and the source of the food: eggs produced by the owner of two very large egg farms in Iowa. It took a couple of months for the company to recall 550 million eggs, and by then they had already been distributed widely under forty brand names across the United States, making it difficult for consumers to know whether their eggs were safe or not.

Around the time of the recall, the egg-producing facilities were inspected by the FDA. The inspectors found flagrant disregard for food safety best practices.[7] Hen barns were infested with rodents, maggots, and wild birds. Chicken manure was improperly piled, pushing open exterior barn doors and allowing wildlife to enter. Not only did samples in the barns test positive for *Salmonella*, but investigators learned that company tests of eggs had detected the bacteria hundreds of times during the previous three years. The company had not the reported the tests.[8]

In response to this unprecedented egg recall, United Egg Producers, an industry advocacy and marketing organization, stepped up its own recommended standards for food safety as well as its communication with consumers. Egg safety begins with industry programs that promote food safety practices on the farm. These practices include the procurement of *Salmonella*-free chicks, biosecurity, pest control, and cleaning and disinfection of poultry houses. Eggs are kept at low temperatures following collection, during transport to the processing plant, and after processing and packing. Education programs have been developed to encourage food preparers to use safe food-handling practices. Scientists continue to conduct research in order to better understand how *Salmonella* gets into flocks and how its presence might be further reduced. United Egg Producers has developed the "5-Star" egg safety program for participating farms to follow (box 12.3).[9]

Food safety specialists emphasize that foodborne illness can happen on farms of any size. Good management is the key to producing food that meets high safety standards. Farms and food processors have at least four reasons to be concerned with food safety — moral responsibility, regulatory compliance, marketing, and fear of litigation. Thus most are highly motivated to produce a safe, high-quality product. The egg company described above was a notable exception: food safety was not a priority, and paying fines and settlements was deemed more cost-effective than running a respectable operation. The result, in addition to making people ill and harming the credibility of an entire industry, was a criminal probe.[10]

When it comes to food safety, most farms and food processors want to do the right things for the right reasons, but they don't always know what to do. Education for farmers and food processors about best practices is critical, and that education is most effective when it is tailored to the farm's products, size, markets, and resources. Best practices work only if they are implemented and carefully followed.

Keeping Food Safe from Farm to Fork

Despite the increase in regulations and guidelines from the FDA and USDA, outbreaks of foodborne illness will continue to occur. Such outbreaks are no longer contained within a small region, affecting just a few people. As farms have consolidated and raw ingredients from many locations are routinely combined and shipped throughout the country, outbreaks have greater potential to sicken thousands throughout the United States.

Fortunately, there is a new generation of food safety specialists working with farmers and food processors across the nation to promote best practices. Just as fortunate, farms and other food businesses of all sizes are typi-

12.3 Requirements of the "5-Star" Egg Safety Program

- Chicks: procure *Salmonella*-free chicks.
- Biosecurity: prevent contamination from coming onto the farm.
- Integrated pest management: control pests in a systematic fashion.
- Cleaning and disinfection of poultry houses: kill microbes.
- Refrigeration: prevent microbial growth.
- Environmental and egg testing: monitor for contamination.
- Vaccination: keep flocks healthy.
- Feed management: prevent contamination.
- Traceability: facilitate recalls if needed.
- Laboratory standards: ensure proper testing.
- Processing plant sanitation: prevent spread of microbes.

United Egg Producers, "Food Safety Programs: UEP '5-Star' Egg Safety Program," Egg Safety Center, 2012. www.eggsafety.org/producers/food-safety-programs.

cally willing, even eager, to embrace reasonable best practices to reduce food safety risks. Farmers and processors recognize the importance of consumer confidence and the need to address the food safety issue head-on, in response to increased media attention, new regulations, and new market expectations.

Meanwhile, consumers can do their part to minimize food safety risks by washing fresh produce, cooking meats thoroughly, and storing foods at the correct temperature. These are simply good food preparation practices in any kitchen. Consumers also need to recognize that visiting a farm is not as simple as it used to be—it poses risks from a food safety standpoint, and farmers have to address these risks. Visitors must follow the rules when visiting a farm, even if that means leaving dogs at home or not letting kids pet the pony before they pick apples without washing their hands in between.

Patronizing small-scale farmers and processors may be one way to build consumer confidence in the face of food safety concerns. Direct markets give consumers the opportunity to ask the people who produce their food questions about their food safety practices. They can see some of the farmers' food-handling practices at the farmers' market or their CSA. They can see a local farm's name on the label at the corner store, then drive by that farm at some point to check it out. Or they can visit the websites of farms and processors to study the information provided about production practices and food safety procedures.

These relationships may reduce food safety risks, but they are certainly no guarantee. In the words of Bill Marler, an attorney specializing in foodborne illness lawsuits, "One of the things the locavore people really have right is the accountability issue. Just because you can shake the hand of the guy who sold you your dinner doesn't mean he is not going to poison you. But it does mean you'll know where to find him if he does."[11]

Fresh food, from known safe sources, processed in clean facilities by knowledgeable handlers, and prepared by informed consumers: that's the kind of food safety program that makes sense for a sustainable food system.

Many more people would choose to farm if they knew what it meant, how to get started, that it's possible to have a social life and a solid business as a farmer. . . . If the young farmer makes it beyond the third year, and still loves it, they'll likely stay a farmer for life. Which is of course what our country desperately needs.

Severine von Tscharner Fleming,
young farmer and activist

13 ❧ *The Next Generation of Farmers*

America's farmers are no spring chickens; their average age is fifty-seven years, and there are five times more farmers seventy-five years of age or older than there are farmers under the age of twenty-five.[1] This situation begs the question, who will farm in the future?

Over the past century the nation has been changing from a rural to an urban and suburban society. Today, only a small percentage of the population is engaged in farming. Yet nearly a million farms remain, and farming continues to play an essential role in rural economic development, food security, and the maintenance of open space and ecosystem services. To ensure a bright future for agriculture, many agencies and organizations have developed efforts to encourage and support new entrants to farming. These people are variously referred to as new farmers, beginning farmers, and next-generation farmers.

The Diversity of New Farmers

New farmers include a wide range of people, not just in terms of their backgrounds but also in terms of where they stand on a continuum from dreaming about farming to being well on the way to a successful enterprise. While the USDA broadly defines a beginning farmer as anyone who has been operating a farm for ten years or less, there is much more nuance to this population.[2]

The Growing New Farmers Project of the New England Small Farm Institute identified a typology of new farmers that describes an evolution of farming intention and experience, as shown in figure 13.1. The first half of the continuum includes types of prospective farmers who have not yet started to farm; the second half is made up of beginning farmers who are in various

Decision-Making Position

Prospective Farmers

Beginning Farmers

Recruits   Explorers   Planners   Start-ups   Re-strategizers   Establishers

FIGURE 13.1 Typology of new farmers. New farmers typically pass through a number of stages as they embark on a career in farming. As their careers progress they face increasing commitment, decision-making responsibility, and risk. A steady progression of farmers moving through each of these stages is necessary to sustain agricultural production.

stages of getting started. Prospective farmers include recruits (people with an aptitude or interest in farming who have not considered it as a career option), explorers (those actively researching farming as a career option), and aspiring farmers (those committed to becoming farmers but haven't started commercially). Beginning farmers include start-up farmers (those in their first few years of commercial production), re-strategizing farmers (those who have completed their first few years and are in the process of reassessing their operation), and establishing farmers (those well on their way to stabilizing production and marketing).[3] Programs and services need to be clear about which type of beginning farmer they are targeting, as these farmers have distinct needs.

Beginning farmers are important for both our current and future food systems. Beginning farms and ranches account for about one-fifth of the nation's family farms and one-tenth of agricultural production by family farms.[4] The good news is that the lifestyle and working environment associated with farming are attractive to many young people as well as to people of all ages seeking a change of career. Despite the fact that the average age of farmers has been increasing steadily, there appears to be an ample pool of people willing and eager to enter into farming as a business.

A study by the Economic Research Service of the USDA found that entry into farming has remained steady in recent decades and that farming entry rates are on a par with those of other industries.[5] The study also found that beginning farmers enter agriculture at all ages and that about a third of beginning farmers are fifty-five years or older. A variety of interests are bringing young people back to the farm:

– interest in local and artisan foods
– environmental awareness
– outdoor and physical activity

– market opportunities

– other successful young farmers[6]

While farm households in general rely on off-farm income, the households of beginning farmers are even more dependent, on average, on financial support from off the farm (fig. 13.2).

Starting a Farm on Leased Land: Paul Bucciaglia, New Milford, Connecticut

Paul Bucciaglia operates Fort Hill Farm, leasing 20 acres of land from Sunny Valley Preserve, a project of the Nature Conservancy.[7] Sunny Valley has 2,050 acres and five working farms as well as 1,400 acres of natural land. It was founded in 1970, when a local philanthropist donated multiple parcels of land to the Nature Conservancy. One condition of the gift was that the farmland be kept in agriculture as long as possible. Today, about 650 acres of the preserve are in active agriculture. The farms, leased by independent farmers, are privately operated businesses, one of which is Paul's. He grows certified organic vegetables, berries, herbs, and flowers for a 400-share CSA program. He also sells at farmers' markets and has a few wholesale accounts. Here, Paul recounts his experience starting a new farm:

> Like many small-scale, direct market farmers, I did not grow up on a farm. I studied agriculture and plant biology, and then worked with a friend in the Midwest who had bought some land and was developing what would become a very successful CSA farm. I enjoyed working with a diversity of crops and cover crops. After a few years I moved back to New England and apprenticed for a season at a CSA farm in Massachusetts. That was a critical year, when I learned skills I would need

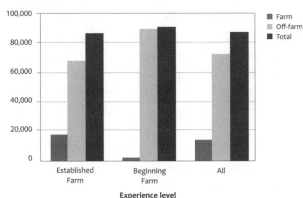

FIGURE 13.2 Farm income relative to off-farm income for beginning and established farm households. Beginning farmers (with ten years or less of farming experience) have about the same household income as established farmers, but on average much more of it comes from off-farm income.

to run a profitable, mechanized, organic vegetable farm. However, I was hesitant to start my own business.

The opportunity emerged to run Holcomb Farm CSA in Granby, Connecticut. The farm was a project of the nonprofit Hartford Food System, and it was the largest CSA in the state. I jumped at the chance, and it was a steep learning curve for me. I made mistakes but on the whole had two successful seasons. Then I felt ready to start my own business. I had a plan which described a pretty clear vision of what my farm would look like. I had saved a small amount of start-up capital, about $20,000, and purchased some very used farm equipment. All I needed was some high-quality farmland. It seemed crazy to think about buying farmland; renting was the only reasonable option. Fate intervened when I met the director of Sunny Valley Preserve, which had a large hayfield of flat, well-drained, stone-free, Class I sandy loam, with a house to boot, that they were looking to rent to an organic farmer. That fall I moved into the house and plowed the first four acres of what would become my farm.

Starting a new farm business comes with huge challenges: capital funding, setting up new markets, developing infrastructure, acquiring equipment, improving soils, and managing people. But starting a farm on rented ground incurs additional problems. One big issue for me was ownership of capital improvements. Farming 20 acres of vegetables can generate far more revenue than 20 acres of hay, but the capital and operating costs are also greater. How landlords and tenants handle this issue can make or break a new farm. Landlords can be reluctant to fund capital improvements for tenants; the funds may not be available, or the landlord may fear that the improvements will not be useful to the next tenant. Tenants are reluctant to finance capital improvements that they cannot own, sell, or move to another farm. This can paralyze a developing farm business.

Our farm lease states that all permanent improvements become property of the Nature Conservancy. There is no provision for ownership, transfer, or sale of the improvements. With no formal plan in place for financing capital improvements, development of the farm has been somewhat piecemeal. Sunny Valley has paid for some capital improvements like building a bare bones pole barn, and repairs and upgrades to the house. I have paid for other permanent capital improvements such as storage and processing sheds, barn doors, and concrete floors. I purchased all farm production equipment, such as machinery, tools, and coolers, through reinvested farm profits.

Critical to the farm's development were several grants from the USDA Natural Resources Conservation Service for irrigation wells, an underground irrigation pipeline, and permanent deer fence. We have also received funds from the Connecticut Department of Agriculture for field and greenhouse equipment and solar power generation. I am very thankful for these grants which helped smooth over the issue around capital improvements and put much needed resources into our business. It is important to note that these critical infrastructure projects could have been financed by us had there been a provision for transfer of ownership in our lease.

Lease tenure is another concern confronting a tenant farmer. I started with a five-year lease. In year three of that first lease, it occurred to me that I only had a two-year lease, which made me uncomfortable. Organic agriculture requires a great deal of long-term investment, such as adding compost, rock minerals, and cover crop residues to fields to maintain soil health. Additionally, if I was unable to retain the lease I would have very little time to locate new land and develop a new farm. Working with Sunny Valley, I was able to address these concerns by developing a five-year rolling lease, so that each year I gain a new five-year lease.

The best news from a farmland preservation perspective is that the farm is permanently conserved. Because the farm's conservation easement requires the land to be in active agriculture, when I move or retire, the land and its infrastructure will be available to another grower.

Leasing farmland has had both positive and negative consequences for me. I've been able to build a successful business in an area that has high demand for fresh, organic produce. There is no other way I could have afforded land in affluent Litchfield County. But not owning land has consequences I didn't fully understand when I built my business. The immediate consequence is that if things don't work out, although you can move to another farm you can't move your local customers with you. Developing market relationships takes a lot of time and effort, so while moving the farm may seem as simple as loading up tractors on a flat bed, the economic costs of doing so are high. In addition, when making necessary capital investments, leasing land puts you in a difficult spot if you cannot recover those costs should you have to leave before they are fully depreciated. This can be managed by amortizing the costs of an improvement over a short time span, say five years, but it still makes investing money into the farm a scarier prospect. The biggest consequence lies down the road, at retirement. Farmers typically can afford to retire by selling their farm business or land. That option is not available to me. I deal with this by budgeting "retirement fund" as a cost in our farm's annual accounting.

Looking to the future, there are many experienced, hard-working young farmers with the knowledge, skills, and intestinal fortitude to start their own farm business. In places like southern New England, where land is prohibitively expensive, leasing land is a much more viable option. I applaud land trusts and other organizations that seek to make farmland available to young farmers. Developing mechanisms to manage the capital and lease tenure needs of a growing farm business will go a long way to ensure the success of these sorely needed new farmers, keep working lands in production, and provide more local food to citizens increasingly aware of and interested in the source of their food.

Joining the Family Farm: Scott Larsen, Audubon, Iowa

Scott Larsen grows corn and soybeans with his father and brother in a rural part of the state halfway between Des Moines and Omaha (see fig. 13.3). As Scott tells it:

I'm extremely happy to be a part of the family farm. I didn't know if there would be room in the operation for me, but I'm glad I pursued it harder as I got older. I'm thirty-seven now and I started getting serious about investing in farming when I was thirty-one.

I grew up on this farm and I've always wanted to stay here and keep farming. This farm has been in my family since the late 1800s. My dad grew up one mile from where he lives now. When his parents died, he bought his brothers' share of the farm. It's a century farm, meaning it's been in the same family for over a hundred years. My entire life, I've watched my father work hard. Some years were very good and others bad. I'm proud of what my father has accomplished, and I would never want to lose what he has built. Instead, I hope to build upon it to be able to pass it on to the next generation.

My brother and I both want the same thing for the farm. We want a decent income to provide for our families by doing what we love but also build a little to help the next generation get started. We both have children who someday may be in the same situation we are in today. I have an eight-year-old son and a five-year-old daughter. Both love helping me out on the farm. It's sometimes hard to pull them away. I could see both of them wanting to be a part of our farm someday. My nephew is five and he is the same way. They are just like my brother and I were. There's something about riding in the tractor with your dad as a child that makes you want to farm.

Our goal is to build a business that will allow any of our children to become a part of it if they wish. My wife and I want our children to go to college to get an education and hopefully even spend some time working for someone else for a while. But if at some point they want to be a part of the farm, we want to be sure there is a place for them to get started.

My dad, my brother, and I farm about 2,000 acres combined. My dad owns 600 acres, and my brother and I rent most of the rest of the land from landlords outside the family. We rent land together and make decisions together. Our income and expenses are split fifty-fifty. Each year, we pay the landowners cash rent and hope the market stays strong to allow us to cover expenses as well as provide for our families.

FIGURE 13.3 Scott Larsen on his farm in Iowa. Scott grows corn and soybeans with his father and brother on land that has been in their family for more than a hundred years. Scott is concerned about keeping the farm viable for future generations of his family.

My dad inherited some land through his family, and he bought the rest little by little over the years. Over the last two years, my brother and I have been able to make a couple of land purchases. One of those was bought from distant family relations, and it ties in with the rest of the land we farm. We are grateful to have been able to buy that piece of land. It was a great feeling to be able to take down that fence.

To a farmer out here in rural Iowa, the dirt means everything. That's how we live; we live off the dirt, the land. Our lives revolve around the land, so keeping it in the same family is tremendously important. When you borrow lots of money to buy land, you constantly worry about the weather, markets, and government programs until you pay off the mortgage and own the land. When you finally own the land, it's a huge accomplishment. It's something to really be proud of.

We grow corn and soybeans, in crop rotation. When I was a kid, we raised hogs and oats too. Six years ago, my dad decided he didn't want to deal with livestock anymore, so we are currently only grain farmers. Our short-term goal is to enter the livestock sector of the business again. However, large-scale units are a must in order to compete with the bigger companies and to be profitable. They have ruined the market. These large companies own the hogs and the packing house. By owning both, they can do it so much cheaper than a small farm on its own. Then that large company signs contracts with the retail giants so they are guaranteed so much money per head. When you're a small farmer, you don't get any guarantees. You can't compete with the large operations.

The main challenge for young farmers like me is larger farmers. It's tough to compete with them. To be profitable, you need so many more acres of land today than were needed even just fifteen years ago. I have friends who would love to farm, but without family who owns land or someone who is willing to help them get started, it is nearly impossible. Because it's so difficult for young families to get started in farming, the small rural communities like we live in suffer. We are losing population, which affects the enrollment in the school system. If five of my friends could come back here and farm, they would each add some more children to the school system and the community would be stronger. Don't get me wrong. I have friends who are large farmers. It's nothing personal. We need to get larger to compete, but we also need to find the right balance to keep our rural communities strong.

It doesn't help that agricultural businesses are fully focused on larger farmers. Equipment manufacturers keep building bigger equipment that makes it easier for large farms. If you take a corn planter, for example, you can plant a field in a fraction of the time with a forty-eight-row compared to the smaller equipment. When it takes less time and effort to cover the ground, farmers want even more land.

My brother and I are in a situation where we need more land to rent in order to provide enough to support both of our families. It has been hard to find more land, though. We can't compete with the high-dollar rent that large farmers can pay. The good news is the baby boomers will eventually retire, and hopefully they won't rent their land to the big guys but instead might rent it to guys like me and my brother. They were young farmers once too and somehow they were given a chance. Hopefully they want to help the next generation get a chance too. Those are the people I love working with.

The reason why it takes so much more land for a farmer to make a profit is because expenses like equipment and fuel costs, cash rent, and seed have skyrocketed. On average, the cash rent my brother and I pay has increased by more than 150 percent since I started farming fifteen years ago. This can work when the market is good, but when it drops it's scary. If you are renting and there are problems, you still have to make the payments. Crop insurance helps but it isn't always enough. It also helps to have a banker who will stick with you during the tough times. In times like these, all we can do is hope for the best.

My advice for new farmers looking to get into corn and soy farming is: contact family members or anyone who might be willing to help you get started. If that's not an option, go to your local Farm Service Agency and look into the possibility of utilizing low-interest loans. It's not easy to get started, but if you can make it work it will be worth it.

I see no end to the consolidation of farms. I wonder sometimes how many people will be left out here in forty years. People buy farms and the first thing they do is tear down the house. In forty years, there might be one house left every 3 miles. Where do you draw the line and stop consolidating? How do we keep our way of life? Farming out here is a way of life. Having grown up here, I think it's the only place to raise a family. I can sit on my porch every morning at 5 a.m. with my cup of coffee and it's quiet and peaceful. My kids can play outside without worrying about anything. I can see the stars at night. I love it out here. I hope I will be able to pass this way of life on to my children.

Needs of New Farmers

A beginning farmer must rapidly acquire information about how to grow crops and/or animals, how to market them, how to manage a farm business, and how to comply with a variety of rules and regulations. People who grow up on a farm can obtain much of this specialized knowledge from their family and from their own experience. For others, this expertise must be acquired. It can come from a combination of experience working on farms, internships, formal education, and technical materials such as books, websites, and videos. Technical advisers, training programs, and educational materials are relatively plentiful, but beginning farmers often struggle with locating the resources that address their specific needs and putting all the information together in a way that helps guide their actions as they seek to establish a farm.

In general terms, beginning farmers need what all farmers need, just in different proportions and delivered in different packages. All farmers, including beginning farmers, need the following:

- access to land;
- a market for their products;
- sufficient capital to build and maintain their business; and
- technical support to help them make sound decisions.

These are described in what follows with a focus on the needs of beginning farmers.

Access to Land

Some farms don't need much land; they produce high-value products on small parcels or grow crops in the small space of intensive greenhouses. But in order to thrive, most farms need a lot of land compared with other types of business. Figure 13.4 outlines some of the ways that new farmers gain access to land.

The average beginning farm in the United States has 200 acres, compared with 434 acres for established farms. The majority of beginning farms include some owned land, but a higher share of beginning farms than established farms rely solely on rented land. The most common way for U.S. farmers to buy land for their operation is to purchase it from a non-relative. This is true for both beginning and established farms. Owners of established farms, however, are more likely than beginning farmers to have inherited or purchased

	from a farm family		from a non-farm family
new farmer status	starting a farm business	moving a farm business	taking over a farm business

	short-term rental	long-term lease	purchase and sale
land status	land never farmed	land formerly farmed	land in farming
	conservation easement	agricultural zoning	unrestricted land

	non-farmers	retiring farmers	farmer's heirs	foundations	land trusts	local government
land owner status	private ownership			non-profit ownership		

FIGURE 13.4 Possible combinations of new farmer, land, and landowner status. There are many paths to land tenure for a new farmer, in part because there are many possible combinations of the status of new farmers, farm land, and farm landowners. New farmers may or may not come from a farm family. They may have their own business or they may be taking over another farmer's business. The land they are considering may have one or several tenure options available, and it may be protected or preserved. The landowners may be farmers, their families, non-farmers, or a nonprofit entity.

their land from relatives. The challenges of acquiring land have been exacerbated by the rising value of farm real estate.[8]

In places where land prices are steadily rising and development is slowly reducing the amount of available farmland, finding an affordable place to farm is a serious challenge for beginning farmers. It's also a challenge for established farmers, who are competing with new farmers for the available farmland. The sale of development rights to land trusts has helped some beginning farmers acquire land, but funding is limited and the smaller parcels desired by many new entrants to agriculture are not usually attractive to land trusts.

While some new farmers have the resources to purchase land as they start their farms, many must find alternative land tenure arrangements that are more affordable. The *Greenhorns' Guide for Beginning Farmers* captures the variety and creativity of this process (box 13.1).[9]

LAND LINK PROGRAMS. Also called "farm link programs," these efforts focus on connecting people who have available farmland, usually retiring farmers, with new farmers who are seeking land to farm. The programs got their start in the Midwest following the 1980s farm crisis, when farmers and service providers were seeing farmers leave the land and were unsure about agriculture's next generation. The Center for Rural Affairs in Walthill, Nebraska, established "Land Link" as a way to encourage new farmers to enter

13.1 Manufacture Some Magic: Many Are the Ways That Folks Have Managed to Get Access to Land

1 Working for a nonprofit organization as farm manager/educational coordinator
2 Renting/leasing land from a land trust
3 Renting/leasing land from non-farming landowners who get an "agricultural tax assessment"
4 Renting a part of a working farm, sharing equipment
5 Farming land owned by a school, restaurant, retreat center, artist-in-residency program, or other institution
6 Collaborative land purchase (siblings, friends, and associations)
7 Farming for a private developer in a "planned development"
8 Starting with a small homestead in a rural town while earning money for eventual farm purchase in outskirts
9 Lottery/inheritance from your family
10 Cannabis cultivation on rented/squatted land to finance your own parcel (*not* recommended)
11 Slowly taking over a farm operation from a retiring farmer
12 Borrowing underutilized private land with a handshake
13 Rooftop farming with corporate partners
14 Renting urban land from the city
15 Farming on the site of an old bedding plant nursery or other compatible space

A note on renting land from estate owners: There are model lease agreements available online. It's critical that you have a leak-proof lease agreement with your landlord. As a lessee with pregnant animals and day-old chickens being delivered tomorrow, you'll want to protect yourself from a landlord who likely has fancier lawyers and faster getaway cars, if and when the winds change.

Adapted from *Greenhorns' Guide for Beginning Farmers*, 4th ed., 2010.
www.thegreenhorns.net/wp-content/files_mf/1335219697greenhorns_guide_sept2010_web.pdf.

farming. Now, there are dozens of similar programs across the country; some are regional or statewide and others are more local.

All matching programs work a little differently, but the basics are the same: the program compiles lists of new farmers and of landowners who want to explore a link; the people make a connection — usually the new farmer contacts the landowner; then both parties get to know each other and decide whether and how to link. Land Link application forms typically ask new farmers about their experience, goals, and assets. Both landowners and beginners need to know what they want to get out of a linking relationship before they start try-ing to work one out.

Getting a good fit is the most important part of land linking, but it's not al-ways easy. Retiring farmers are passing on their life's work; new farmers may be making a very long commitment to an unfamiliar piece of land. Time may be needed to work out financing and legal matters. Everyone involved has to be comfortable with what is happening and work together to communicate com-mon goals and interests. Land Link staff may be available to provide support or to refer seekers and owners to sources of support. Arranging a transfer usually requires assistance to ensure that the land tenure arrangement will work to the benefit of both parties. Seekers and owners may consider a range of tenure ar-rangements that include purchase-and-sale, leasing, and agreements whereby the seeker works for an owner to gain equity in the farm business over time.

Land Link programs have come to realize that the matching component is important but by itself not sufficient to create successful links among partic-ipants. Education and support are critical for success through consultations, publications, and workshops.

Finding a Market

Commodity market prices often pose a serious challenge to farmers, so many beginning farmers look for opportunities in direct markets or special-ized wholesale markets that enable them to build personal relationships and allow some pricing flexibility. It's important for new farmers to have a clear idea of the market niche they will fill and to quickly learn how to produce high-quality products. If they are not in a commodity market, they need to learn customer service skills too.

A primary motivation for many new farmers is a desire to grow things; they see themselves as aspiring food producers. Fewer farmers are motivated by marketing and the other non-production skills needed to run a successful farm business. Thus a lot of new farmers find a place to farm with just a gen-eral idea of what their markets will be. They simply start growing crops or raising animals and let their markets evolve. This can work out, but obviously it's not an ideal approach. That's why most new farmer support programs urge their clients to draft a business plan, even if it's rudimentary, that identifies aspiring farmers' goals and resources as well as their market intentions and financial expectations. It's hard to define specific marketing goals for a new business that lacks production experience and data from previous sales. How-ever, a new farmer's marketing plan should address two central questions: What are you going to sell and how are you going to sell it?

13.2 *Sample Marketing Goals of a Start-up Vegetable Farmer*

I will market my produce as fresh and local. The communication of our values as a farm family is an important part of the marketing strategy. Our customers will know that by supporting our farm they will be supporting the preservation of the local environment and keeping their dollars within the local community. I will attend two winter farmers' markets during my first year of production, and I will offer a CSA-style subscription of weekly greens, storage crops, and herbs in subsequent years, as well as attend markets. I will explore relationships with restaurants and local co-ops but will keep wholesale sales under 30 percent of my total sales. I plan to have gross sales of $20,000 in the first year; this will increase by about $10,000 annually for five years, after which I will have net farm revenues of $25,000. I realize that the summer vegetable CSA/farmers' market arena is saturated with farms and competitors, but there are few local competitors in the winter greens production sector. I will be competing with farms from California and Florida that produce greens during our northern winter. My winter produce will be fresher and of higher quality, and therefore my prices will be slightly higher than those of similar products available from conventional supermarkets. I will target a segment of the population that is interested in increasing the amount of food they consume from local sources and are mindful of this even during the winter. My target market demographic consists of people who are thirty-five to fifty years old, are employed with an annual income between $40,000 and $60,000, are married and have kids, like to entertain at home, and are aware of and concerned about environmental and sustainability issues.

Some new farmers take over existing farms rather than start new enterprises. A new farmer buying the family farm, or someone else's farm, has the benefit of an existing market. That usually comes with historical data showing costs and returns for the farm's products and markets. The new farmer can decide whether to continue with those, to modify, to diversify, or to shift to entirely new products and/or markets. But new farmers starting from scratch must make educated guesses about their markets, their costs, and their returns based on financial data from other farms like theirs, available information about potential customers and competitors, and observations of trends and niches in the market they are interested in. Box 13.2 shows a sample marketing plan for an aspiring vegetable farmer who lays out a clear marketing vision for a brand-new farm but does not yet speculate on expected sales.

Although a new farmer starting from scratch lacks the advantages of taking over an established farm operation with its infrastructure, markets, and real estate, a young farmer taking over a business from a retiring farmer faces a different set of challenges. Farm transfers, especially within a family, can be complicated. They are not simply business transactions but highly interpersonal and emotional transactions. These farm transfers take time, often several years. The younger generation has to learn to manage the business and have reasonable proof that they can be financially viable on their own. The older generation has to have the financial resources necessary for retirement and be willing to let go of managing a business they may have spent their lives building. In addition, there may be siblings of the new farmer or other heirs to the real estate who have interests that must be satisfied in order for the farm to remain intact. A variety of farm transfer programs have been established to help farm families navigate these financial, legal, and personal issues.

Access to Capital

Farm businesses have relatively high capital requirements to pay for the land and infrastructure they need to operate. New farmers can use their own money to pay for these things, if they have it, or they can borrow from others. The lenders may be family or friends, commercial banks, or government lending agencies. Many people who aspire to start a new farm or take over an existing farm are not eligible for loans from conventional lenders, even if they have good experience and references, because they lack sufficient financial assets to secure a loan. A common way that new farmers meet the collateral requirements of a lender is to have a co-signer for a loan.

Another challenge facing new farmers seeking to borrow from banks is the limited number of commercial lenders that are familiar with agricultural businesses, let alone new farm businesses. The Farm Credit System is one bank that is very familiar with agriculture; in fact, that's its specialty. It also has programs that provide financial counseling to assist "young, beginning, and small farmers." Another source of loans for new farmers is the USDA's Farm Service Agency (FSA), which makes and guarantees loans and provides credit counseling and supervision to farmers and ranchers who may not be able to obtain private or commercial credit. The FSA is required to target beginning farmers as borrowers for a portion of the funds Congress gives to it. This means that beginning farmers don't have to compete directly with established farmers for those funds.

"Aggie Bond" loan programs, currently available in seventeen states, are specifically for beginning farmers and ranchers. This federal/state/private partnership, started in 1980, helps new farmers buy land, farm equipment, farm buildings, and breeding livestock through reduced interest rate loans. Each participating state creates a bond that allows lenders to earn federally tax-exempt interest income on loans to beginning farmers and ranchers. The tax savings allow the lenders to offer reduced interest rates. Credit decisions and financial risk remain with the local lending institutions.

A variety of nonprofit organizations also help to provide funding for beginning farmers. For example, the Carrot Project works with lenders in New England and New York to develop alternative financing programs for small and midsize farms, many of whom would be considered beginning farms. By offering technical assistance such as business planning, the program helps increase the success rate of new farms in securing commercial loans.

Some grants are also available to new farmers. The Texas Department of Agriculture has a Young Farmer Grant Program for people eighteen to forty-five years old who are creating or expanding agricultural enterprises. Up to $10,000 may be granted for operating expenses and a match is required. Beginning farmers are eligible for on-farm research grants, though they must compete with established farmers for these funds. The USDA's Sustainable Agriculture Research and Education (SARE) program has farmer/producer grants that support on-farm innovation, and the Organic Farming Research Foundation (OFRF) funds organic farming studies. The USDA's Beginning Farmer and Rancher Development Program supports farmers indirectly by funding organizations that provide programs for beginning farmers.

Some new farmers are also using crowdfunding as a tool for raising money to start their farms or farm enterprises. Crowdfunding platforms like Kickstarter and Indiegogo allow new farmers to post profiles of their projects online and seek donations, from small to large. The farmers may show their appreciation by offering small gifts or samples of their products in return.

Technical Support

A beginning farmer must rapidly acquire information about how to farm, how to market, how to manage money and people, and how to adhere to regulations (box 13.3). Those who grew up on a farm can obtain much of this specialized knowledge from their family and experience. For others, this expertise must be acquired through a combination of employment on farms, education, and technical advice. Technical advisers and training programs are relatively plentiful, but beginning farmers often struggle with locating the resources that address their specific needs.

New farmers get their information from many sources. A study of 286 farmers who received loans from the Iowa Department of Agriculture specif-

13.3 *Information for New Farmers*

The Northeast Beginning Farmer Project housed at the Cornell Small Farms Program developed a set of online tutorials that summarize the knowledge new farmers need to succeed.

- Getting Started—Begin here with goal setting and suggestions for planning.
- Accessing and Evaluating Land—Learn how to find or assess the quality of land for farming.
- Planning and Funding Your Farm Business—Start writing a farm plan and assess funding options.
- Learning How to Farm—Gain the skills you need to produce high-quality products.
- Choosing What to Produce—Consult enterprise budgets, crop ideas, and worksheets.
- Selling What You Produce—Choose the right markets for your products.
- Taking Care of the Land—Cultivate ecologically sound practices.
- Achieving or Improving Profitability—Learn skills to improve your bottom line.
- Understanding Taxes and Regulations—Learn about the benefits and responsibilities of farming.

Cornell University, *Northeast Beginning Farmers Project*, n.d. nebeginningfarmers.org/.

ically for beginning farmers found that the top three sources of information for these farmers were parents, siblings, and relatives; Extension; and agricultural consultants.[10] Recordkeeping, management systems analysis, and marketing strategies were rated among the most important topics they needed information on. A survey of more than a thousand beginning farmers from across the country by the National Young Farmer's Coalition found that apprenticeships were rated the most valuable type of program for young and beginning farmers, followed by local partnerships, community-supported agriculture, Land Link programs, nonprofit training and education, and college and university training and education.[11]

Barriers to Getting Started

The study just cited found three major obstacles for beginning farmers in the United States:

1 Capital: farmers need better access to capital, credit, and small operating loans. These are critical for business start-up and expansion.

2 Land: farmers have great difficulty finding affordable land to purchase or landowners willing to make long-term lease agreements.

3 Health care: it is unaffordable yet absolutely necessary for beginning farmers.[12]

Some barriers to success in farming are external to the individual, and others have to do with the personality and skills of the aspiring farmer. Successful farmers are entrepreneurs; they need to be confident, persistent, and innovative. They must deal with risk, be able to lead people who work for or with them, and be able to manage a business. They need to be organized and able to think long term, even while dealing with day-to-day crises. Farmers must be aware of their own farm as well as their industry as a whole. They must keep abreast of the economy, technology, government, and competitors in order to detect trends that create challenges or opportunities.[13] That's a long list of desirable characteristics. To succeed, new farmers may not need all of them, but they'll need a lot of them.

The Greenhorns offer this advice to young farmers who are in it for the long haul: "Slow down. Don't breathe dust, practice tractor safety, consider long term effects, save your back, keep poise under pressure, maintain graciousness, call your mother for a pep talk, don't swear loudly from the front porch."[14]

14 ∾ *Maintaining Farms and Farmland for the Future*

It's true that plants can be grown without soil, and a hamburger can be made in the laboratory. But in the coming decades human beings will probably continue to derive most of their sustenance from the land. With the exception of some aquaculture, hydroponics, hunting, and fishing, we will get our food from fertile soil, ideally stewarded by competent farmers who make a reasonable profit. Maintaining a critical mass of farms and farmland is essential to a viable food system, yet a variety of factors pose threats to both. Consolidation in food systems, fueled by a lack of true-cost accounting, is squeezing out "farms in the middle" that are too big for direct marketing but too small to compete in wholesale and commodity markets. Destruction of good farmland is being fueled by a lack of land-use planning, dependence on food shipped long distances, and the rising value of farmland for non-farming purposes. To ensure local, regional, and national food security in the future, a combination of strategies for protecting and preserving farms and farmland is needed.

Farmland preservation and farmland protection are not the same thing.[1] Farmland preservation is defined as a voluntary act by an owner who puts his or her land into a permanent conservation easement held by a government agency or a land trust. Farmland protection measures are not necessarily permanent. They include agricultural zoning ordinances, right-to-farm laws, and agricultural tax policies. Farmland preservation and farmland protection complement one another and are most effective for ensuring the long-term success of farms and farmland when used in combination with each other and with programs that promote farm viability and planning for farm transfers to the next generation.

Farm and Farmland Trends

The number of farms in the United States peaked in 1935 at 6.8 million; now there are just over 2 million (fig. 14.1). Today's farmers make up less than 1 percent of the population, and more than half of them claim a principal oc-

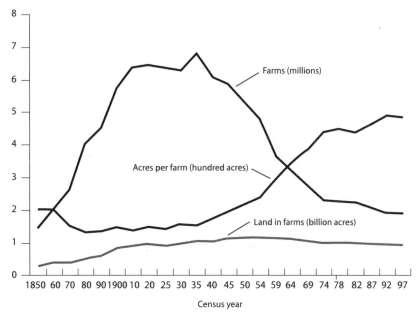

FIGURE 14.1 Change in the number of farms and acreage over time. Since the mid-1900s the number of U.S. farms has declined sharply, average farm size has increased, and land in farms has slowly but steadily declined.

cupation other than farming. Most U.S. farms are small in economic terms: less than a quarter of U.S. farms have gross annual revenues of more than $50,000. A relatively few large farms produce most of our food: 9 percent of farms account for 63 percent of sales of agricultural products.[2]

Of the 2.3 billion acres of land in the United States, about a billion are in agriculture. Cropland accounts for 408 million acres; pastureland and range-land account for 614 million acres. During the past twenty-five years, more than 23 million acres of agricultural land were lost to development. During the past sixty-five years, total cropland area declined nearly 10 percent, while total grazing land declined by 24 percent.[3]

The loss of prime farmland is of particular concern because it has the best combination of physical and chemical characteristics for producing food, feed, forage, fiber, and oilseed crops (fig. 14.2). About a half a million acres of prime farmland are lost to development annually in the United States.[4] Development of prime farmland accounted for approximately 33 percent of all development of rural land from 1982 to 2007; this loss amounts to about 4 percent of all prime farmland.

Agricultural land is under the greatest development pressure when it's

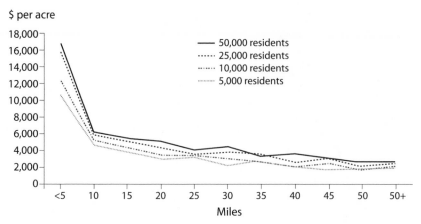

FIGURE 14.2 Loss of prime agricultural land to development. Prime agricultural land is a subset of farmland that has soils best suited for producing crops with the fewest inputs and least amount of erosion. Between 1982 and 2007, a total of 8.7 million acres of prime U.S. farmland were lost to development.

located on the "urban fringe," where there are competing demands for land as cities and suburbs grow (fig. 14.3). Farm fields are well suited to development because they are relatively flat and well drained, and often have access to water. Thus they are ideal locations for housing, industrial buildings, shopping malls, airports, athletic fields, and landfills. Many cities are surrounded by farmland, since they were settled in areas where a local food supply could be created. As our dependence on local food diminished, so did the imperative to keep farmland from being developed.

Development in farming regions drives up the value of farmland and increases the cost of production, as farmers and their commercial partners have to travel farther to exchange products and services. Farms in areas that have become highly developed often have constraints on normal farming operations as a result of their non-farming neighbors' concerns and excessive traffic. This can make it difficult to spread manure, apply farm chemicals, operate machinery early in the morning, drive farm vehicles from field to field, or move cows across the road. The upside of farming on the urban fringe is that it creates opportunities to engage in direct marketing and agritourism due to the proximity of many potential customers.

Why Protect Farmland?

A wide range of benefits warrant the implementation of programs that protect farmland from development. These include food security through a

FIGURE 14.3 Farm real estate values as affected by distance from population centers. The closer farms are to developed areas, the more their land is worth. Imagine how the value would increase for farmland close to large cities (not shown here.)

local food supply, a viable local agricultural economy, maintenance of environmental and rural amenities, and an orderly development process. Other possible benefits include slowing urban and suburban sprawl, keeping a productive land base for agriculture, maintaining open space and rural character, protecting wildlife habitats, and providing an opportunity for groundwater recharge and other ecosystem services.[5]

Studies of farmland protection programs found that they do provide economic value, but the evidence varies with the type of benefit.[6] The strongest evidence of their value has to do with the benefits of public amenities such as scenic enjoyment, wildlife habitats, cultural heritage, and access to on-farm markets and experiences. Research also shows that farmland preservation can benefit the economic viability of agriculture. Farmers often use preservation funds to invest in their operations, suggesting an ongoing commitment to their agricultural businesses. There is indirect evidence that farmland preservation benefits food security in that it supports the market for local agricultural products, but data are lacking to directly link this to the economic impact of local farm products. Farmland preservation appears to have a mixed effect on development overall; in some cases it slows development, but the presence of protected farmland can also raise the value of unprotected land nearby, promoting its development. To contribute most effectively to orderly development, farmland protection programs need to be part of a more comprehensive approach to land-use planning.[7]

Farmland Preservation

Conservation easements are an important tool for preserving farmland. A conservation easement, or covenant, is a legally enforceable agreement between a landowner and a public entity or a nonprofit land trust organization that is created to protect land from development and from specific uses.

An easement may prohibit or restrict the extent of building, commercial use, or specific activities (motorized vehicle use, clear-cutting of trees, etc.). Land under the easement remains the private property of the landowner, who may have donated or sold the "development rights." The decision to put a conservation easement in place is voluntary, but in most cases the restrictions are perpetual, so they are binding on future owners of the property. In the case of so-called term easements, restrictions are put in place for a limited period of time, often in exchange for tax benefits or access to desirable government programs during that period. Conservation easements are used to preserve more than just agricultural land. They also preserve forestland and wildlife habitats, and restrict the development of land, thereby contributing to the maintenance of clean water, clean air, and aesthetic or cultural features.

The earliest conservation easement in the United States was created in 1891 when the first private land trust, the Trustees of Reservations in Massachusetts, was formed to purchase and maintain public parkways in the city of Boston. In the 1930s and 1940s, the U.S. National Park Service bought parcels of land and conserved them for scenic use along parkways in the southeastern part of the country. These scenic easements were intended to facilitate public access to and enjoyment of parks and vistas. Conservation easements today are intended primarily to restrict development.[8] The first U.S. farmland preservation program started in Suffolk County, New York, in the mid-1970s. In 1977 the state of Maryland created the first statewide funding program for the purchase of conservation easements to farmland.[9]

In 1964 the IRS authorized tax deductions for landowners who donated property for scenic easements next to federal highways. A year later, Congress required states to spend a portion of federal highway funds on landscapes along these highways. That spurred states to enact legislation encouraging conservation easements; eventually all fifty states did so. As Congress and the states created incentives and legal authority for the use of conservation easements, their impact increased.[10]

A conservation easement may be donated by the landowner for philanthropic and/or tax benefits, or it may be sold at "fair market value." It may also be sold at a "bargain sale" price that essentially gives away part of its value but still allows the owner to get some compensation. Easement agreements and funding for the purchase of development rights are often put together by a partnership. Some combination of federal, state, and local agencies and non-governmental organizations such as land trusts determine who will hold and enforce the easement and how it will be paid for. Government programs that help pay for easements have acronyms like PDR (purchase of development rights), PACE (purchase of agricultural easements), ACEPP (Agricultural Conservation Easement Purchase Program), and FPP (Farmland Preservation Program).

LAND TRUSTS. Land trusts are often responsible for holding and enforcing conservation easements. The number of U.S. land trusts grew from 53 in 1950 to 1,667 in 2005. At that time they controlled 37 million acres of land. About 9 million acres were held conservation easements; the remainder were likely owned outright by the land trusts. Most of this land is not agricultural; it was preserved for environmental reasons by national organizations such as the Nature Conservancy, the Trust for Public Land, Ducks Unlimited, and the Conservation Fund. The largest of these is the Nature Conservancy, which controls 15 million acres, of which more than 3 million acres are in conservation easements. The nation's local, state, and regional land trusts control 12 million acres of private lands, of which about half are in conservation easements.[11]

State, local, and national land trusts have conserved 47 million acres of many types of land. There are now 1,723 active land trusts, including 1,699 state and local groups and 24 national land trusts. California has the most land trusts with 197, followed by Massachusetts with 159, Connecticut with 137, Pennsylvania with 103, and New York with 97.[12]

At least 4.9 million acres of farm- and ranchland are protected by 192 land trusts plus 119 state-run agricultural easement programs. About three-quarters of protected agricultural land is ranchland rather than cropland. The largest 52 land trusts protect 95 percent of this land, and most of the land was donated to them.[13]

STATE PROGRAMS. States use a variety of approaches to encourage preservation of farmland. Figure 14.4 shows the increase in state purchases of agricultural easements. California's Farmland Conservancy Program provides grants to local governments and nonprofit organizations to support local efforts to establish agricultural conservation easements and planning projects for the purpose of preserving important agricultural land resources. Eligible projects include the voluntary acquisition of conservation easements on agricultural lands that are under threat of being converted to non-agricultural uses; the temporary purchase of agricultural lands in the process of placing conservation easements; conservation policy and technical assistance projects; and improvements to agricultural land already under easement.

The Maryland Agricultural Land Preservation Foundation was established by the Maryland General Assembly in 1977 and is part of the Maryland Department of Agriculture. The Foundation purchases agricultural preservation

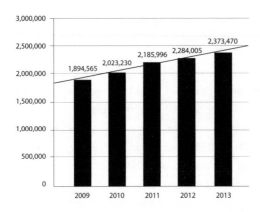

FIGURE 14.4 Acres of farmland protected by state PACE (purchase of agricultural easements) programs. Twenty-eight states have funded agricultural conservation easement programs, investing a total of $3.6 billion to date to protect working farm- and ranchland.

easements that forever restrict development on prime farmland and woodland. The program has invested more than $600 million to permanently protect more than 280,000 acres on approximately 2,100 farms in all of Maryland's twenty-three counties.

Michigan's Farmland and Open Space Preservation Program includes several methods of protecting land. Farmland development rights agreements and local open space easements place a voluntary temporary restriction on the land in exchange for certain tax benefits and exemptions. Conservation easement donations place a permanent restriction on the land. The Agricultural Preservation Fund assists local governments in implementing a local purchase of development rights. A purchase of development rights places a permanent restriction on the land between the state and a landowner, voluntarily entered into by a landowner, preserving his or her land for agriculture in exchange for a cash payment.

New Jersey passed the Farmland Assessment Act of 1964 to mitigate the loss of farmland to rapid suburban development through the use of favorable tax assessments. But by the late 1970s, the value of farmland had outstripped the tax benefits of the act, so the state started to purchase deed restrictions on farms through the Agriculture Retention and Development Act of 1981. Landowners can also choose to voluntarily restrict development on their land for eight years. Although they receive no payment for this, they are eligible to apply for cost-sharing grants for soil and water conservation projects.

Pennsylvania's Farmland Preservation Program was established in 1988 to curb the conversion of prime farmland to non-agricultural land and the loss of productive farm soils. The program allows state, county, and local governments to purchase conservation easements from owners of valuable farmland. The program is funded through an annual allotment of cigarette tax revenue as well as bond funds. More than 4,100 farms have been approved for easement purchases totaling more than 450,000 acres.

The Vermont Housing and Conservation Board was created in 1987 to support a unique coalition of affordable housing, land conservation, and historic preservation. The board is provided with state funding, and it leverages federal and private funds to carry out projects within communities around the state. It has awarded $260 million to in 220 towns, leveraging more than three times that amount from private and public sources to create as many as ten thousand affordable homes, restore dozens of historic buildings, and conserve nearly six hundred farms comprising 143,000 acres of agricultural land.

The USDA's Natural Resources Conservation Service has a Farm and Ranch Land Protection Program that provides up to 50 percent of the fair market easement value in matching funds to help purchase development rights to keep productive farm- and ranchland in agricultural use. This program partners with existing state, tribal, and local governments as well as non-governmental organizations to acquire conservation easements from landowners. The program was originally enacted in 1996 and has been reauthorized and modified since then. More than $1 billion in federal Farm and Ranch Land Protection Program funds have been doubled with matching funds from local and state governments, private donors, and foundations, as well as discounts on the appraised value donated by landowners to place conservation easements on farm- and ranchlands. The indirect economic benefits of these conservation efforts to local communities are often quite significant.[14]

Farmland Protection

AGRICULTURAL ZONING. Conservation easements limit development on a voluntary basis and sometimes compensate the landowner for giving up that option. Uncompensated donations of development rights are usually eligible for income tax charitable deductions. In contrast, agricultural zoning ordinances place development restrictions on land in specific areas, and all landowners in that area must adhere to them, without compensation. Zoning may seem like a negative to some farmers; however, there are many benefits farmers can gain from agricultural zoning that limits development in their area (box 14.1).

For most of our nation's history, land use was determined solely by the property owner, but in 1926 the Supreme Court ruled that zoning may be used to safeguard and promote the health, safety, and general welfare of a community. Zoning has evolved in most communities to reflect different types of land use and thus different kinds of restrictions on its use. Common zoning districts are residential, industrial, commercial, and agricultural. Agricultural zoning, or agricultural protection zoning, refers to ordinances aimed at protecting and encouraging agriculture by maintaining its land base. Usually such zoning is implemented by a town or county in areas where there are many active farming operations and the soil is of high quality.

Agricultural zoning ordinances often restrict or prohibit activities that are not highly compatible with agriculture, such as residential and commercial development; however, they may also restrict a type or scale of agriculture by, for example, limiting the size of large-scale animal operations.[15]

Rural counties in California, Pennsylvania, and Washington began using zoning to protect agricultural land from development during the mid-1970s. In 1981 the National Agricultural Lands Study reported 270 counties with agricultural zoning. Only fifteen years later, an informal survey found agricultural zoning to be in place in almost seven hundred jurisdictions in twenty-four states.[16]

Urban growth boundaries are another type of zoning tool that can be used to protect farmland. These are intended to promote compact development by limiting the extension of sewer and water lines and schools into the countryside.[17] The boundary may be placed so there is enough buildable land within it to accommodate projected growth over the next twenty years. Although a boundary may be changed in the future, protected and preserved farmland outside the boundary helps to maintain viable farms if it is.

Like all local ordinances, agricultural zoning can be altered or eliminated if community attitudes or political leadership shift. As agricultural markets and practices change over time, there may be a need to adjust the ordinance language to accommodate new types of farms and farm activities that were not previously considered part of traditional agriculture, such as on-farm composting, agritourism, and on-farm energy production. If zoning ordinances are not written precisely, it may difficult to interpret the scale and types of practices that are covered.

Agricultural zoning by itself is not sufficient for farmland preservation, and it turns out to be a relatively minor factor. Communities that successfully preserve farmland do so in the context of a culture that values farming and farmers. They are motivated to maintain farmland into the future because of its agricultural importance, not just for its scenic value or as a way to prevent residential or commercial development of land. To be successful, farmland protection and ultimately its preservation require leadership from the agricultural community along with good communication between farmers and non-farmers.[18]

RIGHT-TO-FARM LAWS. From a distance, farming doesn't seem very noisy, smelly, or messy. But up close and personal, it often is. As residential development occurs in farming areas, people who are not familiar or comfortable with normal farming activities become neighbors of farms and are thus exposed to farming activities on a regular basis. Sometimes non-farming neighbors sue their neighboring farms over these practices. "Right-to-farm" laws were established to protect farming operations from nuisance suits. All fifty states have passed right-to-farm laws. The first was passed in 1963 when Kansas enacted a law to protect feedlots from litigation. Several states have enacted right-to-farm legislation.

There are two types of right-to-farm laws.[19] One type immunizes established farms from nuisance suits aimed at practices that are essentially no different from the practices these farms have been following all along. This protects agricultural enterprises that have been operating in a consistent way from being sued by new neighbors. The other type of law is an absolute immunity for a present or future farming operation so long as it is in compliance with applicable laws and regulations. This poses more legal issues than the first type of law because it prevents a neighbor from challenging a farm operation of any type.[20]

Most right-to-farm laws require the use of "generally accepted agricultural practices" in order to be protected from nuisance suits. The law may require the state department of agriculture to establish those standards. Otherwise it may be left to farmers to prove they are following normal practices. Some versions of right-to-farm laws set up agricultural districts. Farms within these districts are protected from nuisance suits and, in some cases, local zoning regulations that would limit normal agricultural practices.

FARMLAND TAX POLICIES. Farmland tax policies are generally aimed at helping farmers stay in business, treating farmers fairly by taxing their land based on its value for farming rather than for "higher-value" uses, and protecting farmland from development by reducing financial pressures on farmers that would cause some to sell their land. These policies are often designed to reduce the amount of property tax on farms. A common approach is differential assessment (also called current use assessment or use-value assessment), whereby farmland is taxed on the basis of its value for agricultural use rather than its fair market value, which is usually higher.

The value for agricultural use of land is what other farmers would pay for it given how much income they expect to make from using it. Fair market value is what the land is worth on the open market, whether for housing, industry, farming, or any other use. A slightly different approach to farmland tax relief, called a "circuit breaker" program, is used by a few states. This allows farmers to claim income tax credits to reduce their local property taxes. The credits are allowable only if property taxes exceed a certain percentage of a farmer's income. These programs are especially important for protecting farmland that remains in highly developed areas, since it is especially vulnerable to being lost. The combination of high land values and high property taxes can lead farmers to quit farming and sell their land for development.[21]

Tax policies that help prevent the sale of agricultural land for development can benefit communities. Converting farmland to residential land increases the demand for, and cost of, local services such as schools, road maintenance, and public safety protection. Thus local governments need to raise their property tax rates as working farm- and forestland gets developed. Studies on the cost of community services show that working farm- and forestlands generate more public revenues than they receive back in public services, and the same was found for commercial and industrial land but not for residential land.[22] It should be noted that converting land to land for commercial and industrial use may indirectly lead to an increase in residential land use since employees will need housing.

One challenge for differential assessment programs is that it can be difficult to determine the value of agricultural land. A market comparison approach can be used if there are sufficient sales of comparable land. Otherwise, the standard practice in the assessment community is to estimate net income generated by the agricultural land and to capitalize that income stream into use value.[23]

Iowa's Agricultural Land Credit Fund, established in 1939, was the first state program to provide farmers with relief from property taxes. Maryland enacted the nation's first differential assessment law in 1956. Between 1959 and 1969, twenty other states adopted differential assessment legislation. Michigan adopted its circuit breaker tax relief program in 1974. By 1989, all fifty states had at least one type of agricultural tax program for farmland owners, and several states had more than one program.[24]

Beyond Farmland: Supporting Farms and Farmers

A profitable farm with a succession plan is less likely to be sold for development than one that does not make (enough) money or one that has not laid the groundwork for intergenerational transfer once the current farmer retires. That's why many programs and organizations work to promote farm viability and farm estate planning. Without these two things, conservation easements and favorable tax policies alone are not likely to protect farms into the future. One might end up with preserved farmland but nobody to farm it.

STATEWIDE FARM VIABILITY PROGRAMS. Several states have programs that provide services to help farms make a profit and provide a decent quality of life for farmers. The Massachusetts Farm Viability Enhancement Program was started in 1996 and is administered by the state's Department of Agricultural Resources. It offers farmers environmental, technical, and business planning assistance to expand, upgrade, and modernize their existing operations. Capital for the implementation of the improvements recommended by the viability plan is available in exchange for an agricultural covenant on the farm property for a fixed term of five or ten years. To date 377 farms have participated in the program, with more than 37,000 acres placed in protective covenants. More than $16 million in grants has been made to these farms.

The New York Farm Viability Institute is a farmer-led nonprofit group that awards grant funds for applied research and education, agricultural innovation, and farm energy projects. Its goal is to help farms increase profits and provide models for other farms. It grew out of a grant to Cornell University in 2003 and in 2005 became an independent organization. It claims a 9:1 return on investment from more than two hundred projects funded, as measured by greater farm profitability, job creation, and business expansion.

The Oklahoma Farm Diversification Program provides grants of up to

$10,000 to support the development of non-traditional crops or livestock, on-farm processing of agricultural commodities, or the development of an agri-tourism venue that will promote access to a new market. Projects cannot be an extension or expansion of existing operations and must show potential to create additional income for the farm unit. Proposals are evaluated by a ten-member advisory board, and its recommendations for funding are submitted to the Oklahoma State Board of Agriculture.

The Tennessee Agricultural Enhancement Program was started in 2005 with tobacco settlement funds. It provides 35 percent cost-share assistance up to $15,000 to producers who make improvements in cattle genetics, livestock equipment, hay storage, livestock feed storage, grain storage, or diversification. Every dollar spent generates another $3.89 in the state's economy, according to a University of Tennessee study. By mid-2012, an investment of $115 million through agricultural grant and cost-share opportunities was estimated to add $447 to the state's economy.[25]

The Vermont Farm Viability Program offers business planning and technical assistance to farmers and agricultural infrastructure businesses that process, store, market, or distribute local farm and forestry products. The program started in 2003 and has worked with more than four hundred farmers and infrastructure businesses across the state. Those who complete their business plans with the program are eligible for grants toward capital expenses or additional technical support.

All of these farm viability programs aim to keep farms profitable now and for the next generation.

FARM TRANSFER PLANNING. Many if not most farms do not have a successor named for the farm business or an estate plan. There are many external threats to the long-term viability of farming and farmland, including urban sprawl, labor shortages, low prices, and complex regulations. But agriculture's self-inflicted wound is the failure of many farm families to plan for the future of their land and their farm businesses. This lack of planning can cause a family to sell their farm, or part of it, to pay inheritance taxes or to distribute the value of the estate among its heirs. Farm transfer planning is a process of decision making that protects agricultural and forest production while preserving family relationships and enhancing community development.[26]

The terms "farm succession" and "farm transfer" both refer to the passing of a farm business from one generation to the next.[27] However, "farm succession" often connotes passing down the farm between generations within a family. Sometimes it involves only handing over the management; or it may include passing down some or all of the assets. "Farm transfer" generally refers to passing the management, assets, and income from one party to another.

Transferring a farm to the next generation is not easy. It involves family interests, legal issues, tax law, personal and business finances, and the different goals and timelines of the people involved. There can be a large cast of characters, including the current farmer(s), their family and heirs, and the next generation of farmers, who may or may not be part of the family.

The process of farm transfer involves the family and the business. Transfer planning and succession planning are important for both. Transfer planning has to do with the legal and economic decisions involved in turning over the ownership of the business, land, and other property to the next generation. Succession planning involves the social decisions around managing interests and conflicts over values and roles that normally arise when farm families discuss the transfer of the business, land, and other property to the next generation.

These processes can be emotionally charged. Many farmers think of their farm as more than a business. It's their life's work, so planning to give it up is stressful. Further, many farm businesses have a lot of assets, like land and buildings, but not much cash. That makes it difficult to divide the assets among heirs without breaking up the farm. There may be tension between heirs who want the farm to stay in production and those who do not, especially if keeping the farm in production would reduce the value of their inheritance. A farm transfer plan can help deal with some of these issues if it's developed well enough in advance of when it will be needed. Each farm and family situation is unique and needs a customized plan.

Farm families that have completed their estate plans often emphasize that communication is key. While the older generation usually holds the cards in terms of ownership of assets and decision-making power, all affected parties should be involved in the discussion. Each generation of the farm family has to identify their goals. For the older generation these may include providing security for their elderly years, minimizing estate taxes, helping the next generation get into or stay in farming, and conserving the land for future generations. The younger generation may have the same goals, or not. Some heirs may want to develop land for cash. Others may want to farm the land, or have it farmed by someone else.

It's critical to determine how much income the farm business really generates, what is needed by the family or families that plan to live on the farm, as well as what income will be needed by the retiring generation. Then a transfer process can be designed that attempts to meet these needs without putting the farm business at risk. Both an estate plan and a farm transfer plan are needed. Box 14.2 outlines the many components that contribute to successful farm transfers.

Farm transfer strategies may include estate planning, such as the drawing up of wills and trusts, as well as making gifts, selling the farm outright, leasing the land to others to farm, and establishing legal entities to own some or all of the farm business assets and farmland. Limited liability companies and farm partnerships are flexible tools for gradually transferring an interest in a farm business or farmland from one part to the other. The right combination of strategies takes time to put together, and it will depend on the finances of the parties, tax considerations, and treatment of non-farm heirs. The last issue can be difficult to resolve. Leaving property to heirs in equal shares may not be appropriate if the goal is to keep the farm viable, because obviously the farming heirs will have a greater need for the farm property than the non-farming heirs. If there is not an equal value of non-farm property, this can lead to the sale of some or all of the farm unless an agreement is reached. Farm transfer planning requires the help of professionals: an attorney with experience doing farm transfers, an accountant, and a financial planner. An Extension farm management specialist can help get the process started, and that's the most immediate need for most farms if they want to remain viable into the future.

Preserving and Protecting Farmland in Montgomery County, Maryland

Agricultural activities occupy about a third of Montgomery County's land. There are 561 farms and 350 horticultural enterprises producing more than $243 million in economic activity. The majority are family-run operations, and they employ more than 10,000 residents. Forty-three percent of the county's farms are farmed as a primary occupation.

The county borders Washington, D.C., and its central and southeastern sections have largely been consumed by the expanding metropolis. The western and northern sections remain predominantly rural and family farms still dominate, with an average size of only 58 acres.

In 1964 the county adopted a planning policy called Wedges and Corridors to concentrate development along transportation corridors with wedges of preserved open space in between. In 1973 the county also adopted a rural zone, encompassing most of the western and northern agricultural areas, which required a minimum 5-acre lot size. Unfortunately, this requirement did not deter suburban development of large-lot housing. Between 1973 and 1979 the county lost 12,268 acres of farmland, mostly in the rural zone. So in 1980 a new master plan was adopted that limited development to one dwelling per 25 acres in the agricultural reserve, which expanded the boundaries of the rural zone from 80,000 to 93,000 acres, encompassing much of the remaining contiguous farmland.

Requiring larger parcels for new houses lowers land prices, especially in areas where land prices have already risen above the agricultural value. With less opportunity for subdivision, the speculative value of farmland decreases. Thus landowners in the agricultural reserve would have suffered an economic loss with the more restrictive zoning and would have strongly opposed it, without a mechanism for compensation. This mechanism, adopted in the master plan, was the transferable development rights (TDR) system. Although, with a few exceptions, properties in the agricultural reserve cannot be developed at more than one dwelling per 25 acres, under the TDR system landowners retain "development rights" at one dwelling per 5 acres that can be used elsewhere, in what are called receiving areas. They can sell the excess development rights, and thus recoup their losses, to developers interested in building at densities higher than otherwise allowed in other parts of Montgomery County. TDR receiving areas are designated by the County Planning Board and Council and conform to local master plans. They are located where more development is appropriate: where schools, roads, and utilities are already in place or along major transportation corridors.

More than 40,000 acres of farmland have been preserved in perpetuity through TDR transfers in Montgomery County. When TDRs are sold, they are permanently removed from the property. Although their market consists only of the receiving areas designated by the county, the TDRs are valued and sold in an open market without government interference. Another 10,000 acres of farmland have been preserved through county and state conservation easement programs that allow farmers to voluntarily limit development on their property in perpetuity. Selling conservation easements to the county on a 150-acre farm, for example, may generate as much as $400,000; there are tax benefits too.

In Montgomery County, farmland preservation programs are not run by the planning or environmental agencies but by the Agricultural Services Division of the Department of Economic Development, which also oversees traditional agricultural economic assistance, such as drought relief, and the county's conservation easement programs. The department also acts as a clearinghouse for the state easement programs. This way, a farmer can do one-stop shopping and compare the multiple state and local easement programs.[28]

Preserving and Protecting Farmland in Skagit County, Washington

The Skagit Valley has highly fertile farmland and produces a variety of crops, livestock, and dairy. It is also a major producer of flower bulbs and vegetable seeds. Located between Seattle and Vancouver, Canada, the area faces growing population and development pressures. More than 150,000 acres were farmed in the 1940s; today that number is down to 93,000.

In 1989 an attempt to develop a theme park on prime farmland led to the founding of Skagitonians to Preserve Farmland (SPF) by five farm families and their friends. One of SPF's first efforts was to advocate for Skagit County's Right to Farm Ordinance, which was enacted in 1991. The following year SPF compiled and published *Farmland Protection in Skagit County: Program Options and Recommendations*, a document that helped shape Skagit County's current development code. By 1995, SPF had a full-time executive director.

A 1996 survey of voters indicated strong support for farmland preservation, including an increase in property taxes to purchase development rights on farmland. The following year the county adopted an ordinance to increase property taxes for the purpose of preserving farmland, which led to the creation of Skagit County's Farmland Legacy Program. Since 2008 the program has preserved nearly 10,000 acres of farmland.

Skagit County also has an Agriculture and Natural Resource Land zoning district that encompasses roughly 80 percent of the county's farmland. The zone allows only one residential dwelling per 40 acres, and it restricts allowable uses to those consistent with agricultural production and businesses.

The county promotes farm viability by co-sponsoring the Festival of Family Farms, and it hosts the Skagit Tulip Festival, which draws hundreds of thousands of visitors annually. Washington State University Extension in Skagit County and its partners offer Sustainable Farm Business Planning courses and workshops for new farmers. The county's Agricultural Advisory Board is another asset; it serves to connect the county with the agricultural community and promote economic opportunities for agriculture.[29]

Farms and Farmland for the Future

While there are many examples of successful farmland protection and preservation programs that enhance the viability of farms, the nation has a long way to go to stabilize its base of farms and farmland for the future. More comprehensive approaches, coupled with more funding, will be needed to achieve this goal. The most successful farmland preservation programs combine significant local and state funding for farmland preservation with a package of different farmland protection techniques.[30] These programs in turn need to be combined with efforts to help farmers maintain profitable businesses and then transfer them to the next generation when they retire.

15 ∾ *Improving Food Systems*

Food systems are like living organisms — always changing. Some parts live on while others die; every part is altered over time, for better or for worse. Individual changes in a complex system are not simply good or bad; they have multiple consequences. This range of effects contributes to diverse perspectives about the positive and negative impacts such changes have. People have vastly different ideas about the best course of action to improve food systems.

For example, pesticides and fertilizers have helped increase food production, but they have also caused environmental degradation. Should we strive to avoid using agrichemicals or to simply use them more safely? Fast foods have increased the availability of low-cost, high-calorie foods that contribute to an obesity epidemic. Should we try to eliminate processed foods or push for healthier junk food?[1] Are food retailers the problem, or are consumers making poor dietary choices? Large farms now produce most of our food, yet small farms account for the majority of farmers, farmland, and agricultural communities. Should we continue to encourage the "efficiency" of large farms or place greater emphasis on other desirable attributes that would favor small-scale food production? The answers to these questions are subjective and based on values to a large extent, although facts may be used for justification.

Around any given food system issue there are numerous strategies for positive change, driven by divergent views. Many of these strategies, despite being based on different philosophies, are not mutually exclusive. For example, we need to develop more effective non-chemical pest control practices *and* we need more judicious use of synthetic pesticides. Fast food chains should offer healthier foods *and* consumers should make better food choices. Both large farms *and* small farms need to be more sustainable.

There will never be consensus on a specific plan to follow, but progress toward just, resilient, and sustainable food systems will be facilitated by clear descriptions of desired outcomes, from aspirational visions down to actions with measurable results. Success will require enthusiasm for the visions and participation in the actions by a critical mass of people from all food system levels: producers, consumers, marketers, scientists, business leaders, policy makers, and educators. Not everyone has to be on board, just enough people from across the food spectrum to create "tipping points" that lead to signifi-

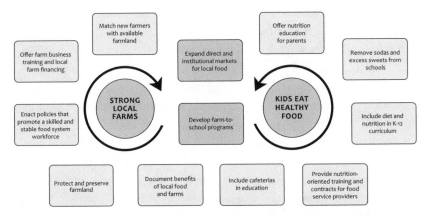

FIGURE 15.1 Nonlinear depiction of food system goals. Fulfilling either of the central goals depends on achieving numerous sub-goals, shown clustered around them. The central goals of strong local farms and kids eating healthier food share two sub-goals: expanding direct and institutional markets for local food and developing farm-to-school programs. These connections suggest that efforts to strengthen local farms and improve kids' diets should be intentionally linked in food system plans.

cant and lasting improvements. It won't be easy, but much work has already been done that can be built upon. And it's not optional; improved food systems are essential for the long-term health of our planet and survival of its growing human population.

Typically, plans for improving food systems include

– a rationale for change based on critical issues to address;
– a compelling vision for the future;
– core principles to guide specific strategies or desired changes;
– actions to implement those strategies and facilitate change; and
– concrete measures of success.

This type of hierarchical plan is useful, but it can lead to linear thinking and approaches that focus on isolated issues. The leverage points of a food system are where interactions occur; therefore, it's also important to identify comprehensive, nonlinear approaches to addressing multiple issues with a set of interconnected strategies (fig. 15.1).

Identifying Critical Issues

The chapters in this book summarize some of the issues that must be addressed to improve food systems for the future, such as climate change, energy use, farm labor, and new farmers. Over the years, many government-sponsored reports have addressed these and other key issues, from the environmental impacts of farming to the effects of diet on human health. Some of these reports offered recommendations that pushed the boundaries of conventional thinking at the time of their publication. These are important to consider as we develop new plans to improve food systems.

With regard to agriculture, the USDA's 1980 *Report and Recommendations on Organic Farming* lent credibility to farming systems that avoided reliance on purchased inputs.[2] It indicated that tens of thousands of farmers were already farming organically and recognized that more research and education were needed to support them. A year later, the USDA issued a report on the condition of farming and its place in the food system, called *A Time to Choose*.[3] The report warned that a few large farms would end up controlling food production unless changes were made to policies and programs.

The National Research Council's 1989 report *Alternative Agriculture* pointed out that "federal polices work against environmentally benign practices and the adoption of alternative agricultural systems, particularly those involving crop rotation, certain soil conservation practices, reductions in pesticide use, and increased use of biological and cultural means of pest control. These policies have generally made a plentiful food supply a higher priority than protection of the resource base."[4]

The USDA's Small Farms Commission 1998 report *A Time to Act* documented the importance of small farms for the nation's food supply, rural economies, and a strong society.[5] It noted that the pace of industrialization had quickened, and time was running out to support something other than a vertically integrated global food processing and distribution system.

Significant reports on the connection between food choices and human health were also released during the same period. In 1977 a U.S. Senate committee report recognized that people needed dietary goals to help make healthier food choices.[6] It suggested that people consume only as much energy as they expended, while increasing their consumption of complex carbohydrates and reducing their consumption of refined and processed sugars and fat.

In 1980 the USDA and Health and Human Services Department issued *Nutrition and Your Health: Dietary Guidelines for Americans* to help people make good daily food choices.[7] This publication has been revised every five years since, to reflect emerging science and emerging public health concerns like obesity. In 1989 the National Research Council published *Diet and Health: Implications for Reducing Chronic Disease Risk*, which identified ways in which diet affects the risk of chronic diseases; it made eating behavior recommendations for reducing those risks.[8]

Taking a more holistic view than previous reports, a 2010 National Research Council report on agricultural systems pointed to the need for integrated research and extension that focuses on the interactions among productivity, environmental, economic, and social sustainability.[9]

Food System Visions and Principles

Improving food systems begins with a vision for an ideal system. Vision statements are meant to be aspirational, not measurable. They are useful for guiding strategies and actions that should have measurable goals. Vision statements tend to frame problems associated with critical issues into positive outcomes—for example, "People will have a healthy diet" rather than "Fewer people will be undernourished or obese." Sustainable farm and food system visions usually contain similar themes, but they vary in how they are worded and which issues are emphasized. Here are some examples.

> We envision a vibrant, just and sustainable food system where: all people, at all times, have physical and economic access to sufficient, safe, nutritious and culturally-acceptable food for an active and healthy life; the principles of ecological sustainability, sustainable livelihoods for food providers, and social justice for all are upheld; the local population actively participates in the decision-making processes related to food at a municipal, regional, and national levels; people have the desire, opportunity, and means to actively engage in all aspects of the food system; and food is celebrated as central to both culture and community. (Just Food, Ottawa)[10]

> We envision a county in which everyone has access to affordable, nutritious food. Local farms and operations play a primary role in producing that food. Each part of the food system, from seed to table and back to soil, is environmentally regenerative, economically viable, and supports a healthy life for all members of our community. (Sonoma County Healthy and Sustainable Food Action Plan)[11]

> Agriculture in the Northeast will be diversified and profitable, providing healthful products to its customers; it will be conducted by farmers who manage resources wisely, who are satisfied with their lifestyles, and have a positive *influence on their communities and the environment.* (Northeast SARE Outcome Statement)[12]

There are four major components or principles that can be found in these and similar visionary descriptions of an "ideal" food system: (1) ecological/environmental sustainability, (2) economic vitality/viability, (3) equal access to healthy, affordable food, and (4) justice/shared power in the food system (box 15.1). These can be subdivided into more specific principles that are easier to align with measurable goals.

15.1 *Principles of a Healthy, Sustainable Food System as Defined by a Coalition of Diet, Health, and Planning Organizations*

1. HEALTH-PROMOTING
- Supports the physical and mental health of all farmers, workers, and eaters.
- Accounts for the public health impacts across the entire life cycle in which food is produced, processed, packaged, labeled, distributed, marketed, consumed, and disposed.

2. SUSTAINABLE
- Conserves, protects, and regenerates natural resources, landscapes, and biodiversity.
- Meets our current food and nutrition needs without compromising the ability of the system to meet the needs of future generations.

3. RESILIENT
- Thrives in the face of challenges, such as unpredictable climate, increased pest resistance, and declining, increasingly expensive water and energy supplies.

4. DIVERSE
- Includes a diverse range of food production, transformation, distribution, marketing, consumption, and disposal practices, occurring at diverse scales, from local and regional to national and global.
- Considers geographic differences in natural resources, climate, customs, and heritage.
- Appreciates and supports a diversity of cultures, socio-demographics, and lifestyles.
- Provides a variety of health-promoting food choices for all.

5. FAIR
- Supports fair and just communities and conditions for all farmers, workers, and eaters
- Provides equitable physical access to affordable food that is health promoting and culturally appropriate.

6. ECONOMICALLY BALANCED
- Provides economic opportunities that are balanced across geographic regions of the country and at different scales of activity, from local to global, for a diverse range of food system stakeholders.
- Affords farmers and workers in all sectors of the system a living wage.

Resilience and Sustainability

Most people would agree that a healthy food system should be both resilient and sustainable (fig. 15.2). Although these goals are complementary, they are not the same. Resilience addresses relatively short-term responses to disturbances; sustainability addresses whole-system management for long-term stability.

For example, resilience is the short-term ability to bounce back from an extreme weather event by re-establishing food production and distribution; sustainability is the longer-term ability to cope with extreme weather conditions in a manner that does not disrupt food production. Resilience is the ability to harvest, process, store, and distribute food for a limited period of time when the electrical grid goes down or when fossil fuel supplies are interrupted. Sustainability is the ability to meet the food system's energy needs for generations to come using renewable, reliable, and affordable energy sources.

Different metrics are needed to assess the resilience and sustainability of food system components. At the field level, resilience measurements might include the water-holding capacity of soil during drought, the ability of land to drain excess rainfall, resistance to wind and water erosion, and the extent of crop insurance coverage. Sustainability measurements might include CO_2 equivalents generated and Btus of fossil energy used per unit of food produced, annual soil erosion rate, and average net profit per acre over many years.

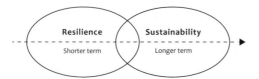

FIGURE 15.2 Resilience and sustainability. These goals are not mutually exclusive, but they occur at different points on the time horizon.

Some metrics can address both resilience and sustainability, since they affect both long- and short-term outcomes. For example, measures of soil heath like compaction and organic matter content affect the ability of land to withstand short-term drought and flooding, and they also affect long-term energy consumption (in the form of fertilizers, tillage, and irrigation) and thus farm viability. Efforts to improve food systems need to account for changes in both resilience and sustainability.

Levels of Food System Change

Three levels of change are adaptation, mitigation, and transformation. These require different levels of rigor, and they contribute to resilience and sustainability over different time horizons. Adaptation is coping with a problem in the short term. Mitigation is reducing the extent of the problem over the medium term. Transformation is solving the problem for the long term.

For example, adaptation to forest fires includes buying fire trucks to help put fires out. Mitigation is using a Smokey the Bear education campaign to change people's behavior so they start fewer forest fires. Transformation is changing the way forests are managed, allowing a natural cycle of burning and regrowth so that forest fires are kept small and are thus no longer a problem.

Another example, adaptation to low yields of continuous corn on a compacted soil means applying a lot of soluble fertilizer; mitigation involves subsoiling or plowing to improve root exploration and nutrient uptake; and transformation entails changing the cropping system to include rotation with perennial sods, timely additions of compost, and reduced tillage. The transformed cropping system no longer needs soluble fertilizer and subsoiling. It is managed in a way that is sustainable over the long term.

Adaptation, mitigation, and transformation can be addressed at the same time, using complementary tactics. The important thing is not to stop at the first two. Without transformation, we'll always be coping with symptoms rather than solving the underlying problems.

Let's use an extreme weather event, such as a flood and its impact on a region's food system, as a context for considering the three levels. The first reaction to such an event is bound to be adaptation: How can we better cope with this kind of disruption? Farms in the floodplains can have better warning systems, testing can be developed to determine whether flooded food and livestock feed are safe to sell, and backup generators can be distributed for short-term power to protect food in storage. Mitigation looks farther ahead: How can the impact of future floods be reduced? Farm structures can be designed to avoid damage from moving water, riparian buffers can be planted to protect fields from erosion, alternative crops can be grown in floodplains that can withstand exposure to floodwater and still be of value, and off-the-grid energy systems can keep the power on indefinitely when the grid goes down. Transformation seeks to avoid the problem entirely. Watershed-level changes in land-use patterns and waterway management can prevent flooding damage if excess rainfall is distributed and absorbed across the landscape. Changes in the type and amount of energy used can reduce greenhouse gas emissions, so climate change is abated along with its contribution to more intense and frequent extreme weather.

Comprehensive combinations of adaptation, mitigation, and transformation are needed to address all of the big food system problems we face, from the childhood diabesity epidemic, to loss of farms and farmland, to excessive consolidation of food production, processing, and sales.

The type of information in box 15.2 wouldn't matter to everyone, but a whole lot of people, probably a critical mass, would start to think more critically about what they were eating and how their food dollars were being "invested." Social media and new communication technologies can create information networks that will help unleash this new level of food awareness and consumer power. "The network, in short, has begun to erode power relationships we had come to believe were permanent features of capitalism: the helplessness of the consumer . . . the power of mainstream media empires to shape ideology . . . and the inevitability of monopolization by large corporations."[13]

The quick response (QR) code is an example of a tool that can be used to disseminate detailed information about food products. Easily recognized by handheld devices, this symbol can instantly connect consumers to a wealth of information on a website. From local cheese, to a loaf of bread or bag of carrots from your region, to a box of pasta from across the continent, to coffee beans from Central America—a little corner of the label could take you to a summary of the farms involved in making the ingredients, the stewardship practices they use, the companies that own the brands, and the benefits they deliver, or not, to the communities where the food is made. The key will be enforcing transparency and honesty, so that labels and linked information can't suggest certain qualities or behaviors without verification.

Food System Plans

Many states, counties, and cities have developed plans to improve their food systems. Some of these contain specific, measurable goals and methods for tracking progress toward the goals (tables 15.1 and 15.2).

15.2 *Examples of Comprehensive Combinations of Adaptation, Mitigation, and Transformation to Address Food System Problems*

Imagine how the diets of children will improve when:
- all schools have staff members who help kids with their diet and health needs;
- limits are placed on children's consumption of sugary beverages;
- farm-to-school education programs are part of the K-12 curricula;
- federal school food programs provide local fresh food rather than excess commodity food;
- school cooks have the capacity and skill to serve delicious, nutritious, whole foods;
- food and health advisory committees are widespread in communities with schools;
- cafeterias are involved in educating kids about food systems.

Imagine how little farmland will be lost when:
- all productive farms with full-time farmers pay reduced property taxes;
- model farmland preservation and protection programs are widely adopted;
- a farmers' retirement fund is set up in every state;
- local and regional food security is a federal policy priority;
- farming is recognized by land-use planners as the best long-term use of fertile soil.

Imagine how many new farmers there will be if:
- young people with documented skills can get zero-interest farm mortgages;
- angel investors are organized to support new farms until they are successfully established;
- non-farming landowners have tax incentives to sign long-term leases with farmers;
- support for programs linking farmland for sale with potential farmers is institutionalized instead of soft-funded;
- new farmers are recognized as essential to public well-being on a par with doctors, firefighters, and teachers.

Imagine how consumer spending on food products will shift when:
- food labels provide point-of-origin information for major ingredients;
- food produced with GMOs, antibiotics, or hormones is clearly identified;
- food products cannot put "farm" in their name unless they are produced by real farms;
- the ratio of fossil energy consumed to calorie content of a food is on the label;

– the condition of workers who harvest and process food is truthfully revealed on labels;

– educational efforts abound that help people understand how their food purchases shape food systems.

Structural Features of Healthy Food Systems

Food system plans often present goals without mentioning the changes in the system's structure that have to be made in order for those goals to be achieved. The structure of relationships plays an important role in a food system. Horizontal relationships built around more than just economic activities can promote the development of values-driven behaviors in a food system, compared with relatively anonymous and narrowly focused vertical relationships that emphasize economic goals while minimizing others. Horizontal relationships are necessary to create added "market value" for food system attributes such as environmental quality, cultural enrichment, and long-term community well-being. Several organizational characteristics of a food system can promote horizontal relationships, and these can be addressed in food system plans. They are distributed systems, economies of scope, and transparency.

Distributed systems is a term used in computer science to describe an arrangement of networked computers that communicate and coordinate their actions in order to achieve a common goal. This design is also everywhere in nature, from ant colonies to bacterial populations (fig. 15.3). The opposite approach is centralization and standardization in a system to create uniformity and simplicity for the sake of low-cost operation.

Distributed systems start new enterprises using models proved to be effective, rather than expanding single, effective enterprises into larger and larger entities. Thus they scale out, or distribute, rather than scale up, or consolidate. This leads to many similar entities doing things just a little bit differently from one another, each with the ability to adapt to the needs and resources of their local environment and the freedom to deviate from the norm through experimentation and innovation. Communication across the entities in the system creates a "learning community" that encourages sharing of new information. In the context of food systems, distributing production and processing across a landscape creates redundancy of capacity, knowledge, and training opportunities, which in the aggregate can provide regional and national food security and resilience.

TABLE 15.1 *Sonoma County Healthy and Sustainable Food Action Plan*

Goal	Measurable Indicators
1. Protect and enhance agricultural land base, farms, and ranches.	Acres in agricultural production, number of farms, number of acres in farmland preservation program
2. Encourage resource management.	Number of organic growers, tonnage of food composted
3. Support local food system jobs and commerce.	Mean annual wages of food system, annual sales of agricultural and food products, number of farmers' markets, number of CSAS
4. Encourage institutional purchasing that supports the local food system.	Number of school districts with farm-to-school programs, net farm income
5. Increase access to healthy, affordable, safe, and culturally appropriate food and beverage choices, while decreasing availability of unhealthy choices.	Percent of adults who are obese, percent of children and teens consuming two or more glasses of soda or sugary drinks daily, number of farmers' markets that accept fresh food coupons
6. Connect the food insecure with food and nutrition assistance programs.	Percent of eligible participation in fresh food coupon programs, percent of eligible students participating in school lunch program
7. Increase education about local agriculture, nutrition, and the impact of food and beverage choices.	Number of public high schools with food and agricultural literacy programs, number of community, school, and private gardens
8. Address root causes of hunger and food insecurity.	Percent of residents that live in households above 300% of the federal poverty level, percent of residents who spend 30% or more of household income on rent; percent of adults in food-secure households
9. Create opportunity and justice for farmers, farm workers, and food system workers.	Average wage paid to farm workers, percent of farms with ethnic minority as principal operator, percent of farms with women as principal operator
10. Increase community resilience.	Number of people served by food banks per month

Ag Innovations Network, "Sonoma County Healthy and Sustainable Food Action Plan," County of Sonoma Department of Health Services and Sonoma County Food System Alliance, Sebastopol, CA, 2012.

TABLE 15.2 *West Virginia Food Economy Scorecard*

Goal		Indicator of Progress	Rate of Change since First Year	Rate of Change since Last Scorecard	Getting Better (+), Worse (−), or Stable (~) since Last Scorecard
Goal 1: Youth and new farmers participate in the agricultural economy	1.1	Average age of farmers	3% older	n/a	n/a
	1.2	Number of farms	5% fewer	4% fewer	−
	1.3	Job placement of high school agricultural program graduates into agricultural fields	51% higher	41% higher	+
	1.4	Participation in Future Farmers of America	unchanged	4% higher	+
Goal 2: Schools and institutions buy healthy local food	2.1	Number of county school systems purchasing local food	n/a	29% higher	+
Goal 3: The public consumes healthy local food at a household level	3.1	Farms making direct sales for human consumption	39% more	n/a	n/a
	3.2	Total value of direct sales	55% more	n/a	n/a
	3.3	Household food insecurity	18% higher	1% higher	~
	3.4	Obesity rate	7% higher	3% higher	−
	3.5	Childhood obesity rate	8% lower	n/a	n/a
	3.6	Diabetes rate	2% lower	6% lower	+
Goal 4: Local farmers increase their income and are profitable	4.1	Market value of agricultural products sold	36% higher	12% higher	+
	4.2	Value of average sales per farm	43% higher	14% higher	+
	4.3	Number of farms where farming is operator's primary occupation	7% fewer	n/a	n/a

Note: Each goal has subgoals that have measurable indicators of progress. Data are available from government or nonprofit sources for each sub-goal, so the rate of positive or negative change can be tracked over time. The 2013 scorecard provides initial answers about whether indicators are getting better or worse; however, rates of change must be interpreted with care. For the purposes of this scorecard, if a rate of change from the last scorecard is 3% or less, it is counted as stable.

West Virginia Food & Farm Coalition, "West Virginia's Road Map for the Food Economy," Oak Hill, WV, 2012.

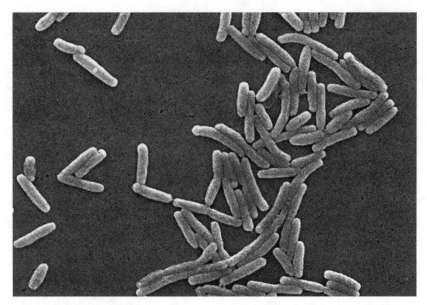

FIGURE 15.3 Bacterial colony. A colony of bacteria is somewhat analogous to a distributed food system. Each bacterium has individual needs, but the organisms work together to achieve well-being for the entire population. They are similar enough in structure and function to cooperate, but some level of individual variation is necessary to allow the whole population to improve and adapt to new conditions. An individual bacterium does not grow ever-larger; it replicates once it has achieved an optimal size.

Economies of scope are derived from value achieved through variety and complementarity rather than simplicity and uniformity, which characterize economies of scale (figs. 15.4 and 15.5). Economies of scope result in advantages when synergy among processes is used to deliver several distinct products or services. Economies of scale result in advantages when standardization of processes is used to deliver large volumes of identical products or services.

In a business context, "economies of scope" typically refers to a company that lowers its costs by making and marketing several different but related products, such as toothpaste, shampoo, and cosmetics, which may contain some of the same ingredients and can be similarly branded. In a food system context, economies of scope derive from multiple market relationships for different forms and uses of a product and its by-products. A simple example is a food processor that peels and packages first-quality vegetables, makes soup with the seconds, and uses the culls and peelings to provide feed for a local pig farmer, who in return provides bacon for some of the soups.

Transparency refers to a robust system for defining, verifying, and communicating the quality and integrity of food, and where and how it is produced and processed. Some of this can and does occur through regulation, and some is the result of an open and democratic process in the marketplace. Regulations already require listing basic ingredients — fat, sugar, and salt content, for example. They also prevent the use of certain practices (e.g., the use of illegal pesticides, uninspected slaughtering) the absence of which is not described on food labels but is expected by consumers. Information about other attributes is revealed when companies perceive a competitive advantage in providing it or when consumers demand it.

Food attributes or claims that are market-driven typically require third-party verification to be credible to consumers. As shown in figure 15.6, these may include unregulated attributes of specific types of foods (e.g., "bird-friendly" coffee) or attributes that exceed minimum regulatory standards (e.g., "animal-welfare-approved" meat); they may also address multiple attributes and foods (e.g., "certified sustainable"). The type of information available to consumers on the label or through the certifier's website can include verification of animal and crop production practices, environmental stewardship, point of origin, food safety, and/or treatment of workers. For all these attributes, the development of standards and methods used to verify compliance are complex and pose both intellectual and logistical challenges.

Local food systems diminish the demand for label information to the extent that knowledge of production practices can be obtained through direct observation and personal relationships. These stem from participation in CSAS, farmers' markets, roadside stands, food cooperatives, and locally owned/operated food businesses. An example of this can be seen in the many small, direct-market vegetable farms that follow organic farming standards but do not feel the need to become certified. Their relationships with local customers are personal, creating sufficient confidence about their commitment to organic production practices to diminish the need for third-party verification or organic labeling. In contrast, organic milk producers generally sell their product to a processor, so documentation through organic certification ensures that the product is indeed organic and allows the retail milk container to be legally labeled as organic.

As in the case of organic milk, which is often sold beyond a purely local market to a wider region, other value chains that do not allow for direct interaction with food producers tend to recruit consumers by being more transparent about production practices and business ownership than is typical of other wholesale products. Labeling and localization or regionalization of food

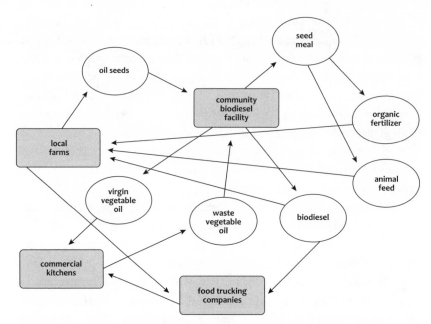

FIGURE 15.4 Economies of scope with community-scale biodiesel production. Local energy, food production, and food retailing are intertwined through the flow of materials. Value is gained by creating many possible uses and markets for products and co-products.

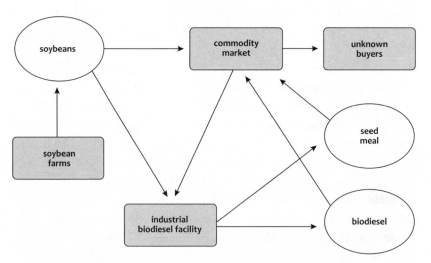

FIGURE 15.5 Economies of scale with industrial biodiesel production. Producers of raw materials are partially disconnected from processors and completely disconnected from end users. Value is gained by increasing production while lowering per unit cost.

FIGURE 15.6 Examples of third-party-verified food attributes. These logos show a range of food attributes that now have third-party verification systems to provide transparency and thus consumer assurance.

can be effective tools for creating greater transparency. Other, emerging tools include external evaluation and online communities. An example of external evaluation is Oxfam's Behind the Brands scorecard, which ranks the world's largest food and beverage companies for the impact of their policies on hunger, poverty, land use, and the environment.[14] It urges consumers to contact the companies about their efforts, or lack thereof, saying, "Change the way the food companies that make your favorite brands do business." As a result of this program, thirty-three major investment funds, representing nearly $1.4 trillion of assets under management, called on the ten biggest food and beverage companies in the world to do more to reduce social and environmental risks in their supply chains.[15]

Online community efforts to promote transparency are relatively new. They include crowdsourced websites such as Real Time Farms, which aims to help consumers trace food back to the farm it came from, whether eating at home or in restaurants.[16] Wiki-spaces are being developed to allow consumers to aggregate their knowledge of farms and food products.

There are many ways to improve transparency, economies of scope, and distributed systems. These are important goals for improving our food systems and can lead to action steps with meaningful outcomes.

Taking Action

It is not possible to change a food system all at once. The challenge is to focus on key issues while recognizing their connection to other aspects of the system. Here, a variety of food system thinkers and activists offer their views on critical issues and how to address them to improve our food system:

The food system is modeled on the plantation system, where labor is seen as a commodity to be obtained at the lowest possible cost to enable greater profit. This is generally true for farming, food processing, and food retailing. Farmworkers are especially vulnerable because they are intentionally excluded by the National Labor Relations Board from protections given to other workers, making it difficult for them to negotiate wages and working conditions by organizing into unions. Furthermore, policies that encourage reliance on foreign labor make it even harder for the food and farm workforce to be treated with the respect. To change this situation requires a food system that not only values healthy, safe food, and respect for the environment but also the dignity of human beings that work to produce food. Food justice should be a priority, supported by certification programs that create the basis for change in consumer buying, so they demand a higher standard for the treatment of food system workers. (Nelson Carrasquillo, General Coordinator, El Comité de Apoyo a Los Trabajadores Agrícolas [Farmworkers Support Committee])

To reach the goals of a reformed food system, universities and nonprofit organizations must have the ability to conduct transformative research that is linked to practical applications. This means that researchers must learn how to carry out systems-oriented inquiry and transdisciplinary projects while educators must utilize both didactic methods and hands-on experience to instill learners with the depth and breadth of knowledge needed to deal with complex problems. There is not nearly enough of this type of research and education going on in food and agriculture programs. Given their historical role and need to stay relevant, land-grant universities should be taking the lead in conducting systems research and putting graduates out into the world with expertise that cuts across disciplinary boundaries. University and college administrators, as well as students, funders, food system businesses, and advocates, have to step up to push these new approaches to research and education to the forefront. (Kate Clancy, Food Systems Consultant; Visiting Scholar, Johns Hopkins School of Public Health; Adjunct Professor, Tufts University)

Perhaps the single most important task facing us to improve our future food system is restoring the biological health of our soils. Relying on external, synthetic inputs to achieve yields instead of incorporating compost, cover crops, etc. for most of the past century, we have degraded and eroded most of our soils. Now that we will soon be entering a time of increased energy costs and depleting fertilizer resources (rock phosphate and potash) we will need to adopt management practices that are necessary to restoring soil health. In addition to restoring soil fertility, biologically healthy soils will also provide food quality and health benefits to our food. (Fred Kirschenman, Distinguished Fellow, Iowa State University Leopold Center; President, Stone Barns, NY; Farmer, North Dakota)

We need to rein in climate change before it is hard for any farmer anywhere to grow us the food we need. When Hurricane Irene dropped record quantities of rain on my Vermont in 2011—the kind of downpours only possible in a globally warmed world—too many farm fields simply turned to rocks and sand as our rivers rampaged. Similarly, it got too hot across the Midwest in 2012 for corn to grow well, even on the most productive soil on the planet. I have great confidence in the ability of farmers, and eaters, to reconstitute a working agricultural system—it's been exhilarating to watch the process over the last fifteen years. But that progress will be overwhelmed by climate change unless, in addition to the hard work of growing food, farmers (and everyone else) take seriously their role as citizens, and join in the spreading movement to stand up to the power of the fossil fuel industry. (Bill McKibben, author and Distinguished Scholar, Middlebury College)

Agricultural policies should be brought in line with health policies. Right now, plenty of federal policies support our existing industrial food production system based on highly concentrated raising of farm animals or commodity monoculture. Production of healthier foods and the sustainable and more conserving methods of agriculture do not get supported to anywhere near the same extent. I'd like to see agricultural policies that encourage production of fruits and vegetables at prices that are affordable, that make a living for farmers, and that maximize health and minimize harm to farmworkers, farm animals, and the environment. We could do this, if only we had the political will. (Marion Nestle, Professor of Nutrition, Food Studies, and Public Health, New York University)

Direct marketing, in all its forms, has grown into a dynamic way to feed people while educating them about the family farms that grow their food. However, it reaches fewer than 5 percent of the population. So it's critical that we build the marketing, logistics, and distribution pathways that enable small- and medium-sized farms to sell to wholesale markets, profitably. This involves transportation, food safety, traceability systems, farm identity promotion, packaging, quality control, and business planning at the farm level. If we get this right, people who don't buy from farmers' markets or CSAs will also be able to eat regional farm-fresh foods they find at their grocery stores and restaurants. (Michael Rozyne, Executive Director, Red Tomato and Co-Founder, Equal Exchange)

Our food system would be healthier if people ate less meat and animal products, and when they did, only products from animals that have been raised with respect and kindness on farms that provide access to the outdoors. Animal factories that confine farm animals in cramped conditions inside windowless buildings, depriving them of basic needs, should be outlawed. This industrial system is not only inhumane, but a danger to human health. The concentration of manure produced by these factories pollutes the environment, while the hormones and drugs administrated to animals enter our food and water systems, putting the public at risk. In addition, human health is jeopardized by the overuse of antibiotics for this type of industrial animal production, which has created "super bugs" that are resistant to antibiotics. (Judy Wick, Founder of White Dog Café and Co-Founder of Business Alliance for Local Living Economies)

Conclusion

Everyone must eat. The call to improve food systems has the potential for widespread impact, well beyond most societal challenges. To date, the many problems posed by modern food systems, whether dietary behavior, farm labor, land use, rural economic development, or water quality, have been addressed in relative isolation. These problems can best be solved by addressing their multiple root causes and by applying knowledge of the complex relationships at work within and among the issues.

The time has come to acknowledge that simple solutions to these problems are rarely effective, whether in business, education, research, or policy. Bold thinking is needed to secure a bright future for food systems, by changing the way people in these systems interact and the measures of success they employ. Practical plans for making these changes must be implemented by coalitions, and the work needs to be done at all levels of the system. Whether the plans focus on local food or international trade, they must have measurable goals that are ambitious but achievable. The result will be enduring sustenance for people, protection of natural resources, and a stronger social fabric stretching from the household to the global food system.

Notes

1. INTRODUCTION TO FOOD SYSTEMS

Epigraph: Peter M. Senge, *The Fifth Discipline: The Art and Practice of the Learning Organization* (New York: Doubleday, 2006).

1. Vern Grubinger, Linda Berlin, Elizabeth Berman, Naomi Fukagawa, Jane Kolodinsky, Deborah Neher, Bob Parsons, Amy Trubek, and Kimberly Wallin, *University of Vermont Transdisciplinary Research Initiative Spire of Excellence Proposal: Food Systems* (Burlington: University of Vermont, 2010).

2. Parke Wilde, *Food Policy in the United States: An Introduction* (New York: Routledge, 2013).

3. University of Connecticut and University of Vermont, *The Bobolink Project: Helping Farmers Protect Grassland Birds*, 2013. www.bobolinkproject.org (accessed April 27, 2014).

4. Peter Morgan, *The Idea and Practice of Systems Thinking and Their Relevance for Capacity Development* (Maastricht: European Centre for Development Policy Management, 2005).

5. Statistic Brain, *Coffee Drinking Statistics*, January 1, 2014. www.statisticbrain.com /coffee-drinking-statistics (accessed April 27, 2014).

6. Jeffery Sobal and Carole A. Bosogi, "Constructing Food Choice Decisions," *Annals of Behavioral Medicine* (December 2009): S37–S46.

7. Frank Newport, "In U.S., 5% Consider Themselves Vegetarians," Gallup Well-Being, 2012.

8. Michael Boland, *Kosher Industry Profile* (Ames: University of Iowa, Agricultural Marketing Resource Center, 2010).

9. Organic Trade Association, *2011 Organic Industry Survey* (Brattleboro, VT: Organic Trade Association, 2011).

10. Hartman Group, Inc., *Beyond Organic & Natural, 2010: Resolving Confusion in Marketing Foods and Beverages* (Bellevue, WA: Hartman Group, 2010).

11. TJH Research and Strategy, *A Survey of Consumer Behavior and Perceptions*, Appalachian Sustainable Agriculture Project, 2011.

12. Alan W. Hodges and Thomas J. Stevens, *Local Food Systems in Florida: Consumer Characteristics and Economic Impacts* (Gainesville: University of Florida, Food and Resource Economics Department, 2013).

13. U.S. Department of Agriculture Economic Research Service, *Ag and Food Statistics: Charting the Essentials / Food Security and Nutrition Assistance*, 2013. www .ers.usda.gov/data-products/ag-and-food-statistics-charting-the-essentials/food -security-and-nutrition-assistance.aspx (accessed January 2014).

14. Alisha Coleman-Jensen, Mark Nord, Margaret Andrews, and Steven Carlson, *Household Food Security in the United States in 2011 (ERR-141)*, Economic Research Report, Economic Research Service (Washington, DC: U.S. Department of Agriculture, 2012).

15. U.S. Department of Agriculture Economic Research Service, *Ag and Food Statistics*.

16. U.S. Department of Agriculture Economic Research Service, *Ag and Food Statistics: Charting the Essentials / Food Prices and Spending*, 2013. www.ers.usda.gov /data-products/ag-and-food-statistics-charting-the-essentials/food-prices-and -spending.aspx (accessed January 2014).

17. Bruce Butterfield, *The Impact of Home and Community Gardening in America* (South Burlington, VT: National Gardening Association, 2009); American Livestock Breeds Conservancy and Tractor Supply Company, "Chicken Ownership in U.S. Has Potential for Significant Growth," Tractor Supply Company press release, April 18, 2012, Mother Earth News website, www.motherearthnews.com/homesteading -and-livestock/chicken-ownership-in-u-s-has-potential-for-significant-growth.aspx (accessed April 27, 2014).

18. Steve Martinez, Michael Hand, Michelle Da Pra, Susan Pollack, Katherine Ralston, Travis Smith, Stephen Vogel, Shellye Clark, Luanne Lohr, Sarah Low, and Constance Newman, *Local Food Systems: Concepts, Impacts, and Issues (ERR-97)*, Economic Research Report, Economic Research Service (Washington, DC: U.S. Department of Agriculture, 2010).

19. Anisha Hingorani and Haan-Fawn Chau, *Los Angeles Food System Snapshot, 2013: A Baseline Report of the Los Angeles Regional Foodshed* (Los Angeles: Los Angeles Food Policy Council, 2013).

20. Kate Clancy and Kathryn Ruhf, "Is Local Enough? Some Arguments for Regional Food Systems," *Choices* 25, no. 1 (2010). www.choicesmagazine.org/magazine /article.php?article=114 (accessed April 27, 2014).

21. Ibid.

22. Ralph Heimlich, *Farm Resource Regions (AIB-760)*, Agriculture Information Bulletin, Economic Research Service (Washington, DC: U.S. Department of Agriculture, 2000).

23. World Bank, *Data by Country: Agricultural Land (% of Land Area)*, World Bank Group, 2014. data.worldbank.org/indicator/AG.LND.AGRI.ZS (accessed April 27, 2014).

24. "The Countries That Eat the Most and the Least," *Huffington Post*, January 10, 2012.

25. UN Food and Agriculture Organization, *Food Outlook, Biannual Report on Global Food Markets* (Rome: FAO), 2013.

26. Ibid.

27. U.S. Department of Agriculture Economic Research Service, *Ag and Food Statistics: Charting the Essentials / Agricultural Trade*, 2013. www.ers.usda.gov/data

-products/ag-and-food-statistics-charting-the-essentials/agricultural-trade.aspx (accessed January 2014).

28. Centers for Disease Control and Prevention, National Center for Health Statistics, *Health, United States, 2011: With Special Feature on Socioeconomic Status and Health* (Washington, DC: U.S. Government Printing Office, 2012).

29. Mark Nord, Margaret Andrews, and Steven Carlson, *Household Food Security in the United States, 2008 (ERR-83)*, Economic Research Report, Economic Research Service (Washington, DC: U.S. Department of Agriculture, 2009).

30. Centers for Disease Control and Prevention, "CDC Estimates of Foodborne Illness in the United States," February 2011. www.cdc.gov/foodborneburden/2011 -foodborne-estimates.html (accessed April 27, 2014).

31. U.S. Department of Agriculture, *2007 Census of Agriculture: United States Summary and State Data (AC-07-A-51)*, National Agricultural Statistics Service (Washington, DC: U.S. Department of Agriculture, 2009).

32. U.S. Environmental Protection Agency, *National Water Quality Inventory: 2000 Report (EPA-841-R-02-001)*, Office of Water (4503F) (Washington, DC: EPA's National Service Center for Environmental Publications, 2002).

2. LOCAL FOOD SYSTEMS

Epigraph: Wendell Berry, *The Unsettling of America: Culture & Agriculture* (San Francisco: Sierra Club Books, 1997).

1. Steven Gorelick, "Is Local Organic Food Elitist?" International Society for Ecology and Culture, 2005. www.localfutures.org/publications/online-articles/is-local -organic-food-elitist (accessed December 4, 2012).

2. Brandon Born and Mark Purcell, "Avoiding the Local Trap: Scale and Food Systems in Planning Research," *Journal of Planning Education and Research* 26 (2006): 195–207.

3. Sarah A. Low and Stephen Vogel, *Direct and Intermediated Marketing of Local Foods in the United States (ERR-128)*, Economic Research Report, Economic Research Service (Washington, DC: U.S. Department of Agriculture, 2011).

4. Jayson L. Lusk and F. Bailey Norwood, "The Locavore's Dilemma: Why Pineapples Shouldn't Be Grown in North Dakota," *Library of Economics and Liberty*, January 3, 2011. www.econlib.org/library/Columns/y2011/LuskNorwoodlocavore.html (accessed December 4, 2012).

5. Adam Diamond and Richard Soto, *Facts on Direct to Consumer Food Marketing*, Agricultural Marketing Service (Washington, DC: U.S. Department of Agriculture, 2009).

6. Philip Ackerman-Leist, *Rebuilding the Foodshed: How to Create Local, Sustainable, and Secure Food Systems* (White River Junction, VT: Chelsea Green, 2013).

7. Food, Conservation, and Energy Act of 2008, Pub. L. No. 110-246, § 6015 (2008).

8. Food Safety Modernization Act, Pub. L. No. 111-353, § 105 (2011).

9. Definition of Local and Locally Grown, 9 V.S.A. § 2465a, Vt., Title 9: Commerce and Trade; Chapter 63: Consumer Protection.

10. Local Food, Farms, and Jobs Act, Illinois Statute 30 ILCS 595.

11. Food and Drugs Act (C.R.C., c. 870), s. B.01.012 (2009) (Can.).

12. Alisa Smith and J. B. MacKinnon, *The 100-Mile Diet: A Year of Local Eating* (New York: Random House, 2007).

13. State of New Jersey Department of Agriculture, "About Jersey Fresh," 2014. jerseyfresh.nj.gov/about (accessed January 2014).

14. Gulf of Maine Research Institute, "Gulf of Maine Responsibly Harvested Program," *Sustainable Seafood Initiative*. www.gmri.org/mini/index.asp?ID=33&p=111 (accessed January 2014).

15. "Eco Apple Program," *Red Tomato*, 2014. www.redtomato.org/ecoapple.php (accessed January 2014).

16. *Ozark Pasture Beef*, 2014. www.ozarkpasturebeef.com (accessed January 2014).

17. Title XVI (Research) of the Food, Agriculture, Conservation and Trade Act of 1990, P.L. 101-624 / 1990 Farm Bill (passed November 28, 1990).

18. Sustainable Agriculture Research & Education (SARE), 2012. sare.org (accessed January 2014).

19. Steve Martinez, Michael Hand, Michelle Da Pra, Susan Pollack, Katherine Ralston, Travis Smith, Stephen Vogel, Shellye Clark, Luanne Lohr, Sarah Low, and Constance Newman, *Local Food Systems: Concepts, Impacts, and Issues (ERR-97)*, Economic Research Report, Economic Research Service (Washington, DC: United States Department of Agriculture, 2010).

20. Lynda Zepeda and Jinghan Li, "Who Buys Local Food?" *Journal of Food Distribution Research* 37, no. 3 (2006): 1–11.

21. www.atkearney.com/documents/10192/709903/Buying+into+the+Local+Food+Movement.pdf/68091049-b5c2-4d2a-a770-ee5b703da8fd.

22. Andrew J. Knight and Hema Chopra, "Perceived Benefits and Barriers to Local Food Procurement in Publicly Funded Institutions," *Journal of Extension* 51, no. 5 (2013).

23. Martinez et al., *Local Food Systems*.

24. Christopher L. Weber and H. Scott Matthews, "Food-Miles and the Relative Climate Impacts of Food Choices in the United States," *Environmental Science and Technology* (2008): 3508–13.

25. Martinez et al., *Local Food Systems*.

26. Ibid.

27. Low and Vogel, *Direct and Intermediated Marketing*.

28. Marcus Wohlsen, "How Store Shelves Stay Stocked Even after a Sandy-Sized Disaster," *Wired*, November 1, 2012.

29. Thomas A. Lyson, *Civic Agriculture: Reconnecting Farms, Food and Community* (Lebanon, NH: University Press of New England, 2004).

3. THE BUSINESS OF FOOD AND FARMING

1. U.S. Department of Agriculture Economic Research Service, *Ag and Food Sectors and the Economy*, 2013. www.ers.usda.gov/data-products/chart-gallery/detail.aspx ?chartId=40045 (accessed January 2014).

2. U.S. Department of Agriculture Economic Research Service, *Ag and Food Statistics: Charting the Essentials / Food Prices and Spending*, 2013. www.ers.usda .gov/data-products/ag-and-food-statistics-charting-the-essentials/food-prices-and -spending.aspx (accessed January 2014).

3. Ibid.

4. Richard Volpe and Abigail Okrent, *Assessing the Healthfulness of Consumers' Grocery Purchases (EIN-102)*, Economic Information Bulletin, Economic Research Service (Washington, DC: U.S. Department of Agriculture, 2012).

5. U.S. Department of Agriculture Economic Research Service, *Ag and Food Statistics: Charting the Essentials / Food Security and Nutrition Assistance*, 2013. www.ers.usda.gov/data-products/ag-and-food-statistics-charting-the-essentials/food -security-and-nutrition-assistance.aspx (accessed January 2014)..

6. Ibid.

7. Jean C. Buzby, Hodan Farah Wells, and Jeanine Ben, *ERS's Food Loss Data Help Inform the Food Waste Discussion*, Amber Waves, Economic Research Service (Washington, DC: U.S. Department of Agriculture, 2013).

8. Dana Gunders, *Wasted: How America Is Losing Up to 40 Percent of Its Food from Farm to Fork to Landfill* (New York: Natural Resources Defense Council, 2012).

9. Ibid.

10. Don Hofstrand, *Commodities versus Differentiated Products* (Ames: University of Iowa, Agricultural Marketing Resource Center, 2007).

11. Robyn van En Center, "CSA Database search," Wilson College, Chambersburg, PA, 2011. www2.wilson.edu/CsaSearch (accessed November 5, 2013).

12. New Hampshire Farmers' Market Association, *Definitions, Rules & Laws*, 2013. www.nhfma.org/about/definitions-rules-laws (accessed November 5, 2013).

13. Iowa State University, Agricultural Marketing Resource Center, *Farmers' Markets*, 2002–14. www.agmrc.org/markets__industries/food/farmers-markets (accessed November 5, 2013).

14. Enrolled House Bill No. 4732. Mich., Act No. 125 (passed October 1, 2013).

15. North Carolina Department of Agriculture and Consumer Services, "North Carolina Certified Roadside Farm Market Program," *North Carolina Farm Fresh*. www.ncfarmfresh.com/CertifiedCriteria.asp (accessed November 2013).

16. Sarah A. Low and Stephen Vogel, *Direct and Intermediated Marketing of Local Foods in the United States (ERR-128)*, Economic Research Report, Economic Research Service (Washington, DC: U.S. Department of Agriculture, 2011).

17. U.S. Department of Agriculture Economic Research Service, *Food Markets & Prices / Food Service Industry / Market Segments*, 2013. www.ers.usda.gov/topics/food -markets-prices/food-service-industry/market-segments.aspx (accessed January 2014).

18. U.S. Department of Agriculture Economic Research Service, *Food Expenditures*, 2013. www.ers.usda.gov/data-products/food-expenditures.aspx (accessed January 2014).

19. Mary Holz-Clause and Malinda Geisler, *Grocery Retailing Profile* (Ames: Iowa State University, Agricultural Marketing Resource Center, 2012).

20. U.S. Department of Agriculture Economic Research Service, *Food Markets & Prices / Food Service Industry / Market Segments*, 2013. www.ers.usda.gov/topics /food-markets-prices/food-service-industry/market-segments.aspx# (accessed January 2014).

21. U.S. Department of Agriculture Economic Research Service, *Food Markets & Prices / Retailing & Wholesaling / Wholesaling*, 2013. www.ers.usda.gov/topics/food -markets-prices/retailing-wholesaling/wholesaling.aspx# (accessed January 2014).

22. Ibid.

23. Robert A. Hoppe and David E. Banker, *Structure and Finances of U.S. Farms: Family Farm Report, 2010 Edition (EIB-66)*, Economic Information Bulletin, Economic Research Service (Washington, DC: U.S. Department of Agriculture, 2010).

24. U.S. Department of Agriculture, *2007 Census of Agriculture: United States Summary and State Data (AC-07-A-51)*, National Agricultural Statistics Service (Washington, DC: U.S. Department of Agriculture, 2009).

25. Robert Hoppe and James MacDonald, *Updating the ERS Farm Typology (EIB-110)*, Economic Information Bulletin, Economic Research Service (Washington, DC: U.S. Department of Agriculture, 2013).

26. Jorge Fernandez-Cornejo, *Off-Farm Income, Technology Adoption, and Farm Economic Performance (ERR-36)*, Economic Research Report, Economic Research Service (Washington, DC: U.S. Department of Agriculture, 2007), 53.

27. Hoppe and Banker, *Structure and Finances of U.S. Farms*.

28. U.S. Department of Agriculture Economic Research Service, *Farm Income and Wealth Statistics*, 2013. www.ers.usda.gov/data-products/farm-income-and-wealth -statistics.aspx (accessed January 2014).

29. U.S. Department of Agriculture Economic Research Service, *Agricultural Production Practices and Prices*, 2013. www.ers.usda.gov/data-products/ag-and-food -statistics-charting-the-essentials/agricultural-production-and-prices.aspx (accessed January 2014).

30. U.S. Department of Agriculture Economic Research Service, *Sugar and Sweeteners Yearbook Tables: Table 44—U.S. Maple Syrup Production and Value, by State, Calendar Years*, 2013. www.ers.usda.gov/data-products/sugar-and-sweeteners-yearbook -tables.aspx (accessed January 2014).

31. National Chicken Council, *Vertical Integration*, 2012. www.nationalchicken council.org/industry-issues/vertical-integration (accessed January 2014).

32. Chris Laughton and Roberto Lopez, *The Overlooked Economic Engine: Northeast Agriculture*, Farm Credit East, 2010.

33. Michael Brady and Justin Taylor, *Agriculture's Contribution to Washington's*

Economy, IMPACT Center Fact Sheet (Pullman: Washington State University, School of Economic Sciences, 2011).

34. Ruby Ward, Paul Jakus, and Dillon Feuz, *The Economic Impact of Agriculture on the State of Utah*, Economic Research Institute Report 2010-02 (Logan: Utah State University, Department of Applied Economics, 2010).

35. Titus Awokuse, Tomas Ilvento, and Zachary Johnston, *The Impact of Agriculture on Delaware's Economy* (Newark: University of Delaware, Department of Food and Resource Economics, 2010).

36. Michelle Marquez, *Agriculture Value Chain for California*, Research Brief, Centers of Excellence, Economic and Workforce Development, Chancellor's Office of California Community Colleges, 2011.

37. Vern Grubinger, Kenneth Mulder, and Dave Timmons, *Vermont's Agriculture: Generating Wealth from the Land* (Montpelier:Vermont Sustainable Agriculture Council, 2005).

38. U.S. Department of Agriculture, *2007 Census of Agriculture: Vermont State and County Data (AC-07-A-45)*, National Agricultural Statistics Service (Washington, DC: U.S. Department of Agriculture, 2009).

39. Vermont Sustainable Jobs Fund, *Farm to Plate Strategic Plan*, Executive Summary (Burlington, VT: Queen City Printers, 2011).

40. Grubinger, Mulder, and Timmons, *Vermont's Agriculture*.

41. Vermont Sustainable Jobs Fund, *Farm to Plate Strategic Plan*.

42. Roger Doiron, "What's a Home Garden Worth?" *Kitchen Gardeners International*, March 2, 2009. kitchengardeners.org/blogs/roger-doiron/home-garden -worth (accessed November 30, 2012).

43. Economic & Policy Resources, Inc., *The Vermont Travel & Tourism Industry — 2009*, Summary information adopted from "A Benchmark Study of the Economic Impact of Visitor Expenditures on the Vermont Economy — 2009," Vermont Department of Tourism and Marketing, 2010.

44. New Hampshire Coalition for Sustaining Agriculture and UNH Cooperative Extension, "Is Your Town Farm Friendly? A Checklist for Sustaining Rural Character," University of New Hampshire. cecf1.unh.edu/sustainable/farmfrnd.cfm (accessed November 30, 2012).

45. Errol Castens, "Salad Days Are Here Again," *Northeast Mississippi Daily Journal*, May 4, 2012. djournal.com/news/errol-castens-salad-days-are-here-again (accessed January 2014).

4. VALUES IN FOOD SYSTEMS

1. Park Wilde, *Food Policy in the United States: An Introduction* (New York: Routledge, 2013).

2. Marty Strange, *Family Farming: A New Economic Vision* (Lincoln / San Francisco: University of Nebraska Press / Institute for Food and Development Policy, 1988), 174.

3. ETC Group, *Putting the Cartel before the Horse . . . and Farm, Seeds, Soil, Peasants, etc.*, Communiqué 111 (Ottowa: ETC Group, 2013).

4. Mary Hendrickson and William Heffernen, *Concentration of Agricultural Markets* (Columbia: University of Missouri, Department of Rural Sociology, 2007).

5. Reinvestment Fund, "Understanding the Grocery Industry," in *Financing Healthy Food Options: Implementation Handbook*, by Community Development Financial Institutions Fund (Washington, DC: U.S. Department of the Treasury, 2011).

6. Food & Water Watch, *Consolidation and Buyer Power in the Grocery Industry*, Fact sheet (Washington, DC: Food & Water Watch, 2010).

7. Nation's Restaurant News, *U.S. Top 100* (New York: Penton Restaurant Group, 2011).

8. U.S. Department of Agriculture, *Food Expenditures, Food Away from Home: Total Expenditures*, Food Expenditure Series, Economic Research Service (Washington DC: U.S. Department of Agriculture, 2012).

9. Food Processing, *Food Processing's Top 100, 2012 Rankings*, Putman Media, Inc., 2012. www.foodprocessing.com/top100/index.html (accessed December 2012).

10. Aldo Leopold, *A Sand County Almanac* (New York: Oxford University Press, 1949), viii.

11. Rachel Carson, *Silent Spring* (Boston: Houghton Mifflin, 1962).

12. Frances Moore Lappé, *Diet for a Small Planet* (New York: Ballantine Books, 1985).

13. Wendell Berry, *What Are People For?* (San Francisco: North Point Press, 1990).

14. Fred Magdoff, "Ecological Agriculture: Principles, Practices, and Constraints," *Renewable Agriculture and Food Systems* 22, no. 2 (2007): 109–17.

15. Michael Pollan, *The Omnivore's Dilemma: A Natural History of Four Meals* (New York: Penguin Press, 2007).

16. Paul Thompson, *The Agrarian Vision: Sustainability and Environmental Ethics* (Lexington: University of Kentucky Press, 2010).

17. Patricia Allen, *Together at the Table: Sustainability and Sustenance in the American Agrifood System* (University Park: Pennsylvania State University Press, 2004).

18. Brewster Kneen, *From Land to Mouth: Understanding the Food System*, 2d ed. (Toronto: NC Press, 1995).

19. Brandon Born and Purcell, Mark, "Avoiding the Local Trap: Scale and Food Systems in Planning Research," *Journal of Planning Education and Research* 26 (2006): 195–207.

20. Brewers Association, *Craft Brewing Statistics: Facts*, 2012. www .brewersassociation.org (accessed August 2013).

21. G.W. Stevenson, Kate Clancy, Robert King, Larry Lev, Marcia Ostrom, and Stewart Smith, "Midscale Food Value Chains: An Introduction," *Journal of Agriculture, Food Systems, and Community Development* (2011): 27–34.

22. www.sustainableharvest.com/ (accessed January 2014).

23. John Talberth, Clifford Cobb, and Noah Slattery, *The Genuine Progress Indicator, 2006: A Tool for Sustainable Development* (Oakland, CA: Redefining Progress, 2007).

24. Minnesota Planning Environmental Quality Board, *Smart Signals: An*

Assessment of Progress Indicators (St. Paul: Minnesota Planning, 2000); State of Maryland, *Maryland's Genuine Progress Indicators*, n.d. www.green.maryland.gov /mdgpi/indicators.asp (accessed September 2013).

25. Linda Pannozzo and Ronald Colman, *New Policy Directions for Nova Scotia: Using the Genuine Progress Index to Count What Matters* (Glen Haven, NS: GPIAtlantic, July 2009).

26. National Research Council of the National Academies, *Toward Sustainable Agricultural Systems in the 21st Century* (Washington, DC: National Academies Press, 2010).

27. Renée Johnson, Randy A. Aussenberg, and Tadlock Cowan, *The Role of Local Food Systems in U.S. Farm Policy* (Washington, DC: Congressional Research Service, March 12, 2013).

5. THE AGRICULTURAL WORKFORCE

Epigraph: Matt Milkovich, "Hiring Farm Workers More Complicated Than Ever," *Fruit Growers News*, May 2011.

1. William Kandel, *Profile of Hired Farmworkers: A 2008 Update (ERR-60)*, Economic Research Report, Economic Research Service (Washington, DC: U.S. Department of Agriculture, 2008).

2. National Center for Farmworker Health, Inc., "Facts About Farm Workers," 2012. www.ncfh.org/docs/fs-Facts%20about%20Farmworkers.pdf. (accessed April 27, 2014).

3. U.S. Department of Agriculture Economic Research Service, *Rural Labor and Education: Farm Labor*, 2012. www.ers.usda.gov/topics/farm-economy/farm-labor.aspx (accessed July 2013).

4. Daniel Baker and David Chappelle, "Health Status and Needs of Latino Dairy Farmworkers in Vermont," *Journal of Agromedicine* 17, no. 3 (July 2012): 277–87.

5. Alice C. Larson, "California Migrant and Seasonal Farmworker Enumeration Profiles Study," prepared for the Office of Migrant Health, Bureau of Primary Health Care, U.S. Department of Health and Human Services, Rockville, MD, 2000.

6. Gregorio Billikopf, "Labor Management in Agriculture: Cultivating Personnel Productivity, ANR Publication 3417," Agriculture and Natural Resources Agricultural Issues Center, University of California, Modesto, 2003.

7. T. Maloney, personal communication, December 2012.

8. U.S. Bureau of Labor Statistics, *Occupational Outlook Handbook, 2012–2013 edition, Agricultural Workers* (Washington, DC: Office of Occupational Statistics and Employment Projections, 2012).

9. U.S. Department of Labor, *Fact Sheet #71: Internship Programs Under the Fair Labor Standards Act* (Washington, DC: U.S. Department of Labor, Wage and Hour Division, 2010).

10. Ibid.

11. Washington State Department of Labor and Industries, "Small Farm Internship Pilot Project 2011 Final Report for the Washington Legislature," 2011.

12. Phillip Martin, *Promise Unfulfilled: Unions, Immigration, and the Farm Workers* (Ithaca, NY: Cornell University Press, 2003).

13. Andorra Bruno, *Immigration of Temporary Lower-Skilled Workers: Current Policy and Related Issues* (Washington, DC: Congressional Research Service, 2012).

14. Alfonso Serrano, "Bitter Harvest: U.S. Farmers Blame Billion-Dollar Losses on Immigration Laws" *Time*, September 21, 2012. business.time.com/2012/09/21/bitter -harvest-u-s-farmers-blame-billion-dollar-losses-on-immigration-laws (accessed April 27, 2014).

15. Matt Milkovich, "Hiring Farm Workers More Complicated Than Ever," *Fruit Growers News*, May 2011.

16. Ibid.

17. Vermont Sustainable Jobs Fund, *Farm to Plate Strategic Plan*, Executive Summary (Burlington, VT: Queen City Printers, 2011).

18. Vermont Folklife Center and Chris Urgan, *The Golden Cage: Mexican Migrant Workers and Vermont Dairy Farmers*, n.d. goldencageproject.org/voices/index.htm (accessed April 27, 2014).

19. North Carolina Department of Labor, *Gold Star Grower Housing Program*, n.d. www.nclabor.com/ash/goldstar.htm (accessed April 27, 2014).

20. Agricultural Justice Project, *Food Justice Certification*, n.d. agriculturaljusticeproject.org/ (accessed January 2014).

6. FARMING AND THE ENVIRONMENT

Epigraph: National Research Council of the National Academies, *Toward Sustainable Agricultural Systems in the 21st Century* (Washington, DC: National Academies Press, 2010).

1. Joseph A. Tainter, *The Collapse of Complex Societies* (Cambridge: Cambridge University Press, 1990).

2. Liberty H. Bailey, *The Holy Earth* (New York: Scribner, 1915).

3. Albert Howard, *An Agricultural Testament* (New York: Oxford University Press, 1943).

4. Evelyn B. Balfour, *The Living Soil* (London: Faber & Faber, 1943).

5. Miguel Altieri, "Ecological Impacts of Industrial Agriculture and the Possibilities for Sustainable Farming," in *Hungry for Profit: The Agribusiness Threat to Farmers, Food, and the Environment*, edited by F. Magdoff and J. B. Foster F. H. Buttel (New York: Monthly Review Press, 2000), 77–92; Stephen R. Gliessman, *Agroecology: The Ecology of Sustainable Food Systems*, 2d ed. (Boca Raton, FL: CRC Press [Taylor & Francis Group], 2007); Fred, Magdoff, "Ecological Agriculture: Principles, Practices, and Constraints," *Renewable Agriculture and Food Systems* 22, no. 2 (2007): 109– 17; David Pimentel, H. Acquay, M. Biltonen, P. Rice, M. Silva, J. Nelson, V. Lipner, S. Giordano, A. Horowits, and M. D'Amore, "Environmental and Economic Costs of Pesticide Use," *Bioscience* 42, no. 10 (1992): 750–60.

6. U.S. Department of Agriculture Economic Research Service, *U.S. Agricultural*

Trade, Export Share of Production, 2012. www.ers.usda.gov/topics/international
-markets-trade/us-agricultural-trade/export-share-of-production.aspx (accessed April
27, 2014).

7. Nancy M.Trautmann, Keith S. Porter, and Robert J. Wagenet, *Modern Agriculture:
Its Effects on the Environment* (Ithaca, NY: Cornell University, Pesticide Safety
Education Program, 1985).

8. Carolyn Dimitri, Anne Effland, and Neilson Conklin, *The 20th Century
Transformation of U.S. Agriculture and Farm Policy (EIB-3)*, Economic Information
Bulletin, Economic Research Service (Washington, DC: U.S. Department of
Agriculture, 2005).

9. Arthur Grube, David Donaldson, Timothy Kiely, and La Wu, *Pesticide
Industry Sales and Usage, 2006 and 2007 Market Estimates* (Washington, DC:
U.S. Environmental Protection Agency, Office of Pesticide Programs, 2011).

10. USDA Pesticide Data Program, *Annual Summary, Calendar Year 2010*,
Agricultural Marketing Service (Washington, DC: U.S. Department of Agriculture,
2012).

11. U.S. Department of Agriculture Economic Research Service, *Fertilizer Use and
Price*, 2013. www.ers.usda.gov/data-products/fertilizer-use-and-price.aspx (accessed
April 27, 2014).

12. Natural Resources Conservation Service, *2007 National Resources Inventory,
Soil Erosion on Cropland* (Washington, DC: Natural Resources Conservation Service,
2010).

13. National Water Quality Assessment Program, *Selected Findings and Current
Perspectives on Urban and Agricultural Water Quality by the National Water-Quality
Assessment Program* (Washington, DC: U.S. Geologic Survey, 2001).

14. Viney P. Aneja, William H. Schlesinger, and Jan Willemerisman, "Effects of
Agriculture upon the Air Quality and Climate: Research, Policy, and Regulations,"
Environmental Science & Technology 43, no. 12 (2009): 4234–40.

15. National Research Council of the National Academies, *Toward Sustainable
Agricultural Systems in the 21st Century* (Washington, DC: National Academies Press,
2010).

16. Megan Stubbs, *Agricultural Conservation: A Guide to Programs* (Washington,
DC: Congressional Research Service, 2013).

17. Environmental Protection Agency, *National Water Quality Inventory: Report to
Congress 2004 Reporting Cycle* (Washington, D.C.: Environmental Protection Agency,
2009).

18. Robert J. Gilliom, "Pesticides in the Nation's Streams and Ground Water,"
Environmental Science and Technology 41, no. 10 (2007): 3408–14.

19. David Pimentel, H. Acquay, M. Biltonen, P. Rice, M. Silva, J. Nelson, V. Lipner,
S. Giordano, A. Horowits, and M. D'Amore, "Environmental and Economic Costs of
Pesticide Use," *Bioscience* 42, no. 10 (1992): 750–60.

20. Louisiana Universities Marine Consortium, "What Is Hypoxia?" *Hypoxia in the*

Northern Gulf of Mexico, 2013. www.gulfhypoxia.net/Overview (accessed September 2013).

21. Margaret Walsh, Greg Johnson, Ron Heavner, Roel Vining, Greg Zwicke, and Susan O'Neill, *Agricultural Air Quality at NRCS: Air Quality Workshop Proceedings* (Washington, DC: Natural Resources Conservation Service, 2006).

22. Viney P. Aneja, William H. Schlesinger, and Jan Willemerisman, "Effects of Agriculture upon the Air Quality and Climate: Research, Policy, and Regulations," *Environmental Science & Technology* 43, no. 12 (2009): 4234–40.

23. UN Environment Programme, "Conference on Biological Diversity, Conference of Parties, Decision V/5," Nairobi, 2000.

24. Alison McLaughlin and Pierre Mineau, "The Impact of Agricultural Practices on Biodiversity," *Agriculture, Ecosystems & Environment* 55 (1995): 201–12.

25. Economic Research Service, *Adoption of Genetically Engineered Crops in the U.S.* (Washington, DC: U.S. Department of Agriculture, 2013).

26. JoAnn Burkholder, Bob Libra, Peter Weyer, Susan Heathcote, Peter S. Thorne, and Michael Wichman, "Impacts of Waste from Concentrated Animal Feeding Operations on Water Quality," *Environmental Health Perspectives* 115, no. 2 (2007): 308–12.

27. U.S. Environmental Protection Agency, *Potential Environmental Impacts of Animal Feeding Operations* (Washington, DC: U.S. Environmental Protection Agency, 2012).

28. Curtis E. Beus and Riley E. Dunlap, "Conventional versus Alternative Agriculture: The Paradigmatic Roots of the Debate," *Rural Sociology* 55, no. 4 (1990): 590–616.

29. National Research Council of the National Academies, *Toward Sustainable Agricultural Systems*.

30. Gyles Randall, Michael Schmitt, Jeffrey Strock, and John Lamb, *Validating N Rates for Corn on Farm Fields in Southern Minnesota: Recommendations to Optimize Profits and Protect Water Quality* (St. Paul: University of Minnesota, 2004).

31. Marcel Aillery, Noel Gollehon, Robert Johansson, Jonathan Kaplan, Nigel Key, and Marc Ribaudo, *Managing Manure to Improve Air and Water Quality*, Economic Research Report 9 (Washington, DC: U.S. Department of Agriculture, 2005).

32. Lester E. Ehler, "Integrated Pest Management (IPM): Definition, Historical Development and Implementation, and the Other IPM," *Pest Management Science* 62 (2006): 787–89.

33. National Research Council of the National Academies, *Toward Sustainable Agricultural Systems*.

34. Organic Trade Association, *2011 Organic Industry Survey* (Brattleboro, VT: Organic Trade Association, 2011).

35. U.S. Department of Agriculture, *2011 Certified Organic Production Survey*, National Agricultural Statistics Service (Washington, DC: U.S. Department of Agriculture, 2012).

36. National Research Council of the National Academies, *Toward Sustainable Agricultural Systems.*

37. Title XVI (Research) of the Food, Agriculture, Conservation and Trade Act of 1990. P.L. 101-624 / 1990 Farm Bill (passed November 28, 1990).

38. Coen Reijntjes, Bertus Haverkort, and A. Waters-Bayer, *Farming for the Future* (London: Macmillan Press, 1992).

39. Altieri, "Ecological Impacts of Industrial Agriculture."

7. CLIMATE CHANGE AND AGRICULTURE

1. U.S. Environmental Protection Agency, *Climate Change Indicators in the United States*, 2013. www.epa.gov/climatechange/science/indicators/weather-climate /temperature.html (accessed January 2014).

2. Pieter Tans and Ralph Keeling, "Trends in Atmospheric Carbon Dioxide: Full Mauna Loa CO_2 Record," U.S. Department of Commerce / National Oceanic & Atmospheric Administration/NOAA Research, n.d. www.esrl.noaa.gov/gmd/ccgg /trends (accessed January 2014).

3. NCAR, UCAR (University Corporation for Atmospheric Research), *Global Warming & Climate Change: Frequently Asked Questions*, n.d. www2.ucar.edu/climate /faq (accessed July 11, 2013).

4. U.S. Environmental Protection Agency, *Causes of Climate Change*, January 2014. www.epa.gov/climatechange/science/causes.html (accessed January 2014).

5. U.S. Environmental Protection Agency, *Climate Change Indicators*, 2013.

6. U.S. Environmental Protection Agency, *Climate Change Indicators in the United States*, 2012. www.epa.gov/climatechange/pdfs/CI-summary-2012.pdf (accessed January 2014).

7. Cameron Wake, *Indicators of Climate Change in the Northeast over the Past 100 Years*, (Durham: University of New Hampshire, Climate Change Research Center, 2005).

8. Timothy D. Perkins, "Statement of Timothy D. Perkins, Ph.D., Director, UVM Proctor Maple Research Center," testimony, June 4, 2007, before the U.S. House Select Committee on Energy Independence and Global Warming. globalwarming.house.gov /tools/assets/files/0101.pdf (accessed July 11, 2013).

9. M. L. Parry, O. F. Canziani, J. P. Palutikof, P. J. van der Linden, and C. E. Hanson (eds.), *Climate Change, 2007: Impacts, Adaptation, and Vulnerability—Contribution of Working Group II to the Fourth Assessment Report of the Intergovernmental Panel on Climate Change* (Cambridge: Cambridge University Press, 2007).

10. C. L. Walthall et. al. *Climate Change and Agriculture in the United States: Effects and Adaptation*, Technical Bulletin 1935, Agricultural Research Service, Climate Change Program Office (Washington, D.C: U.S. Department of Agriculture, 2012).

11. David W. Wolfe, "Climate Change Impacts on Northeast Agriculture: Overview," Cornell University, 2005.

12. Susan G. Spierre and Cameron Wake, *Trends in Extreme Precipitation Events for*

the *Northeastern United States, 1948–2007* (Durham: University of New Hampshire, Carbon Solutions New England, 2010).

13. John L. Jifon and David W. Wolfe, "High Temperature-Induced Sink Limitation Alters Growth and Photosynthetic Acclimation to Elevated CO_2 in Bean (*Phaseolus vulgaris* L.)," *Journal of the American Society for Horticultural Science* 130, no. 4 (2005): 515–20.

14. Lewis H. Ziska and Jeffrey S. Dukes, *Weed Biology and Climate Change* (Oxford: Wiley-Blackwell, 2010).

15. Curtis Petzoldt and Abby Seaman, *Climate Change Effects on Insects and Pathogens* (Geneva: New York State Agricultural Extension Station, 2005).

16. U.S. Environmental Protection Agency, *Inventory of U.S. Greenhouse Gas Emissions and Sinks: 1990–2009* (Washington, DC: U.S. Environmental Protection Agency, 2011).

17. Council for Agricultural Science and Technology (CAST) Task Force, *Climate Change and Greenhouse Gas Mitigation: Challenges and Opportunities for Agriculture* (Ames, IA: Council for Agricultural Science and Technology, 2004).

18. Paustian, Keith, John M. Antle, John Sheehan, and Eldor A. Paul, *Agriculture's Role in Greenhouse Gas Mitigation* (Arlington, VA: Pew Center on Global Climate Change, 2006).

19. Anthony Leiserowitz, Edward Maibach, Connie Roser-Renouf, and Jay Hmielowski, *Global Warming's Six Americas, March 2012 & November 2011* (New Haven, CT: Yale Project on Climate Change Communication, 2012).

20. Ibid.

21. J. Gordon Arbuckle, *Iowa Farm and Rural Life Poll: 2011 Summary Report* (Ames: Iowa State University Extension and Outreach, 2011).

8. ENERGY, FOOD, AND FARMS

1. Patrick Canning, Ainsley Charles, Sonya Huang, Karen R. Polenske, and Arnold Waters, *Energy Use in the U.S. Food System (ERR-94)*, Economic Research Report, Economic Research Service (Washington, D.C.: U.S. Department of Agriculture, 2010); John Hendrickson, *Energy Use in the U.S. Food System: A Summary of Existing Research and Analysis* (Madison: University of Wisconsin, Center for Integrated Agricultural Systems, 1996).

2. Canning et al., *Energy Use.*

3. Michael Pollan, *The Omnivore's Dilemma: A Natural History of Four Meals* (New York: Penguin Press, 2006).

4. David Pimental, Sean Williamson, Omar Gonzalez-Pagan, Caitlin Kontak, and Steven E. Mulkey, "Reducing Energy Inputs in the U.S. Food System," *Human Ecology* 36 (2008): 459–71; John S. Steinhart and Carol E. Steinhart, "Energy Use in the U.S. Food System," *Science* (1974): 307–16.

5. Christopher L. Weber and H. Scott Matthews, "Food-Miles and the Relative Climate Impacts of Food Choices in the United States," *Environmental Science and*

Technology, 2008: 3508–13; Richard Heinberg and Michael Bomford, *Food and Farming Transition: Toward a Post-Carbon Food System* (Sebastopol, CA: Post Carbon Institute, 2009).

6. Matthew J. Mariola, "The Local Industrial Complex? Questioning the Link Between Local Foods and Energy Use," *Agriculture and Human Values* 25 (2008): 193–96.

7. Heinberg and Bomford, *Food and Farming Transition*.

8. Eric Garza, *The Energy Return on Invested of Biodiesel in Vermont* (Montpelier: Vermont Sustainable Jobs Fund, 2011).

9. Frederick Magdoff, "The Political Economy and Ecology of Biofuels," *Monthly Review* 60, no. 3 (2008).

9. ACCESS TO HEALTHY FOOD

Epigraph: Kathleen Merrigan, "Increasing Access to Locally Grown and Healthy Food," *White House Blog*, March 22, 2012. www.whitehouse.gov/blog/2012/03/21.

1. U.S. Department of Agriculture Economic Research Service, *Ag and Food Statistics: Charting the Essentials / Food Prices and Spending*, 2013. www.ers.usda .gov/data-products/ag-and-food-statistics-charting-the-essentials/food-prices-and -spending.aspx (accessed January 2014).

2. Alisha Coleman-Jensen, Mark Nord, Margaret Andrews, and Steven Carlson, *Household Food Security in the United States in 2011 (ERR-141)*, Economic Research Report, Economic Research Service (Washington, DC: United States Department of Agriculture, 2012).

3. Cynthia Ogden and Margaret Carroll, *Prevalence of Obesity Among Children and Adolescents: United States, Trends 1963–1965 Through 2007–2008*, Centers for Disease Control and Prevention, 2010.

4. Rachel Schattman, Virginia Nickerson, Linda Berlin, Ellen Kahler, and Heather Pipino, "Appendix D, Dissolving the Double Bind: Strategies for Expanding Food Access and Developing Vermont's Local Food System," in *Farm to Plate Strategic Plan*, by Vermont Sustainable Job Fund (Burlington, VT: Queen City Printers, 2011).

5. Food Research and Action Center (FRAC), "Hunger and Obesity? Making the Connections," February 2010. www.frac.org/pdf/Paradox.pdf (accessed December 20, 2012).

6. Christine Delsol, "Farm Tours and Fresh Veggies in California's 'Salad Bowl,'" *San Francisco Chronicle*, August 23, 2011.

7. Schattman et al., "Appendix D, Dissolving the Double Bind."

8. Robert S. McElvaine, *The Great Depression: America, 1929–1941* (New York: Three Rivers Press, 1993).

9. Mark Winne, *Closing the Food Gap: Resetting the Table in the Land of Plenty* (Boston: Beacon Press, 2008).

10. Second Harvest Food Bank of Northwest North Carolina, *The History of Food Banking*, n.d. www.hungernwnc.org/about-us/history%20of%20food%20banking.html (accessed December 20, 2012).

11. Capital Area Food Bank, *ProgramsI*, n.d. www.capitalareafoodbank.org
/programs/ (accessed December 20, 2012).

12. Steven Gorelick, "Is Local Organic Food Elitist?" *International Society for
Ecology and Culture*, 2005. www.localfutures.org/publications/online-articles/is-local
-organic-food-elitist (accessed December 4, 2012).

13. Steve Martinez, Michael Hand, Michelle Da Pra, Susan Pollack, Katherine
Ralston, Travis Smith, Stephen Vogel, Shellye Clark, Luanne Lohr, Sarah Low, and
Constance Newman, *Local Food Systems: Concepts, Impacts, and Issues (ERR-97)*,
Economic Research Report, Economic Research Service (Washington, DC: U.S.
Department of Agriculture, 2010).

14. Jake Claro, *Vermont Farmers' Markets and Grocery Stores: A Price Comparison*,
Northeast Organic Farming Association of Vermont, 2011.

15. Alisha Coleman-Jensen, Mark Nord, Margaret Andrews, and Steven Carlson,
Household Food Security in the United States in 2010 (ERR-125), Economic Research
Report, Economic Research Service (Washington, DC: United States Department of
Agriculture, 2011).

16. Adam Diamond and Richard Soto, *Facts on Direct to Consumer Food Marketing*,
Agricultural Marketing Service (Washington, DC: U.S. Department of Agriculture,
2009).

17. Sarah A. Low and Stephen Vogel, *Direct and Intermediated Marketing of Local
Foods in the United States (ERR-128)*, Economic Research Report, Economic Research
Service (Washington, DC: U.S. Department of Agriculture, 2011).

18. Alison Gustafson, David Cavallo, and Amy Paxton, "Linking Homegrown
and Locally Produced Fruits and Vegetables to Improving Access and Intake in
Communities through Policy and Environmental Change," *Journal of the American
Dietetic Association* 107, no. 4 (April 2007): 584–85.

19. Kimberley Hodgson, "Planning for Food Access and Community-Based Food
Systems: A National Scan and Evaluation of Local Comprehensive and Sustainability
Plans," American Planning Association, 2012.

20. The national average of annual household expenditures on fresh produce
was $429 in 2009. For comparison, families earning $100,000 or more per year
spent $712, while families with household incomes of less than $15,000 spent $254
per year. See Roberta Cook, "Tracking Demographics and U.S. Fruit and Vegetable
Consumption Patterns," Department of Agricultural and Resource Economics,
University of California, Davis, 2011.

21. Alanna Moshfegh, "Research to Advance Understanding of the Interrelationship
of Poverty and Nutrition," *Journal of the American Dietetic Association* 107, no. 11
(November 2007): 1882–85.

22. Steve Sexton, *The Inefficiency of Local Food*, November 14, 2011. www
.freakonomics.com/2011/11/14/the-inefficiency-of-local-food (accessed December 19,
2012).

23. Gorelick, "Is Local Organic Food Elitist?"

24. Rich Pirog and Nick McCann, *Is Local Food More Expensive? A Consumer Price Perspective on Local and Non-Local Foods Purchased in Iowa* (Ames, IA: Leopold Center for Sustainable Agriculture, 2009).

25. John Hendrickson and Marcy Ostrom, "CSA: More for Your Money Than Fresh Vegetables," Research Brief 52, University of Wisconsin–Madison, Center for Integrated Agricultural Systems (CIAS), 2001.

26. wholesomewave.org/ (accessed December 20, 2012).

27. Angela Berkfield and Richard Berkfield, "Getting Everyone to the Table: Brattleboro's Community Food Security Project," *Local Banquet*, Fall 2009.

28. Mark Bittman, "Local Food: No Elitist Plot," *New York Times*, November 1, 2011.

29. Dawn Thilmany McFadden and Sarah A. Low, "Will Local Foods Influence American Diets?" *Choices, A publication of the Agricultural & Applied Economics Association*, First Quarter 2012.

10. FARM TO SCHOOL

Epigraph: First Lady Michelle Obama, "Remarks by the First Lady at the School Nutrition Association Conference," March 1, 2010. www.whitehouse.gov/the-press -office/remarks-first-lady-school-nutrition-association-conference.

1. U.S. Department of Agriculture, *Program Data, Child Nutrition Tables*, August 6, 2013. www.fns.usda.gov/pd/cnpmain.htm (accessed August 20, 2013).

2. Seventeen percent of children and adolescents aged two to nineteen years are obese; see Cynthia Ogden and Margaret Carroll, *Prevalence of Obesity Among Children and Adolescents: United States, Trends 1963–1965 Through 2007–2008*, Centers for Disease Control and Prevention, 2010. www.cdc.gov/nchs/data/hestat/obesity_child _07_08/obesity_child_07_08.pdf (accessed April 27, 2014).

3. Ibid.

4. Allison A. Hedley, Cynthia L. Ogden, Clifford L. Johnson, Margaret D. Carroll, Lester R. Curtin, and Katherine M. Flegal, "Prevalence of Overweight and Obesity Among US Children, Adolescents, and Adults, 1999–2002," *Journal of the American Medical Association* 291, no. 23 (2004): 2847–50.

5. Maria R. Signorino and William E Winter, "Childhood Obesity and Diabetes," *Current Medical Literature: Diabetes* 25, no. 1 (2008): 1–16.

6. Centers for Disease Control and Prevention, *Strategies to Prevent Obesity and Other Chronic Diseases: The CDC Guide to Strategies to Increase the Consumption of Fruits and Vegetables* (Atlanta, GA: U.S. Department of Health and Human Services, 2011).

7. National Farm to School Program, "Farm to School: Case Studies and Resources for Success," 2004. agmarketing.extension.psu.edu/Wholesale/PDFs/farm_school _success.pdf (accessed December 27, 2012).

8. National Farm to School Network, "Farm to School Chronology," 2009. www .farmtoschool.org/files/F2SChronology3.09.pdf (accessed December 27, 2012).

9. National Farm to School Network. *About Us*, n.d. www.farmtoschool.org/aboutus .php (accessed December 18, 2012).

10. Vermont FEED (Food Education Every Day), *About Us: What Is Vermont Feed?* n.d. www.vtfeed.org (accessed October 11, 2013).

11. A. Nelson, personal communication, October 2013.

12. www.greenmountainfarmtoschool.org/ (accessed December 27, 2012).

13. www.burlingtonschoolfoodproject.org (accessed December 27, 2012).

14. Ibid.

15. Windham County Farm to School, *About WCFTS: History,* n.d. brattf2s .wordpress.com/home/about/history/ (accessed December 27, 2012).

16. Anupama Joshi, Andrea Misako Azuma, and Gail Feenstra, "Do Farm-to-School Programs Make a Difference? Findings and Future Research Needs," *Journal of Hunger & Environmental Nutrition* 3, no. 2 (2008): 229–46.

17. Ibid., 233.

18. Ibid., 237–38.

19. Ibid., 240.

20. Ibid., 239.

21. Ibid., 233.

22. Tara L. LaRowe, Andrea B. Bontrager Yoder, Amanda Knitter, Amy Meinen, Janice L. Liebhart, and Dale Schoeller, *Wisconsin Farm to School: One Year Evaluation Report* (Madison: University of Wisconsin, Department of Family Medicine, 2011).

23. Ibid., 2.

24. Gretchen Geotz, "USDA Releases First Farm to School Evaluation," *Food Safety News,* July 19, 2011. www.foodsafetynews.com/2011/07/usda-releases-first-farm-to -school-evaluation-1/ (accessed December 27, 2012).

25. Ibid.

11. AGRITOURISM AND ON-FARM MARKETING

1. Jack Kloppenburg, Jr., Sharon Lezberg, and Kathy DeMa, "Tasting Food, Tasting Sustainability: Defining the Attributes of an Alternative Food System with Competent, Ordinary people," *Human Organization* (2000): 177–86.

2. Rich Pirog, Timothy Van Pelt, Kamyar Enshayan, and Ellen Cook, *Food, Fuel, and Freeways: An Iowa Perspective on How Far Food Travels, Fuel Usage, and Greenhouse Gas Emissions* (Ames, IA: Leopold Center for Sustainable Agriculture, 2001).

3. L. C. Chase, "Agritourism," 2008, in *Encyclopedia of Rural America: The Land and People,* 2d ed., edited by G. A. Goreham (Millerton, NY: Grey House, 2008), 70–74. Copyright 2008 by Grey House Publishing. Reprinted with permission.

4. Kim Jensena, Megan Bruch, Jamey Menard, and Burt English, *Agritourism, 2103 Update,* (Knoxville: University of Tennessee, 2013), 31.

5. adamsfamilyfarm.com/farm-history/ (accessed July 2013).

6. World Food Travel Association, "What Is Food Tourism?" n.d. www .worldfoodtravel.org/our-story/what-is-food-tourism/ (accessed July 2013).

7. Mandala Research, "New Study of Traveler Eating Interests Shows Promoting

Culinary Activities Can Pay Off: Almost a Third of Travelers Choose Destinations Based on Eating Opportunities," Press release, August 27, 2013. www.prnewswire.com /news-releases/new-study-of-traveler-eating-interests-shows-promoting-culinary -activities-can-pay-off-221375241.html.

8. U.S. Department of Agriculture, "2007 Census of Agriculture: Table 7. Income from Farm-Related Sources: 2007 and 2002." National Agricultural Statistics Service, 2009. www.agcensus.usda.gov/Publications/2007/Full_Report/Volume_1,_Chapter_1 _US/st99_1_006_007.pdf (accessed January 2014).

9. C. E. Carpio, M. K. Wohlgenant, and T. Boonsaeng, "The Demand for Agritourism in the United States," *Journal of Agricultural and Resource Economics* 33, no. 2 (2008): 254–69.

10. U.S. Department of Agriculture, "2007 Census of Agriculture: Table 7."

11. National Survey on Recreation and the Environment (NSRE): 2000–2002, Interagency National Survey Consortium, Coordinated by the USDA Forest Service, Recreation, Wilderness, and Demographics Trends Research Group, Athens, GA, and the Human Dimensions Research Laboratory, University of Tennessee, Knoxville, 2002.

12. Hawaii Agricultural Statistics Office, *Hawaii Ag-Tourism*, U.S. Department of Agriculture, Hawaii Department of Agriculture, Hawaii Agricultural Statistics, 2004.

13. National Agricultural Statistics Service, *Vermont Agri-tourism, 2002*, New England Agricultural Statistics Service, National Agricultural Statistics Survey (Concord, NH: U.S. Department of Agriculture, 2004).

14. U.S. Department of Agriculture, "2007 Census of Agriculture: Table 7."

15. Thomas Allen, Todd Gabe, and James McConnon, "The Economic Contribution of Agri-Tourism to the Maine Economy," Staff Paper 563, University of Maine, Department of Resource Economics and Policy, 2006.

16. D. Kuehn and D. Hilchey, *Agritourism in New York: Management and Operations* (Oswego, NY: New York Sea Grant, 2001).

17. Jensena et al., *Agritourism, 2103 Update.*

18. J. Wilson, D. Thilmany, and M. Sullins, *Agritourism: A Potential Economic Driver in the Rural West*, Colorado State University Cooperative Extension, 2006.

19. Rachel Carter and Daryl Jones, *Agritourism in Mississippi: Effects and Impacts*, Publication 2676, Extension Service of Mississippi State University, 2011.

20. Holly A. George, Christy Getz, Shermain Hardesty, and Ellen Rilla, "California Agritourism Operations and Their Economic Potential Are Growing," *California Agriculture*, April–June 2011: 57–65.

21. Stonebridge Research, "Economic Impact of the Napa Valley Wine Industry," 2008.

22. Mandala Research, "New Study of Traveler Eating Interests"

23. www.vtfarms.org/ (accessed August 27, 2013).

24. Lisa Chase, Varna M. Ramaswamy, Steven W. Burr, Jascha Zeitlin, Gary P. Green, and Michael Dougherty, "Checklist: Successes and Challenges in Agritourism," *University of Vermont: Agritourism: A Web-Based Resource for Farmers:*

Resources, June 2012. www.uvm.edu/tourismresearch/agritourism/agchecklists
/AgritourismSuccessesChallenges.pdf (accessed July 2013).

25. U.S. Department of Agriculture, *2007 Census of Agriculture*, (Washington, DC:
U.S. Department of Agriculture, 2009).

12. FOOD SAFETY FROM FARM TO FORK

Epigraph: Michael R. Taylor, "Succeeding on Produce Safety," *FDA Voice*, April 17,
2012. blogs.fda.gov/fdavoice/index.php/tag/produce-safety/.

1. Centers for Disease Control and Prevention, "CDC Estimates of Foodborne
Illness in the United States," February 2011. www.cdc.gov/foodborneburden/2011
-foodborne-estimates.html.

2. Ben Hewitt, *Making Supper Safe: One Man's Quest to Learn the Truth about Food
Safety* (New York: Rodale, 2011).

3. Rich Pirog, Timothy Van Pelt, Kamyar Enshayan, and Ellen Cook, *Food, Fuel, and
Freeways: An Iowa Perspective on How Far Food Travels, Fuel Usage, and Greenhouse
Gas Emissions* (Ames, IA: Leopold Center for Sustainable Agriculture, 2001).

4. Megan Baxter, "Agritourism and Food Safety," Interview by Keith Silva, *Across the
Fence*, Burlington, VT, August 25, 2011.

5. Centers for Disease Control and Prevention, "Salmonella Serotype Enteritidis:
General Information," November 23, 2010. www.cdc.gov/nczved/divisions/dfbmd
/diseases/salmonella_enteritidis/.

6. Lyndsey Layton, "As Egg Producers Consolidate, Problems of Just One Company
Can Be Far-Reaching," *Washington Post*, August 24, 2010.

7. U.S. Food and Drug Administration, *Hillandale Farms, New Hampton, IA, 483
Issued 8/26/2010 (UCM224174)*, 483 Inspectional Observations Report (Lenexa: FDA
Kansas City District Office, 2010); U.S. Food and Drug Administration, *Quality
Egg LLC (Wright County Egg), Galt, IA, 483 Issued 8/30/2010 (UCM224399)*, 483
Inspectional Observations Report (Lenexa: FDA Kansas City District Office, 2010).

8. Ryan J. Foley, "ISU Lab Warned of Salmonella in Eggs," *Ames Tribune*, June 4, 2012.

9. United Egg Producers, "Food Safety Programs: UEP '5-Star' Egg Safety Program,"
Egg Safety Center, 2012. www.eggsafety.org/producers/food-safety-programs.

10. "Egg Baron 'Jack' DeCoster: Focus of Criminal Probe," *Food Safety News*, May
17, 2012.

11. Hewitt, *Making Supper Safe*, 67.

13. THE NEXT GENERATION OF FARMERS

1. U.S. Department of Agriculture, "2007 Census of Agriculture: Farmers by Age,"
National Agricultural Statistics Service (NASS), 2008. www.agcensus.usda.gov
/Publications/2007/Online_Highlights/Fact_Sheets/Demographics/farmer_age.pdf
(accessed January 2014).

2. Mary Ahearn and Doris Newton, *Beginning Farmers and Ranchers (EIB-53)*,

Economic Information Bulletin, Economic Research Service (Washington, DC: U.S. Department of Agriculture, 2009).

3. Sue Ellen Johnson, Marion Bowlan, Jane McGonigal, Kathryn Ruhf, and Cathleen Sheils, *Listening to New Farmers: Findings from New Farmer Focus Groups* (Belchertown, MA: New England Small Farm Institute, 2001).

4. U.S. Department of Agriculture Economic Research Service, "Agricultural Resource Management Survey (ARMS)," May 2012. www.ers.usda.gov/data-products /arms-farm-financial-and-crop-production-practices.aspx (accessed October 2013).

5. Ahearn and Newton, *Beginning Farmers and Ranchers*.

6. Lindsey L. Shute, *Building a Future with Farmers: Challenges Faced by Young, American Farmers and a National Strategy to Help Them Succeed* (Tivoli, NY: National Young Farmers' Coalition, 2011).

7. This section is adapted from B. Bowell, C. Coffin, and J. Martin, "Farmland ConneCTions: A Guide for Connecticut Towns, Institutions and Land Trusts Using or Leasing Farmland," American Farmland Trust and University of Connecticut Cooperative Extension System, 2011. Copyright 2011 by American Farmland Trust. Used by permission.

8. U.S. Department of Agriculture, *Beginning Farmers and Ranchers at a Glance, 2013 Edition*, Economic Brief No. 22, Economic Research Service (Washington, DC: U.S. Department of Agriculture, 2012).

9. *Greenhorns' Guide for Beginning Farmers*, 4th ed,. 2010. www.thegreenhorns.net /wp-content/files_mf/1335219697greenhorns_guide_sept2010_web.pdf.

10. Larry D.Trede and Scott Whitaker, "Beginning Farmer Education in Iowa: Implications to Extension," *Journal of Extension* 36, no. 5 (1998). www.joe.org /joe/1998october/a3.php (accesssed April 27, 2014.)

11. Shute, *Building a Future with Farmers*.

12. Ibid.

13. Canadian Farm Business Management Council, "So You Want to Be a Farmer," Ontario, 1999.

14. *Greenhorns' Guide for Beginning Farmers*.

14. MAINTAINING FARMS AND FARMLAND FOR THE FUTURE

Epigraph: Aldo Leopold, "Conservation Economics" (1934), in *The River of the Mother of God and Other Essays*, edited by Susan L. Flader and J. Baird Callicott (Madison: University of Wisconsin Press, 1991), 202.

1. Tom Daniels, "Farmland Preservation Policies in the United States: Successes and Shortcomings," Conference Paper, University of Pennsylvania, City and Regional Planning, 2004.

2. U. S. Environmental Protection Agency, *Ag 101: Demographics*, 2013. www.epa .gov/agriculture/ag101/demographics.html (accessed October 2013).

3. Cynthia Nickerson, Robert Ebel, Allison Borchers, and Fernando Carriazo,

Major Uses of Land in the United States, 2007 (EIB-89), Economic Information Bulletin, Economic Research Service (Washington, DC: U.S. Department of Agriculture, 2011).

4. Natural Resources Conservation Service, *2007 National Resources Inventory: Development of Non-Federal Rural Land* (Washington, DC: Natural Resources Conservation Service, 2013).

5. Nickerson et al., *Major Uses of Land in the United States, 2007.*

6. Lori Lynch and Joshua M. Duke, "Economic Benefits of Farmland Preservation: Evidence from the United States," Paper WP 07-04, University of Maryland, Department of Agricultural and Resource Economics, 2007.

7. Ibid.

8. Dana Joel Gattuso, "Conservation Easements: The Good, the Bad, and the Ugly," Working Paper 569 (Washington, DC: National Center for Public Policy Research, 2008).

9. Daniels, "Farmland Preservation Policies."

10. Gattuso, "Conservation Easements."

11. Ibid.

12. Katie Chang, *National Land Trust Census Report* (Washington, DC: Land Trust Alliance, 2010).

13. American Farmland Trust, *A Nationwide Survey of Land Trusts That Protect Farm and Ranch Land* (Washington, DC: American Farmland Trust, 2012).

14. Kendall Slee, *Power of Leveraging Local and Federal Dollars to Strengthen Agricultural Land Easement Investments* (Washington, DC: Farmland Alliance, 2012).

15. Stephen J. Hudkins, *Agricultural Zoning Fact Sheet* (Columbus: Ohio State University, 2009).

16. American Farmland Trust, *Saving American Farmland: What Works* (Washington, DC: American Farmland Trust, 1997).

17. Daniels, "Farmland Preservation Policies."

18. Joel Russell, *How Well Has Agricultural Protection Zoning Worked? Practicing Planner, Winter 2009* (Chicago: American Planning Association, 2009).

19. Christine Kellett, "Understanding 'Right to Farm' Laws," Penn State University Law School, 1999.

20. Ibid.

21. American Farmland Trust, *Differential Assessment and Circuit Breaker Tax Programs* (Northampton, MA: American Farmland Trust, 2008).

22. American Farmland Trust, *Cost of Community Services Studies* (Northampton, MA: American Farmland Trust, 2010).

23. John E. Anderson, "Estimating Agricultural Use Value for Property Tax Purposes: How Do State Programs Assess Use Value?" Social Science Research Network, University of Nebraska at Lincoln, Department of Economics, January 14, 2011. ssrn.com/abstract=1743754 (accessed April 27, 2014).

24. American Farmland Trust, *Differential Assessment.*

25. Jamey Menard, Kim Jensen, and Burton C. English, "How TAEP Strengthens the

State's Economy: 2011 Update," University of Tennessee, Department of Agricultural and Resource Economics, 2011.

26. Robert A. Brannan, *Planning the Future of Your Farm: A Workbook on Farm Transfer Decisions* (Blacksburg: Virginia Polytechnic Institute and State University, 2012).

27. Kathy Ruhf, Jerry Cosgrove, and Adriana Eliot, *Farm Succession and Transfer: Strategies for the Junior Generation* (Keene, NH: Land for Good, 2012).

28. Adapted from Natural Resources Defense Council, *Montgomery County Agricultural Reserve, The Country's Largest Farmland Protection Program.* Solving Sprawl, Montgomery County, Maryland, Natural Resources Defense Council, n.d.; adapted from Montgomery County Maryland. *Agricultural Facts.* The Montgomery County Department of Economic Development, Agricultural Services Division, Derwood, MD: Montgomery County Government, 2012.

29. American Farmland Trust, "Skagit County Agricultural Protection," in *An Evaluation of County Farmland Protection Programs in the Puget Sound Basin: Appendix B*, 17–18 (Seattle: American Farmland Trust, 2012); Skagitonians to Preserve Farmland, *Mission, Vision, History*, 2013. www.skagitonians.org (accessed October 2013).

30. Daniels, "Farmland Preservation Policies."

15. IMPROVING FOOD SYSTEMS

1. David H. Freedman, "How Junk Food Can End Obesity," *Atlantic*, July/August 2013.

2. USDA Study Team on Organic Farming, *Report and Recommendations on Organic Farming* (Washington, DC: U.S. Department of Agriculture, 1980).

3. U.S. Department of Agriculture, *A Time to Choose: Summary Report on the Structure of Agriculture* (Washington, DC: U.S. Department of Agriculture, 1981).

4. National Research Council of the National Academies, *Alternative Agriculture: Committee on the Role of Alternative Farming Methods in Modern Production Agriculture, Board on Agriculture* (Washington, DC: National Academy Press, 1989).

5. USDA National Commission on Small Farms, *A Time to Act* (Washington, DC: U.S. Department of Agriculture, 1998).

6. U.S. Senate Select Committee on Nutrition and Human Needs, *Dietary Goals for the United States*, 2d ed. (Washington, DC: U.S. Government Printing Office, 1977).

7. U.S. Department of Agriculture and U.S. Department of Health and Human Service, *Nutrition and Your Health: Dietary Guidelines for Americans*, Home and Garden Bulletin No. 232 (Washington DC: U.S. Department of Agriculture, 1980).

8. National Research Council, *Diet and Health: Implications for Reducing Chronic Disease Risk* (Washington, DC: National Academies Press, 1989).

9. National Research Council of the National Academies, *Toward Sustainable Agricultural Systems in the 21st Century* (Washington, DC: National Academies Press, 2010).

10. Just Food, *Our Projects*, 2014. www.justfood.ca/about/ (accessed January 2014).

11. Ag Innovations Network, *Sonoma County Healthy and Sustainable Food Action Plan*, County of Sonoma Department of Health Services and Sonoma County Food System Alliance, Sebastopol, CA, 2012.

12. Northeast SARE (Sustainable Agriculture Research & Education), *Northeast SARE Outcome Statement*, 2012. www.nesare.org/About-Us/Northeast-SARE-Outcome -Statement (accessed January 2014).

13. Paul Mason, *Why It's Still Kicking Off Everywhere: The New Global Revolutions* (London: Verso Books, 2012).

14. Oxfam America, *Behind the Brands*. www.behindthebrands.org/en-us.

15. Oxfam International, *Investors Push Food Industry Giants For Urgent Action On Transparency*, September 16, 2013. www.oxfam.org/en/grow/pressroom /pressrelease/2013-09-17/investors-push-food-industry-giants-urgent-action -transparency (accessed January 2014).

16. Real Time Farms, *Know Where Your Food Comes From*, 2012. www .realtimefarms.com (accessed January 2014).

Figure and Map Credits

FIGURES

1.1 Vern Grubinger, Linda Berlin, Elizabeth Berman, Naomi Fukagawa, Jane Kolodinsky, Deborah Neher, Bob Parsons, Amy Trubek, and Kimberly Wallin, *University of Vermont Transdisciplinary Research Initiative Spire of Excellence Proposal: Food Systems* (Burlington: University of Vermont, 2010).

1.2 Adapted from Jim Bower, Ron Doetch, and Steve Stevenson, *Tiers of the Food System: A New Way of Thinking about Local and Regional Food* (Madison: University of Wisconsin Center for Integrated Agricultural Systems, 2010).

1.3 Mary Story, Karen M. Kaphingst, and Karen Glanz, "Creating Healthy Food and Eating Environments: Policy and Environmental Approaches" *Annual Review of Public Health* 29 (2008): 253–72.

1.4 MetroVancouver, *Regional Food System Strategy*, 2011; www.MetroVancouver.org.

1.5 Adapted from the Michigan State University Center for Regional Food Systems, 2010; www.michiganfood.org.

1.6 Paul J. Burgess and Joe Morris, "Agricultural Technology and Land Use Futures: The UK Case," *Land Use Policy* 26, Suppl. 1 (2009): S222–29.

1.7 Courtney Johnson, Greg Albrecht, Quirine Ketterings, Jen Beckman, and Stockin Kristen, *Agronomy Fact Sheet Series: Nitrogen Basics — The Nitrogen Cycle*, Nutrient Management Spear Program (Ithaca, NY: Cornell University Cooperative Extension, 2005). Developed through the Faculty Innovation in Teaching Program, Office of the Provost, Cornell University.

1.8 Kenneth Hanson, Elise Golan, Stephen Vogel, and Jennifer Olmsted, *Tracing the Impacts of Food Assistance Programs on Agriculture and Consumers (FANRR-18)*, Food Assistance and Nutrition Research Report, Economic Research Service (Washington, DC: U.S. Department of Agriculture, 2002).

1.9 Robert Dahni, *Southeast Asian Flavors* (El Segundo, CA: Mortar & Press, 2008).

2.1 Sarah A. Low and Stephen Vogel, *Direct and Intermediated Marketing of Local Foods in the United States (ERR-128)*, Economic Research Service (Washington, DC: U.S. Department of Agriculture, 2011).

2.2 Photo by Vern Grubinger.

2.6 Photo by Vern Grubinger.

2.7 U.S. Department of Agriculture Economic Research Service, *Ag and Food Statistics: Charting the Essentials / Food Availability and Consumption*, 2013. www.ers.usda .gov/data-products/ag-and-food-statistics-charting-the-essentials/food-availability -and-consumption.aspx.

2.8   Photo by Vern Grubinger.

3.1   Carolyn Dimitri and Lydia Oberholtzer, *Marketing U.S. Organic Foods: Recent Trends from Farms to Consumers (EIB-58)*, Economic Information Bulletin, Economic Research Service (Washington, DC: U.S. Department of Agriculture, 2009).

3.2   U.S. Department of Agriculture Economic Research Service, *Charting the Essentials / Food Prices and Spending*, 2013. www.ers.usda.gov/data-products/ag-and-food-statistics-charting-the-essentials/food-prices-and-spending.aspx.

3.3   U.S. Department of Agriculture Economic Research Service, *Charting the Essentials / Food Prices and Spending*, 2013. www.ers.usda.gov/data-products/ag-and-food-statistics-charting-the-essentials/food-prices-and-spending.aspx.

3.4   U.S. Department of Agriculture Economic Research Service, *Ag and Food Statistics: Charting the Essentials / Food Prices and Spending*, 2013. www.ers.usda.gov/data-products/ag-and-food-statistics-charting-the-essentials/food-prices-and-spending.aspx.

3.5   U.S. Department of Agriculture Economic Research Service, *Ag and Food Statistics: Charting the Essentials / Food Prices and Spending*, 2013. www.ers.usda.gov/data-products/ag-and-food-statistics-charting-the-essentials/food-security-and-nutrition-assistance.aspx.

3.6   Richard Volpe and Abigail Okrent, *Assessing the Healthfulness of Consumers' Grocery Purchases (EIN-102)*, Economic Information Bulletin, Economic Research Service (Washington, DC: U.S. Department of Agriculture, 2012).

3.7   U.S. Department of Agriculture Economic Research Service, *Ag and Food Statistics: Charting the Essentials / Farming and Farm Income*, 2013. www.ers.usda.gov/data-products/ag-and-food-statistics-charting-the-essentials/farming-and-farm-income.aspx.

3.8   U.S. Department of Agriculture Economic Research Service, *Ag and Food Statistics: Charting the Essentials / Farming and Farm Income*, 2013. www.ers.usda.gov/data-products/ag-and-food-statistics-charting-the-essentials/farming-and-farm-income.aspx.

3.9   U.S. Department of Agriculture Economic Research Service, *Ag and Food Statistics: Charting the Essentials / Farming and Farm Income*, 2013. www.ers.usda.gov/data-products/ag-and-food-statistics-charting-the-essentials/farming-and-farm-income.aspx.

3.10 National Chicken Council, *Vertical Integration*, 2012. www.nationalchickencouncil.org/industry-issues/vertical-integration.

3.11 Vern Grubinger, Kenneth Mulder, and Dave Timmons, *Vermont's Agriculture: Generating Wealth from the Land* (Montpelier: Vermont Sustainable Agriculture Council, 2005).

3.12 Photo by Vern Grubinger.

4.1   Philip H. Howard, "Visualizing Consolidation in the Global Seed Industry: 1996–2008," *Sustainability* (2009): 1266–87.

4.2 "Food Manufacturing NAICS 311," U.S. Department of Commerce Industry Report, 2008.

5.1 William Kandel, *Profile of Hired Farmworkers, A 2008 Update ERR-60*, Economic Research Report, Economic Research Service (Washington, DC: U.S. Department of Agriculture, 2008).

5.2 U.S. Department of Agriculture Economic Research Service, *Rural Labor and Education: Farm Labor*, 2012. www.ers.usda.gov/topics/farm-economy/farm-labor .aspx.

5.3 Photo by Laurie Bombard.

6.1 U.S. Department of Agriculture, Economic Research Service, *Adoption of Genetically Engineered Crops in the U.S.*, 2013. www.ers.usda.gov/data-products /adoption-of-genetically-engineered-crops-in-the-us.aspx.

6.2 Adapted from Geoff Zehnder, *Overview of Monitoring and Identification Techniques for Insect Pests*, eOrganic, 2010. www.extension.org/pages/19198 /overview-of-monitoring-and-identification-techniques-for-insect-pests.

6.3 Photo by Vern Grubinger.

7.1 U.S. Environmental Protection Agency, *Climate Change Indicators in the United States*, 2013. www.epa.gov/climatechange/science/indicators/weather-climate/ temperature.html.

7.2 Pieter Tans and Ralph Keeling, "Trends in Atmospheric Carbon Dioxide: Full Mauna Loa CO_2 Record," U.S. Department of Commerce/National Oceanic & Atmospheric Administration/NOAA Research. www.esrl.noaa.gov/gmd/ccgg /trends.

7.3 Photo by Vern Grubinger.

7.4 Photo by Vern Grubinger.

7.5 U.S. Environmental Protection Agency, *Inventory of U.S. Greenhouse Gas Emissions and Sinks: 1990–2009* (Washington, DC: U.S. Environmental Protection Agency, 2011).

7.6 U.S. Department of Agriculture Economic Research Service, *Natural Resources & Environment / Climate Change / Background*, 2012. www.ers.usda.gov/topics/natural -resources-environment/climate-change/background.aspx.

7.7 Anthony Leiserowitz, Edward Maibach, Connie Roser-Renouf, and Jay Hmielowski, *Global Warming's Six Americas, March 2012 & November 2011* (New Haven, CT: Yale Project on Climate Change Communication, 2012).

8.1 Adapted from Martin C. Heller and Gregory A. Keoleian, "Assessing the Sustainability of the US Food System: A Life Cycle Perspective," *Agricultural Systems* 76, no. 3 (2003): 1007–41.

8.2 Adapted from a presentation given by Gustavo Camargo, Penn State University, October 2013.

8.3 Photo by Vern Grubinger.

8.4 Photo by Glenn Cook. North Carolina State University, *Database of State Incentives for Renewables and Efficiency*, n.d. dsireusa.org/solar/solarpolicyguide/?id=17.

9.1 Alisha Coleman-Jensen, Mark Nord, Margaret Andrews, and Steven Carlson, *Household Food Security in the United States in 2011 (ERR-141)*, Economic Research Report, Economic Research Service (Washington, DC: U.S. Department of Agriculture, 2012).

9.2 Photo by Vern Grubinger.

10.1 Steve Martinez et al., *Local Food Systems: Concepts, Impacts, and Issues (ERR-97)*, Economic Research Report, Economic Research Service (Washington, DC: U.S. Department of Agriculture, 2010).

10.2 Photo by Vern Grubinger.

10.3 Photo by Vern Grubinger.

11.1 Photo by Vern Grubinger.

11.2 Wholesale photo used under Creative Commons License: Attribution-ShareAlike 2.0 Generic (CC BY-SA 2.0) by Beatrice Murch, "Root Vegetables," June 13, 2007. www.flickr.com/photos/blmurch/558723935. Direct Sales photo used under Creative Commons License: Attribution 2.0 Generic (CC BY 2.0), by Church Street Marketplace, "Burlington Farmers Market, Burlington Vermont," July 17, 2004. www.flickr.com/photos/churchstreetmarketplace/4130120037/in/photostream/. Education photo by Lisa Chase.

11.3 Photo by Vern Grubinger.

12.1 Photo by Vern Grubinger.

13.1 From C. Sheils, *Growing New Farmers: Professional Development Discussion Series 101: What Does the Term "New Farmer" Mean?* (Belchertown, MA: New England Small Farm Institute, 2002), pp. 2–4. Copyright 2011 by New England Small Farm Institute. Reprinted with permission.

13.2 U.S. Department of Agriculture Economic Research Service, *Farm Economy / Beginning & Disadvantaged Farmers / Beginning Farmers & Age Distribution of Farmers*, 2013. www.ers.usda.gov/topics/farm-economy/beginning-disadvantaged -farmers/beginning-farmers-age-distribution-of-farmers.aspx.

13.3 Photo by Scott Larsen.

14.1 U.S. Department of Agriculture, Office of Communications, *Agriculture Fact Book, 2001–2002* (Washington, DC: U.S. Government Printing Office, 2003).

14.2 Photo by Lynn Betts, USDA Natural Resources Conservation Service.

14.3 Cynthia Nickerson, Robert Ebel, Allison Borchers, and Fernando Carriazo, *Major Uses of Land in the United States, 2007 (EIB-89)*, Economic Information Bulletin, Economic Research Service (Washington, DC: U.S. Department of Agriculture, 2011).

14.4 Farmland Information Center, "Status of State PACE Programs," USDA Natural Resources Conservation Service and American Farmland Trust, Farmland Information Center, 2013.

15.3 Photo by Janice Haney Carr. Used with permission from the U.S. Centers for Disease Control, Public Health Image Library.

MAPS

2.1 U.S. Department of Agriculture, *2007 Census of Agriculture: Agricultural Diversification*, National Agricultural Statisics Service, 2009. www.agcensus.usda .gov/Publications/2007/Online_Highlights/Fact_Sheets/Economics/agricultural _diversification.pdf.

11.1 U.S. Department of Agriculture, "2007 Census of Agriculture: Table 7. Income from Farm-Related Sources: 2007 and 2002," National Agricultural Statistics Service, 2009. www.agcensus.usda.gov/Publications/2007/Full_Report/Volume_1, _Chapter_1_US/st99_1_006_007.pdf.

Index

access to healthy food: affordable local
food, 141–48; cheap food health conundrum, 138–41, *141*; increasing access,
147–48; as measure of progress, 69; Post
Oil Solutions, 145–47; subsidized school
lunches, 149; Wholesome Wave, 144–45.
See also food security
Adams Farm, 169–70
adaptation approach, 111–17, *114*, 236, 238
affordability. *See* access to healthy food
"Aggie Bond" loan programs, 208–9
agrarian ethic, 59–60
agricultural census, 42–45
agricultural ecosystems, 14, 88, 98–99
Agricultural Justice Project, 87
agricultural use vs. fair market value, 222
agricultural zoning, 219–20, 229
agriculture: alternative paradigm, 21–23,
98–99, 101–7, 144, 199–200; climate
change implications, 110–11; connecting
children to, 152–53, 154–55, 157–58;
GHG emissions share, *118*; industrial
paradigm, 54–57, 59, 98–99, 247–48.
See also farmland; farms and farmers
agritourism: benefits and challenges,
177–80, *178*; and consumer–farmer
connections, 180–81; defined, 165;
evolution, 168–71, 175–77; impacts and
trends, 171–75, *172*; Liberty Hill Farm,
175–77; overview, 165–68
agroecology, 98–99, 103–4, 107
air quality, 91, 94–95, 100
alternative agricultural paradigm, 21–23,
98–99, 101–7, 144, 199–200. *See also*
direct-to-consumer markets; farm-to-
school programs
Altieri, Miguel, 107

anaerobic digestion, 131, *131*
animal factories, elimination of, 247
animal wastes, 97–98, 100, *106*, 131
anonymity of food for consumers, 60, 74
apprenticeships, farm, 77–78
Arctic sea ice melting, 109–10
Arethusa Farm, 155–56
average annual temperature changes,
108–9, 110

Bacillus thuringiensis, 97
Bailey, Liberty Hyde, 89
Baldwin Dairy, 115
Balfour, Lady Eve, 89
Baxter, Megan, 188–90
bed-and-breakfast, farm as, 175–77
Beginning Farmer and Rancher Development Program, 209
beginning farmers. *See* new farmers
Berkfield, Richard, 145
Berry, Wendell, 59
biodiesel, 130, 133
biodiversity, 95–96
biofuels, 130–36
biogas, 131
biomass fuels, 131–34, 136
Bombard, Gary, 79, 81
Bombard, Laurie Mazza, 81
borrowing for farm capital, 208
Brattleboro Farm to School Program,
156–59
broad-line (full-line) grocery distributors,
41
Bt (insect-resistant) crops, 97
Bucciaglia, Paul, 197–200
Burlington School Food Project, 154–55
business of food: agricultural census,

42–45; consolidation in, 55–57, *56–57*, 202; and economics of food systems, 45–46; food consumption and waste, 33–34, *35*, 36–37; marketing of food, 37–41; retail food stores, 41, 50, 56, 57; Vermont food system, 46–53. *See also* economic systems

Buy Local campaigns, 21

Cabot Creamery, 50–51
CAFOs (concentrated animal feeding operations), 95, 97–98, 100
capital, new farmer's need for, 208–9, 210
carbon dioxide (CO_2), 108, *109*, 112
Carman Brook Maple & Dairy Farm, 180
Carrot Project, 209
Carson, Rachel, 58
Case, Thomas, 155–56
Cedar Circle Farm, 188–90
Chávez, César, 58
Circle Mountain Farm, 146–47
circuit breaker programs, 222, 223
civic agriculture, *31*, 31–32
Clancy, Kate, 12
climate change: adaptation to, 111–17, *114*; Baldwin Dairy, 115; beliefs about, 120–22, *122*; consumer's role in mitigation, 119–20; Edgewater Farm, 115–17; GHG emissions, 25–28, 108, *109*, 112, 117–20, *118*; implications for agriculture, 110–11, 246; measures of, 108–10; mitigation approach, 111, 117–20, *118*
commodity food system, 22, 23, 26–27, 37, 42, *43*, 45, 64–65, 206
community factor in food system, 3, *4*, *31*, 31–32, 98, 147. *See also* access to healthy food; local food systems
community gardens, 148
community-supported agriculture (CSA), 27, 38, 116, 167
concentrated animal feeding operations (CAFOs), 95, 97–98, 100
conservation easements/covenants, 52, 212, 215–19

conservation of resources, 52, 91–92, 128, 136–37
Conservation Stewardship Program, 92
conservation tillage, 91, 100
consolidation in food production, 55–57, *56–57*, 202
consumers: agritourism and connecting to farmers, 180–81; anonymity of food for, 60, 74; benefits of food system change for, 238–39, 243; climate change mitigation role, 119–20; energy conservation practices, 136–37; experience of on-farm shopping, 167; and farmworker working conditions, 87; food safety role, 190, 193; information's empowerment of, 237, 243, 245; local food systems role for, 17, 24–25, *26*, 51–52; local "plus" connection between food and, 21–22; nutritional recommendations vs. consumption preferences, 29, 34–35; power of choice, 51–52; spending on food by, 34, *34, 35*, 264n20; transparency's benefits for, 57, 71; types of food consumed, 36; waste from consumption patterns, 33–34, *35*, 36–37; "willingness to pay" and food markets, 37–38. *See also* human health; values in food systems
conventional agricultural paradigm, 54–57, 59, 98–99, 247–48
Cook, Glenn and Karen, 134–35
cooperative networks, 29, 49–50, 71–73, 86. *See also* horizontal networks
corn as energy source, 132–33
cost of food, 24–25, *35*, 54–57, 60. *See also* access to healthy food
cover cropping, 23, 104, 199
crowdfunding for new farmers, 209
CSA (community-supported agriculture), 27, 38, 116, 167
culinary tourism, 170, 174–75
cultural experience, on-farm visit as, 166–67

dairy farms, 83, 84–85, 104–7, 115, 180
Davis, Jed, 50–51

Deep Root Co-op, 49–50

demand for food in U.S., 33

development pressure on farmland, 213–15, *214*, 215–16, 227–28

diet and nutrition: benefits of food system change for, 238; cost benefits of healthy food for society, 148; farm-to-school programs' contribution, 149–50, 152, 158; food choice impact on environment, 27–28; fresh produce accessibility, 142–43; local food as behavior modification, 29–30; recommendations vs. American consumption preferences, *29*, 34–35; tracking student dietary behaviors, 159–60, 162; updated federal guidelines, 232–33

differential tax assessment programs, 222–23

differentiated product, food as, 37, 72

direct-to-consumer markets: and affordable local food, 142–43, 145–46; economic role of, 38–39; experiential value for consumer, 167; farmers' markets, 30, 38–40, 145–46; food safety issue for, 189–90, 193; local food system's role in, 11, 16, 17–18, 38–39; national distribution of, *18*; new farmers' preference for, 206; and values-driven food economy, 71, 247; in Vermont, 46–48. *See also* agritourism

distancing of food from consumers, 60, 74

distributed systems, 239, *242*

diversity in food system, 234

drought, climate effects on farming, 113

EBT (Electronic Benefit Transfer), 30

ecological agriculture, 98–99, 103–4, 107

economic injury level (EIL), 101

economic systems: and anonymity of food in marketplace, 60; balance in improved food system, 234; civic agriculture, *31*, 31–32; externalities, 2–3, 6, 54; importing/exporting foods, 13; local food system benefits, 16, 28; modeling

perspective, 1–2, 6, *7*; and protection of farmland benefits, 215; and social connections in local food markets, 22; values in, 54, 60; willingness to pay more for local food, 24–25. *See also* business of food; direct-to-consumer markets

economic threshold (ET), 101

economies of scope vs. economies of scale, 54, 242, *244*

Edgewater Farm, 115–17

education, food system, 147, 149, 152–53, 167, 176–77, 193. *See also* farm-to-school programs

educational performance, effect of nutrition on, 150

egg industry and *Salmonella*, 190–92, 193

EIL (economic injury level), 101

electricity, 129, 131–32

Electronic Benefit Transfer (EBT), 30

emergent properties, defined, 9

energy return on investment (EROI), 130

energy systems: biofuels, 130–36; conservation and efficiency, 128, 136–37; consumers' role, 136–37; EROI, 130; fossil fuels, 14, 70, 124–25; introduction, 123–25, *124*; local food systems, 125–28; quality of energy, 128–30, *129*; solar, 123, 135–36; usage by local vs. commodity food producers, 26–27; wind, 134–35, *135*

Environmental Protection Agency (EPA), 92, 99, 100

Environmental Quality Incentives Program, 92

environmental systems: air quality, 91, 94–95, 100; alternative farming systems, 102–4; benefits of system thinking for, 8; biodiversity, 95–96; Evergreen Farms, 104–5; excess manure, 97–98; and food system models, 2; GMOs, 96–97; Happy Cow Creamery, 105–7; herbicides, 97, 100; and hidden costs of food, 57; historical perspective, 88–90;

increasing productivity, inputs, and impacts, 90–91; local food systems, 25–28; mitigation approaches, 98–102; pesticides, 55, 91, 92–93, 99, 100–101, *101*; quality of environment as measure of progress, 69; relationship to food systems, 5, *6*; resource conservation and protection, 52, 91–92, 128, 136–37; soil quality, 89, 91, 93–94, *94–95*, 113, 246; sustainable agriculture practices, 23; transformational change, 105–7; valuing of, 58–59; water quality, 92–93. *See also* climate change

EPA (Environmental Protection Agency), 92, 99, 100

erosion, 91, 93–94, *94*, 113

estate planning, 223, 224–26

ET (economic threshold), 101

ethanol as energy source, 133–34

Europe, agritourism in, 179

Evergreen Farms, 104–5

experience vs. product focus, 167–68, *168*

exporting foods, 14

externalities, economic, 2–3, 6, 54

fairness value, 54, 69, 230, 234, 245–46

family farm, as start for new farmers, 200–203. *See also* small farms

Farm and Ranch Land Protection Program, 219

Farm Credit System, 208

farmers' markets, 30, 38–40, 145–46. *See also* direct-to-consumer markets

farm-gate output, 46

farmland: amount of, 213; benefits of food system change, 238; development pressure on, 213–15, *214*, 215–16, 227–28; farm-to-school impact on, 161–62; loss of, 213–14, *214*; Montgomery County, MD, 227–28; percentage of cover, 70; preservation of, 212, 215–19, 227–29; protection of, 212, 214–15, 219–23, 227–29; Skagit County, WA, 228–29; tax policies to support, 222–23; trends

for future, 212–14, *213–14*; Vermont's conservation, 52

farm link programs, 204–6

farms and farmers: and climate change, 111, 112–13, 121–22, *122*; cooperative structures, 49–50, 71–73, 86; farmers as small minority of population, 212–13; farm-to-school impact on, 161–62; food safety practices, 186–88; hired farmworkers as operating expense share, 75; income for, 42, 43–44, *44*; and increased productivity, 90–91; increase in size and decline in number, 42, *43*, 90, *213*; local food sales and distribution, *19*; measuring well-being and viability, 70; mitigating GHG emissions, 118–20; model for, 5, *5*; and pricing of commodity foods, 37; production data, 43–53, *44–45*, *47*; programs to support, 223–27; size classes of farms, *43*; succession planning, 223, 224–26; transfers of assets and operations, 208, 223, 224–26. *See also* business of food; local food systems; small farms

Farm Service Agency (FSA), 208

farms-in-the-middle, horizontal networks in, 62–63

Farm to Plate Initiative, Vermont, 48–49

farm-to-school programs: challenges for, 159–63; evolution of, 152–53; overview, 149–52, *150*; strengthening programs, 163–64; in Vermont, 153–59

farm transfers, 208, 223, 224–26

farm viability programs, 223–24

FDA (Food and Drug Administration), 183, 184, 186

FEED (Food Education Every Day), 153–54, 157

feedback loops, defined, 9

fertilizers, 91, 92, 99–100. *See also* nutrient management

financing systems, 208–9, 210

food access. *See* access to healthy food

food action plan, *240*

food banks, 140–41, 147

food-borne illness, 14

food-buying behavior. *See* consumers

Food Connects, 156

food culture, model of, *7*

food economy scorecard, *241*

Food Education Every Day (FEED), 153–54, 157

food festivals, 170–71

food hubs, 20, 72–73, 148

food insecurity. *See* food security

Food Justice certification, *86*, 87

food-miles concept, 125–26

food processing, 48, 55–56. *See also* business of food

food safety: Cedar Circle Farm, 188–90; as challenge to farm-to-school programs, 163; evolution of regulation, 183–88; introduction, 182–83, *183*; promoting best practices, 192–94; *Salmonella* in eggs, 190–92

food security: benefits from protection of farmland, 214–15; and cheap food conundrum, 138–41, *141*; and food waste, 37; global level, 13; and local food systems, 29–31; passively cooled crop storage, *30*; U.S. levels of insecurity, 10, 14. *See also* access to healthy food

food service establishments, 41. *See also* farm-to-school programs

food systems: action steps in improving, 246–48; adaptation approach, 111–17, *114*, 236, 238; critical issues for, 231–33; defined, 1; energy use in, 123–25, *124*, 129; food system plans, 237–39; hierarchy of, *3*, 4–7; levels of, *9*, 9–14; levels of change in, 236–37; mitigation approach, 98–102, 111, 117–20, *118*, 237, 238; models for, 1–3; overview of improvement approaches, 15, 230–31, *231*; reasons for studying, 14; resilience and sustainability in, 230, 234, 235–36; structural features of healthy, 239–46, *244–45*; systems thinking to analyze, 8–9;

transformational change, 68–70, 105–7, 236–37, 238, 243, 245–47; visions and principles for improving, 233–35. *See also* local food systems; sustainability of food systems; values in food systems

food tourism, 170, 174–75

foreign farmworkers, 74, 75–76, *75–76*, 81–85

Fort Hill Farm, 197–200

Fortin, Karen, 180

fossil fuels, 14, 70, 124–25

fresh produce, 142–43, 160, 185–87, 264n20

Frost, Amy, 146–47

GAPs (Good Agricultural Practices), 186

GDP (Gross Domestic Product), 70

genetically modified organisms (GMOs), *96*, 96–97

genetic engineering (GE), *96*, 96–97

Genuine Progress Indicators (GPIs), 70

geographic proximity factor in local food definition, 16–17, 18, 19–21

GHG (greenhouse gas) emissions, 25–28, 108, *109*, 112, 117–20, *118*, 131

Gillespie, Katherine, 156–59

global food systems level, 13–14, 32

global warming. *See* climate change

GMFTS (Green Mountain Farm-to-School), 154

GMOs (genetically modified organisms), *96*, 96–97

Good Agricultural Practices (GAPs), 186

governmental role in food system: direct payments to farmers, 44, *44*; EPA, 92, 99, 100; FDA, 183, 184, 186; local governments and costs of local food, 25; model for, *3*, *4*. *See also* policy systems; state governments; USDA

GPIs (Genuine Progress Indicators), 70

grasses as energy sources, 132

Great Depression, food insecurity during, 140

greenhouse gas (GHG) emissions, 25–28, 108, *109*, 112, 117–20, *118*, 131

Green Mountain Farm-to-School
(GMFTS), 154
Gross Domestic Product (GDP), 70
Growing New Farmers Project, 195–96
growth vs. progress, and food system value,
68–70
guest worker program, 78–81
Gulf of Mexico, dead zone in, 93

H-2A guest worker program, 78–81
HACCP (Hazard Analysis and Critical
Control Points), 184, 185
Happy Cow Creamery, 105–7
Harpster, Andy, 104
Harpster, R. Wayne, 104
health. See human health
health care availability, new farmers' need
for, 211
Hellen family, 180
herbicides, 97, 100
herbicide-tolerant (HT) crops, 97
hierarchical networks, 45, 45, 60–62, 61,
191, 239
hierarchy of systems, defined, 9
hired farmworkers, 74–85, 75–76, 245–46
horizontal networks, 60–68, 61, 67, 71–73,
239
household food systems level, 10–11, 49
Howard, Sir Albert, 89
HT (herbicide-tolerant) crops, 97
human health: cheap food health conundrum, 138–41, 141; as externality for
economics of food production, 3; food
system models, 3, 4; food system's impact on, 14; healthy food as cost savings,
148; local food systems impact, 28–29;
as measure of progress, 69; and school
meal programs, 149–52; structural
features of food system for, 239–46,
244–45; and vision for improved food
system, 234. See also access to healthy
food; diet and nutrition
human resource management practices,
76–77

hunger, challenge of world, 13.
See also food security
hypoxic seas, 93

illegal immigrants. See undocumented
farmworkers
immigration policy, 75–76
importing foods, 13
individual food systems level, 10.
See also consumers
industrial agricultural paradigm, 54–57, 59,
98–99, 247–48
information networks, importance to food
system transformation, 237, 243, 245
inputs, reducing purchased non-renewable,
107, 232
inputs and outputs in systems thinking, 9
insect pest populations, climate change
effects, 112
insect-resistant (Bt) crops, 97
integrated pest management (IPM),
100–101, 101
intergenerational farm transfer, 223,
224–26. See also new farmers
Intergovernmental Panel on Climate
Change (IPCC), 110
intermediary food markets, 40–41
internships, farm, 77–78
IPM (integrated pest management),
100–101, 101

Jamaican immigrants as farmworkers,
79–81
justice, food system, 69, 230, 234, 245–46

Kennett, Beth, 175–77
Kingsolver, Barbara, 21
knowledge and attitudes, farm-to-school
impact on, 160, 162
Kupers, Karl, 63–65

La Mota Ranch, 179–80
land. See farmland
land access for new farmers, 203–6, 211

land link programs, 204–6
land trusts, 204, 217
land-use planning, 215
Lappé, Francis Moore, 58–59
large farms, share of production, 43, *43*.
    See also industrial agricultural
    paradigm
Larsen, Scott, 200–203
leased land startup for new farmers,
    197–200, 203, 205
Leopold, Aldo, 58
Liberty Hill Farm, 175–77
Lincoln, Abraham, 184
liquid biomass fuels, 129, 131
LISA (Low Input Sustainable Agriculture)
    program, 23. *See also* SARE
livestock farming, 45, 95, 97–98, 100, 101–2,
    106, *106*, 131, 217
local food systems: affordability issue,
    141–48; community outcomes, 31–32;
    consumers and incentives, 17, 24–25,
    51–52; defined, 11, 16–22; economic
    benefits, 16, 28; energy's role in, 125–28;
    and enhanced information about food
    sourcing, 243, 245; environmental
    values in, 25–28, 54–55; fluid boundaries
    of, 16–17; and food security, 29–31;
    horizontal networks in, 62; human
    health impact, 28–29; introduction, 16;
    and regional systems, 12; as school ed-
    ucation and meal sources, 149, 152–53;
    social values in, 54–55; and sustainable
    agriculture, 22–24; Vermont's role
    in, 47. *See also* direct-to-consumer
    markets; farm-to-school programs
local governments, and costs of local food,
    25
local "plus" connection between food and
    consumers, 21–22
locavores, 20
low-income communities, farm connec-
    tions to, 138. *See also* access to healthy
    food
Lyson, Thomas, 31

Magdoff, Fred, 59
management-intensive grazing (MIG),
    101–2
manufacturers' wholesalers, 41
manure management, 97–98, 100, *106*, 131
maple syrup production, 169, 180
market-based food system model, 2, 37–41,
    71–73. *See also* direct-to-consumer
    markets
market information, challenges for new
    farmers, 206–8
Matthews, H. Scott, 27
Mazza, Sam, 79–81
merchant wholesalers, 41
Merrigan, Kathleen, 138, 163
methane (CH_4), 118, 131
midsize family farms, defined, *43*
MIG (management-intensive grazing),
    101–2
migrant farmworkers, 74–75, 78–81, 82
mitigation approach, 98–102, 111, 117–20,
    118, 237, 238
Montague, Hepburn, 79, 80

National Farm to School Network, 153
national food system level, 13
Native Americans, 169
natural gas as energy source, 136
Natural Resources Conservation Service
    (NRCS), 91
Nature Conservancy, 197, 217
NCAT (National Center for Appropriate
    Technology), 77
Nelson, Abbie, 154
net metering, *135*
new farmers: barriers to getting started,
    210–11; benefits of food system change
    for, 238; diversity of, 195–96; income
    sources, 196–97, *197*; as indicator of
    farm viability, 70; joining the family
    farm, 200–203; leased land startup,
    197–200; needs of, 203–10
nitrogen-based fertilizer pollution, 99–100
nitrogen cycle, *6*

nitrous oxide (N$_2$O), 118
nonprofit funding for new farmers, 209
no-till field management, 100, 106
NRCS (Natural Resources Conservation Service), 91
nutrient management, 97–98, 99–100, *106*, 131, 132
nutrition. *See* diet and nutrition

obesity, 14, 138–39, 150–52, 160, 162
ocean waters, agricultural runoff effects, 93
off-farm income, new farmers' reliance on, 197
OFRF (Organic Farming Research Foundation), 209
oligopoly model for food production, 55–56
on-farm marketing. *See* agritourism
online communities and transparency, 245–46
organic food production, 21–22, 102–3, 144
overweight and obesity, 14, 138–39, 150–52, 160, 162

PACE (purchase of agricultural easements) programs, *218*
parent behaviors, farm-to-school impact on, 160–61
pathogens and food safety, *183*
payback period for adopting new energy resources, 128, 135–36
pesticides, 55, 91, 92–93, 99, 100–101, *101*
phosphorus-based fertilizer pollution, 99–100
pick-your-own (PYO) operations, 40, *166*, *167*, 189–90
policy systems: and accountability for hiring farmworkers, 85–86; consumer's power to affect, 52; Davis's criticism of dairy pricing, 51; evolution of regulation, 183–88; Farm Bill (2008) and local food, 19; genetically engineered crops, 97; and hired farmworkers, 75–76; local food purchasing promotions, 26;

manure management, 100; mitigation approach, 98–102; model for, *4*; national food system level, 12–13; nutrient management, 99–100, 132; organic agriculture, 102–3; pesticide regulation, 99; right-to-farm laws, 221–22, 228–29; Roosevelt's soil conservation initiative, 91; taxes, 52, 222–23. *See also* governmental role in food system
Pollan, Michael, 59
Post Oil Solutions (POS), 145–47
precipitation patterns, 110, 112–13
preservation of farmland, 212, 215–19, 227–29
price of food. *See* cost of food
primary production, defined, 123
producer cooperatives, 49–50, 71–73, 86
productivity, increased food, 90–91
progress vs. growth, and food system value, 68–70
property taxes, 52, 222–23
protection of farmland, 212, 214–15, 219–23, 227–29
purchase of agricultural easements (PACE) programs, *218*
purchasing cooperatives, 29, 71
PYO (pick-your-own) operations, 40, *166*, *167*, 189–90

quick response (QR) codes, 237

rainfall patterns, 110, 112–13
ranchland, protection of, 217
real estate values, 204, 214, 227–28
reductionist vs. system thinking, 8
regional food systems level, 12, 17, 19, 21, 22, 48, 50, 72
renewable energy sources, 123, 127, 131, 134–35, *135*, 135–36
resiliency, food system, 230, 234, 235–36
retail food stores, 41, 50, 56, 57
return on investment for energy used (EROI), 130
right-to-farm laws, 221–22, 228–29

Robin, Vicki, 21
Rodale, J. I., 89
rotational grazing, 101–2, 106
Ruhf, Kathryn, 12

Salmonella in eggs, 190–92, 193
SARE (Sustainable Agriculture Research
    and Education) program, *23*, 209
scenic easements, 216
schools, state incentives for local food
    purchasing, 26. *See also* farm-to-school
    programs
self-employed farmers and families, 74, *75*
SES (Soil Erosion Service), 91
Shea, Erin, 83–84, 85–86
shell corn as energy source, 132–33
Shepherd's Grain, 63–66
short-term profit value, 54, 55
Skagit County, Washington, 228–29
small farms: in agritourism, 173; benefits
    of local food system for, 16; challenge
    of larger farms for new farmers, 201–2;
    direct marketing by, 48; ethanol pro-
    duction on, 134; food safety strategies,
    188–90; internship option for, 77;
    number of, 213; official definition, 42,
    43; revitalizing of, 43
Small Farms Commission report (1998),
    232
SNAP (Supplemental Nutrition Assistance
    Program), 142
social capital, 74, 161–62
social systems, 6–7, *7*, 22, 23, 54–55, 57, 70,
    107
social values, 54–55, 58–59
Soil Conservation Service, 91
Soil Erosion Service (SES), 91
soil quality, 89, 91, 93–94, *94–95*, 113, 246
solar energy, 123, 135–36
solid fuels, 129–30
specialty grocery distributors, 41
spending on food by consumers, 34, *34*, 35
Sprague, Pooh, 108, 115–16
state governments: agritourism variations,

171–74, *172*, 177; certification of organic
    foods, 22; circuit breaker programs,
    222, 223; definitions of local food in,
    20; direct market sales, 47; and farmers'
    markets, 39–40; farm-to-school
    programs, 153, 159; farm viability
    programs, 223–24; food and forestry
    system-friendly states, 52; food produc-
    tion by state, 44–46; incentives for local
    food buying, 25, *26*; land preservation,
    216, 217–18, *218*; manure management,
    100; nutrient management, 99–100;
    pesticide regulation, 99
stewardship concept, 89, 104–5
Strange, Marty, 55
student dietary behaviors, 159–60, 162
Sunny Valley Preserve, 197
Supplemental Nutrition Assistance
    Program (SNAP), 142
supply chain, food, 33–34, 60–68, *67*, 72
sustainability of food systems: and
    agrarian ethic, 59–60; contribution
    to community, 147; elements in path
    to, 230; and environmental impact,
    103–4; local food systems, 22–24;
    measuring progress in, 70; overview, 15;
    supply chains, 60–68, 72; and vision for
    improved food system, 234, 235–36
Sustainable Agriculture Research and
    Education (SARE) program, *23*, 209
Sustainable Harvest Coffee, 66–68, *67*
system boundaries, defined, 8
systems thinking, 8–9, 14

tax policies to support farming, 52, 222–23
TDR (transferable development rights)
    system, 227–28
technical support, new farmer's need for,
    209–10
temperature changes (global warming),
    108–9, 110
tenant farmer, new farmer as, 197–200
term easement, defined, 216
Thompson, Paul, 59

tourism, and Vermont's food production, 49. *See also* agritourism
transformational approach, 68–70, 105–7, 236–37, 238, 243, 245–47
transgenic crops, *96*, 96–97
transparency in food system, 57, 65, 71, 235, 237, 243, 245–46
transportation energy usage, 26–27, 125–27
Trantham, Tom, 105–7

undifferentiated product, food as. *See* commodity food system
undocumented farmworkers, 74, *75*, *76*, 81–85
United Egg Producers, 191–92, 193
U-pick operations, 40, *166*, 167, 189–90
Urban, Chris, 84
urban growth boundaries, 220–21
urban/suburban encroachment on farmland, 213–15, *214*, 215–16, 227–28
USDA (U.S. Department of Agriculture): farm-to-school initiatives, 162–63; food safety role, 183, 184; land preservation programs, 91–92, 219; organic food production regulation, 102–3; pesticide regulation, 99; SARE, 209; Small Farms Commission report (1998), 232; Small Farms/School Meals Initiative, 153; support for beginning farmers, 209
use-value taxation, 52

values-based supply chains, 63–68, 72
values in food systems: consolidation and narrowing of values, 55–57, *56–57*; economic, 54, 55, 60; environmental, 25–28,

54–55; expanding of, 58–60; fairness, 54, 69, 230, 234, 245–46; introduction, 54–55; market-based approaches, 71–73; measures of progress, 68–70; Shepherd's Grain, 63–66; social, 54–55, 58–59; Sustainable Harvest Coffee, 66–68, *67*; sustainable supply chains, 60–68, 72
Vermont Farms! Association, 177
vertical networks, 45, *45*, 60–62, *61*, 191, 239
Vrieze, John, 115

wages, hired farmworkers, 77
Wallace, Henry, 58
Washington State, 77–78, 228–29
water quality, 92–93
Weber, Christopher L., 27
weed management, 112
wholesalers, food, 41, *51*, 247
Wholesome Wave, 144–45
wind energy, 134–35, *135*
wood energy, 132
wood gasifiers, 136
workforce: H-2A guest worker program, 78–81; internships and farm apprenticeships, 77–78; overview, 74–77; undocumented farmworkers, 74, *75*, *76*, 81–85; win-win labor conditions, 85–87, 245–46
World Wide Opportunities on Organic Farms (WWOOF), 78

Young Farmer Grant Program, Texas, 209

zoning for land protection, 219–20, 229